——PATH THROUGH——
CATHOLICISM

Mark Link, S.J.

TABOR®
PUBLISHING

Allen, Texas

IMPRIMI POTEST
Robert A. Wild, S.J.

NIHIL OBSTAT
Rev. Glenn D. Gardner, J.C.D.
Censor Liborum

IMPRIMATUR
†Most Rev. Charles V. Grahmann
Bishop of Dallas

January 11, 1991

The *Nihil Obstat* and *Imprimatur* are official declarations that
the work contains nothing contrary to Faith and Morals. It is
not implied thereby that those granting the *Nihil Obstat* and
Imprimatur agree with the contents, statements, or opinions
expressed.

ACKNOWLEDGMENTS

Excerpts from *The Documents of Vatican II,* Walter M. Abbott,
S.J., Gen. Ed. Copyright © 1966 by The America Press.
Reprinted by permission of The America Press.

All Scripture quotations are from the *Good News Bible,* in
Today's English Version. Copyright © American Bible Society
1966, 1971, 1976. Used by permission.

Excerpts from the English translation of *The Roman Missal* ©
1973, International Committee on English in the Liturgy, Inc.
(ICEL); excerpts from the English translation of *Pastoral Care
of the Sick: Rites of Anointing and Viaticum* © 1982, ICEL. All
rights reserved.

ILLUSTRATIONS
Lora Lutz

CALLIGRAPHY
Bob Niles

Send all inquiries to:
Tabor Publishing
One DLM Park
Allen, Texas 75002

Printed in the United States of America

ISBN 1-55924-543-3 (Student Text)
ISBN 1-55924-544-1 (Resource Manual)

1 2 3 4 5   95 94 93 92 91

Preface

The film *The Heart Is a Lonely Hunter* contains a moving scene. A teenage girl is listening to a record. With her is a deaf friend. At one point, the girl tries to communicate to her friend what music sounds like.

To do this, the girl stands in front of her friend so that he can read her lips. She also makes movements with her body and hands.

After a while, the friends laugh and give up. They realize that trying to describe music to a deaf person is like trying to describe color to a blind person. It is next to impossible.

Describing the Catholic faith poses a similar problem. Trying to express it in words is like trying to describe sound to a deaf person or color to a blind person. It is like trying to catch a moonbeam in your hand, or like trying to capture the song of a bird and give it to a loved one.

To put it in yet another way, Catholicism is not simply a creed to be memorized; it is a faith to be lived. It is not a book to be read; it is a spirit to be caught.

Mark Link, S.J.

Contents

Part One

Catholic Revelation

Introduction
FAITH JOURNEY

Listen! I stand at the door and knock.
REVELATION 3:20

Every faith journey begins
with God knocking at the door of our heart.
That knock can take many forms:
a spiritual hunger,
an inspiring person,
a loving friend.

Our faith journey continues
with God walking with us every step of the way.
God lights our path when it grows dark.
God lifts our spirit when it wanes.
God helps us up when we stumble and fall.
God's grace embraces us every inch of the way.

But God respects our freedom.
God does not force us.
This means that if God's grace
is to touch and transform us,
we must open ourselves to it.
We must work as if all depends on us,
but trust as if all depends on God.

Looking Ahead
REVELATION:
God's Self-communication of Love

The path we will travel in the weeks ahead
is made up of three parts:

- Revelation: God's self-communication of love to us
- Worship: God's ongoing initiative of love— and our response
- Morality: God's invitation to love and live as Jesus did—and our response

In Part One
we will explore God's self-communication
of love:

1 *Faith*
2 *Tradition and Scripture*
3 *Hebrew Scriptures*
4 *Christian Scriptures*
5 *God*
6 *Jesus*
7 *Holy Spirit*
8 *Church*
9 *Afterlife*

1 Faith

Father John Powell of Loyola University was watching the students file into his room on the first day of his theology course. That's when he first met Tommy.

Tommy was combing his long flaxen hair, which hung six inches below his shoulders. Father knew that it's what is in your head—not on it—that counts. But he was unprepared for Tommy. So he wrote him off as strange—very strange.

Faith Journey

Tommy turned out to be Father's "atheist in residence," but they managed to live together in relative peace. At the end of the course Tommy asked Father somewhat cynically, "Do you think I'll ever find God?"

Father decided on a little shock therapy. "No, Tommy," he said emphatically, "I don't think you'll ever find God, but I am certain God will find you." Tommy shrugged and left. Father felt a little disappointed that Tommy had apparently missed his clever line.

Then Came Sad News

About a year later, Father Powell learned that Tommy had terminal cancer. Father writes:

> *Before I could search him out,*
> *he came to me.*
> *When he walked into my office,*
> *his body was badly wasted,*
> *and his long hair had fallen out*
> *because of chemotherapy. . . .*
> *"Tommy, I've thought about you so often.*
> *I hear you are sick!" I blurted out.*
>
> *"Oh, yes, very sick. I have cancer.*
> *It's a matter of weeks."*

Tommy asked, "Do you think I'll ever find God?"

"Can you talk about it?"

"Sure, what would you like to know?"

*"What's it like to be only twenty-four
and know that you are dying?"*

"Well, it could be worse."

"Like what?"

*"Well, like being fifty
and having no values or ideas," Tom said,
"like being fifty and thinking booze,
seducing women, and making money
are the real 'biggies' in life.*

*"But what I really came to see you about
is something you said to me
on the last day of class.
I asked if you thought
I would ever find God and you said, 'No!'
which surprised me.
Then you said, 'But God will find you.'*

*"I thought about that a lot,
even though my search for God
was hardly intense at that time."
(My "clever" line.
He thought about that a lot!)*

Tommy Makes a Decision

Tommy went on to tell Father that after the doctors removed a malignant lump from his groin, he got serious about trying to locate God.

*"I really began banging against
the bronze doors of heaven.
But nothing happened.
Well, one day I woke up,
and instead of throwing
a few more futile appeals to a God
who may or may not be there,
I just quit. . . .*

*"I decided to spend what time I had left
doing something more profitable.
I thought about something else you said:
'The essential sadness
is to go through life without loving.
But it would be almost equally sad
to leave this world
without ever telling those you loved
that you loved them.'*

*"So I began with the hardest one: my dad.
He was reading the newspaper
when I approached him.*

" 'Dad, I would like to talk with you.'

" 'Well, talk.'

" 'I mean, it's really important.'

*"The newspaper came down three slow inches.
'What is it?'*

*" 'Dad, I love you.
I just wanted you to know that.'*

*"The newspaper fluttered to the floor.
Then my father did two things
I couldn't remember him doing before.
He cried and hugged me.
And we talked all night,
even though he had to go to work
the next morning.*

*"It was easier
with my mother and little brother.
They cried with me, too,
and we hugged one another,
and we shared the things
we had been keeping secret for so many years.*

*"I was only sorry that I had waited so long.
Here I was, in the shadow of death,
and I was just beginning to open up
to all the people
I had actually felt close to."*

God Finds Tommy

Tommy then shared with Father Powell what happened next. It was something he had not anticipated. Tommy said, "I turned around and God was there. . . . You were right. He found me."

Tommy discovered that God had always been there waiting for him. While he had been "banging against the bronze doors of heaven," God had been patiently knocking at the door of Tommy's heart. And so, when Tommy opened the door of his heart to love, he found God standing there.

The surest way to find God is by opening to love.

Father Powell was silent for a moment. Then, in a low voice, choked with emotion, he said:

"Tommy . . .
I think you are saying something
much more universal than you realize.
You are saying the surest way to find God
is not to make him a private possession
or an instant consolation in time of need,
but rather by opening to love.
You know, Saint John said that:
'God is love, and whoever lives in love
lives in God and God in him.'

"Tom, could I ask a favor?
Would you come to my theology-of-faith course
and tell my students what you just told me?"

Though we scheduled a date
he never made it. . . .

Before he died, we talked one last time.
"I'm not going to make it to your class,"
he said.

"I know, Tom."

"Will you tell them for me?
Will you . . . tell the whole world for me?"

"I will, Tom. I'll tell them."*

Faith Difficulties

The beautiful story of Tommy's faith journey illustrates an important point about faith. Like most things in life, it grows and develops by stages. The three main stages through which our faith passes in its growth process are:

- the childhood stage: faith by birth,
- the adolescent stage: faith in transition,
- the adult stage: faith by choice.

Of these three stages, the adolescent stage is normally the most critical and the most painful. It is the most critical stage because at this time in our lives we begin the important transition from being a Christian by *culture* (physical birth) to being a Christian by *conviction* (personal choice).

Likewise, the adolescent stage is the most painful stage because during this stage our childhood faith must die in order that our adult faith can be born. The *dying* of our childhood faith is what causes all the pain.

John Kirvan's book *The Restless Believers* contains a moving description of how the death of our childhood faith affects us. He quotes a young person as saying:

"I don't know what's gone wrong,
but I just don't believe like I used to.
When I was in grade school
and for the first couple years of high school
I was real religious,
and now I just don't seem to care."

The death of our childhood faith makes us feel sick of heart—even guilty. This is unfortunate, for our faith is simply going through an important growth stage. It is changing from being a cultural faith to being a convictional faith.

The transition from being a Christian by *culture* (birth) to being a Christian by *conviction* (choice) is a gradual process. Moreover, it is a process that is never *fully* complete. It goes on all of our lives.

---

*Paraphrased from John Powell, *Unconditional Love* (Allen, Texas: Tabor Publishing, 1978), pp. 117–23.

Faith Growth

The transition from childhood faith to adult faith takes place at three levels: mind, heart, and soul. (By soul we mean the deepest dimension of our being.)

Before we take a closer look at each of these levels, it will help to clarify what we mean by faith.

First, faith involves belief in *someone,* not something. Saint Paul says:

> *I live by faith in the Son of God,*
> *who loved me*
> *and gave his life for me.*
> GALATIANS 2:20

Second, faith also involves belief in *what* Jesus tells us. Because Jesus loved us and gave his life for us, we trust him. Therefore, faith involves

Faith involves belief in someone, not something.

not only belief *in Jesus* but also belief *in what Jesus tells us* about his Father. Jesus said:

> *"I have told you everything*
> *I heard from my Father. . . .*
> *I have told you this*
> *so that my joy may be in you*
> *and that your joy may be complete."*
> JOHN 15:15, 11

Finally, faith involves entering into a relationship of friendship with Jesus. Jesus said:

> *"I love you*
> *just as the Father loves me. . . .*
> *I call you friends,*
> *because I have told you everything*
> *I heard from my Father."*
> JOHN 15:9, 15

And so faith involves saying yes to—

- Jesus (God in the flesh),
- Jesus' teaching, and
- Jesus' invitation to friendship

Let us now take a look at the three levels at which the *transition* from childhood faith to adult faith takes place.

First Is the Mind Level

Young people often find themselves questioning things about their faith that they once took for granted. For example, they ask: "Is there really a God, or is God simply a figment of our imagination?" "Is Jesus really the Son of God, or is he simply a noble leader?" "Is the Church really the Body of Christ, or is it just another human organization?"

Questions like these are not only understandable but necessary. But questioning our faith in God does not mean there is no God. It simply means that our perspective of God (or Jesus and the Church) is often incomplete and sometimes even erroneous. Thus Leo Tolstoy observes correctly:

> *When a savage ceases to believe*
> *in his wooden God,*
> *this does not mean that there is no God,*
> *but only that the true God is not made of wood.*

In other words, questioning our childhood view of God is necessary. Equally important, however, we must also open ourselves to an adult view of God. And this is where an open mind is so necessary, even though it is not always easy. For the birth of new ideas is often as difficult and painful as the death of old ones.

Second Is the Heart Level

The transition to adult faith involves not just opening the mind to truth, but also opening the heart to love.

Father Powell puts it this way: "The surest way to find God is . . . by opening to love. 'God is love, and whoever lives in love lives in God and God in him.' " A story will help to illustrate his point.

Albert Schweitzer was a concert pianist in Europe. He gave up his musical career to become a missionary doctor in Africa. Commenting on the importance of opening the heart to love, he said:

Do you really want to believe in Jesus?
Then you must do something for him.
In this age of doubt
there is no other way to him.
And if for Jesus' sake . . .
you have given your neighbor a morsel of bread
or a sip of water or a piece of garment—
those smallest acts of kindness
which he promises to bless
as though they were done to him—
you will see then
that you have really done it for him.
For then he will come nearer to you,
as one who is alive.
REVERENCE FOR LIFE

In other words, when we open our heart to another in love, we automatically open it to God as well. As in Tommy's case, an inability to find God is frequently traceable to an inability to open to love.

Third Is the Soul Level

Of the three levels at which the transition to adult faith occurs, the soul level is the hardest to understand. This is because the faith journey is

a mystery of *gift* and of *freedom*. Again, a story will illustrate.

Dorothy Day died in 1980 at the age of eighty-four. Reporting her death, the *New York Times* called her one of the most influential Catholics in America. Since her death, there has been a movement to canonize her for her personal life and work among New York City's poor and destitute.

In her book *From Union Square to Rome*, Dorothy describes her faith journey to God. Concerning a critical step of the journey, she writes:

Many a morning
after sitting all night in taverns . . .
I went to early Mass
at St. Joseph's Church on Sixth Avenue.
It was just around the corner
from where I lived, and seeing people
going to an early weekday Mass attracted me.
What were they finding there?
I longed for their faith.
My own life was sordid
and yet I had occasional glimpses
of the true and the beautiful.
So I used to go and kneel
in the back pew of St. Joseph's.

This brings us back to our point that the faith journey is a mystery of *gift* and *freedom*.

First of all, faith is a mystery of *gift* in that God's grace—

■ prepares us for the journey,
■ invites us to embark on the journey, and
■ embraces us every step of the journey.

Second, faith is a mystery of *freedom* in that God does not force the gift of faith upon us. God respects our freedom. Concretely, this means that we are free to respond to God's invitation to enter into a relationship of love and trust. Or we are free to reject it.

In brief, the faith journey is a *team effort:* a mystery of *gift* (on God's part) and of *freedom* (on our part).

And so the transition from childhood faith to adult faith takes place at three levels:

■ mind: openness to truth,
■ heart: openness to love, and
■ soul: openness to faith.

Faith Dynamic

The story of Dorothy Day introduces us to the dynamic of faith. That is, it introduces us to how we experience our faith as it *grows* and *matures.* Briefly, we experience it as—

- involving risk,
- involving process, and
- involving periods of darkness.

Faith Involves Risk

The clearest example of what we mean when we say that faith involves risk is marriage. When two people marry, neither is *absolutely* sure that the other will remain faithful, should a major problem arise. In other words, they have no *absolute* certainty about how the other will respond. This is the risk involved. But they take this risk because they love and trust each other.

Faith is something like that. It too involves risk, not in the sense that God may be unfaithful (God is always faithful). Rather, it involves risk in the sense that we are not sure where a faith response to God will lead us. And this risk can be overcome only by trust—the kind of loving trust that one lover has in another.

Faith Involves Process

The biggest mistake we can make is to think that someday we will "get the faith" and never have to worry about it again. To illustrate, consider this statement by a young woman:

One day
I decided to make Jesus the center of my life.
This decision
gave me unbelievable peace and joy.
But two days later,
I found myself doing something
that no true follower of Jesus should do.
I concluded
that I had not really committed my life
to Jesus at all.
I had only psyched myself into thinking I had.
But then I realized something important.
I realized
that when we commit our lives to Jesus,
we commit only that part of ourselves
that we are conscious of at the moment.
That's all we can do.

This young woman's experience illustrates what psychologists tell us: the greater part of ourselves lies below our consciousness. It surfaces only gradually with each new experience.

This brings us back to why faith involves *process.* It is because we constantly evolve and change as persons. Because of this, we must

We are not sure where a faith response to God will lead us.

constantly recommit ourselves to God as we change and evolve. Our faith can never be a *one-time* decision to believe. It must always remain an *ongoing* decision, a lifelong *process.*

Faith Involves Darkness

Faith has a way of going in and out of focus. What was once clear to us becomes fuzzy for a while. Worse yet, there are times when our faith seems to go behind a cloud and disappear in darkness. This darkness is usually caused by one of three things:

- human nature,
- ourselves, or
- God.

First, it may be caused by *human nature,* which has "highs" and "lows." In other words, the darkness simply reflects the natural highs and lows, or mood swings, of everyday human life. Commenting on these mood swings, Anthony Padovano says:

> On one day, life is beautiful. . . .
> We appreciate everything and everyone. . . .
> On such a day it is difficult to know
> why we ever thought life was difficult.
> On another day, however, nothing is right. . . .
> It is a time
> when we number more enemies than we have
> and find fault with every friend.
> On such a day, it is difficult
> to know why we ever thought life was easy.

BELIEF IN HUMAN LIFE

Questioning Our Faith

We can question our faith in two ways: constructively or destructively. Questioning our faith *constructively* means we want to know what is true so we can do what is right. Questioning our faith *destructively* means we want to prove it false so we can do what we want. For example, we suddenly begin to behave in a way that conflicts with our faith, as when our faith tells us that it is wrong to cheat and steal but we do it on a regular basis anyway.

When our faith and our behavior are in conflict, we realize that we must resolve the conflict. If we don't, we won't be at peace with ourselves. So we try to change our behavior. If we can't change it, we may be tempted to question our faith destructively. That is, we may try to prove it false so that we can continue our behavior—and be at peace with ourselves.

What should we do if we discover ourselves questioning our faith destructively? First, we should be honest and admit it. Once we admit it, it ceases to control us and we control it. Second, we should understand that because we are human, our faith and our behavior will always be in conflict to some extent. This is why Jesus came into the world: because we need help to do what is right and because we need forgiveness when we do what is wrong. Finally, we should understand that faith questioning if done *constructively* is healthy and leads to faith maturity. How so?

First, it *produces faith clarity.* For example, we have a question about God. Probing the question constructively, we see God in a new light. We get a clearer picture of God in our mind.

Second, faith questioning *widens faith horizons.* For example, we wonder if the theory of evolution contradicts the Bible. So we investigate the matter and discover that the biblical teaching on creation and the theory of evolution are compatible. As a result, our faith is widened to embrace new horizons.

Finally, constructive faith questioning *deepens faith commitment.* Take the case of God, again. Before our questions about God, we may have prayed to God out of habit. After our questions, we see God in a new light and begin to pray to God in a more personal way.

Our faith is like that. It also has its mood swings. These mood swings simply go with the territory of being a human person.

Second, the periods of darkness may be caused by *ourselves.* We can bring them on by neglecting our faith. That is, we can let our faith grow weak from sin or from lack of spiritual nourishment. In other words, just as our body grows weak from abuse or lack of physical nourishment, so our soul grows weak from sin and lack of spiritual nourishment.

Third and finally, the periods of darkness may be caused by *God.* That is, God allows them to happen in order to strengthen and deepen our faith. In other words, God uses them to help us grow in our faith (Genesis 22:1–12).

Regardless of the cause of these periods of darkness, the agony they can produce is great. In his novel *The Devil's Advocate,* Morris West has a person who is experiencing "darkness" ask:

> *How does one come back to belief?*
> *I tried to reason myself*
> *back to . . . a parent. . . .*
> *All children have parents. . . .*
> *I groped for God and could not find God.*
> *I prayed to God . . . and God did not answer.*
> *I wept at night for the loss of God.*
> *Lost tears and fruitless grief.*

> *Then one day, God was there again. . . .*
> *I had a parent and God knew me. . . .*
> *I had never understood till this moment*
> *the meaning of the words "gift of faith."*
> (slightly adapted)

Recap

The faith journey is a mystery of *gift* (on God's part) and of *freedom* (on our part). Faith involves a free response of our total self to—

- Jesus (God in the flesh),
- Jesus' teaching, and
- Jesus' invitation to friendship.

Many young people experience faith problems because their faith is in a *transitional* stage. It is undergoing a change from being a *cultural* faith (faith by birth) to being a *convictional* faith (faith by choice).

The transitional stage is a time when young people should strive for a special openness of *mind* (to truth), *heart* (to love), and *soul* (to faith).

Our *faith journey* never ends, but continues until we die. It involves *risk* (trust in God), *process* (constant recommitment), and *periods of darkness* (times of questioning).

Faith involves risk and periods of darkness.

Understanding Faith

Review

Faith Difficulties

1. Explain (a) the three stages through which faith passes as it grows, (b) why the second stage is the most critical and the most painful.

Faith Growth

2. To what three things does faith involve saying yes to?

3. List and explain the three levels at which the transition from childhood faith to adult faith takes place.

4. What do we mean when we say that faith is a mystery of *gift* and *freedom,* a team effort between God and ourselves?

Faith Dynamic

5. Explain in what sense our journey of faith involves (a) risk, (b) process, (c) periods of darkness.

6. List and explain three reasons why we sometimes experience periods of darkness in our faith journey.

Questioning Our Faith

7. Explain the difference between constructive and destructive faith questioning.

8. Explain how a conflict between belief and behavior sometimes leads to destructive faith questioning.

9. List and explain three ways constructive faith questioning can lead to faith maturity.

Exercises

1. As a child, Nancy used to believe in God with all her heart. But as she grew older, her belief in God weakened. By the time she was nineteen, she was no longer sure that she believed in God. Then, a few years later, something unexpected happened. Nancy experienced "the miracle" of her daughter's birth. As if someone pushed a button inside her, the idea of God flashed in her head. Her mind asked, "How can such a miraculous thing as a child be the product of pure chance?"

But then something else unexpected happened. Nancy's husband and her mother died within a month of each other. These two tragedies sent her faith in God reeling again. Her doubts swarmed back. The whole idea of a good God seemed preposterous! How could an all-loving God permit such a horrible thing

to happen. Nancy's mind and heart almost closed themselves to the idea of God.

At this critical point, Nancy decided to put God to the test. In the midst of her darkness and confusion, she began to pray. She begged for a ray of light—just a tiny one. But it never came.

Next, Nancy tried to woo faith into her tortured soul, as a lover woos a beloved. But faith rejected her overtures. Then, in desperation, she began to claw for faith, as a person dying of thirst claws the desert sand for water. But, again, nothing happened. Finally, she fell back exhausted. Nancy later wrote to a friend:

> *That's when it happened. Suddenly, out of nowhere, God entered my soul. There were no signs in the sky, no voices in the night. But I knew in the depths of my being that God was there. How did I know? I can't explain it. I just knew it with all my being.*

Using actual passages from the story about Nancy, show how it illustrates (a) the three main stages through which faith normally passes, (b) the three levels at which faith takes place, (c) the three dynamics that characterize faith. Then respond to the following questions:

- Did your faith ever seem to disappear for a while, as Nancy's did? If so, when (year of grade school or high school)?
- What things did you begin to question, especially, about your faith?
- How did you resolve these questions, or are they still with you?
- On a scale of one (low) to ten (high), evaluate your present faith in (a) God, (b) Jesus, (c) the Church.

2. In *The Empire Strikes Back,* Luke Skywalker flies his X-wing plane to a swamp planet. There he seeks out a guru, named Yoda, to teach him how to become a Jedi warrior. Luke wants to help free his galaxy from the tyranny of Darth Vader. The novel says, "Luke felt ready to unlearn all his old ways ... to learn all this Jedi master had to teach." So Luke didn't complain when Yoda told him to concentrate on trying to lift rocks with his mind. Luke trusted his master. If Yoda said this could be done, then Luke would do it. He tried and succeeded. Then came the day when Yoda told him to concentrate on lifting his X-wing plane with his mind. Luke was skeptical but agreed to try. Slowly the plane budged a little. But then, Luke fell back, exhausted from the concentration. "I can't do it," he said. "It's too big!" "Size has nothing to do with it," Yoda said. With that Yoda began to concentrate. Slowly, the plane floated up into the air. Luke exclaimed, "I don't believe it!" Yoda replied, "That's why you failed."

Explain how this episode is like a faith relationship with God and Jesus. What are some things that keep you from believing more firmly in God? In Jesus? In Jesus' teaching?

3. John Newton was a British sea captain and slave trader. One night a violent storm threatened his ship and his cargo of slaves en route from Africa to America. Newton promised God that he would give up the slave trade and become God's slave forever if his ship made it to port safely. It did, and Newton kept his promise. He studied for the ministry and eventually became a great preacher and composer of hymns. One of his most moving hymns celebrates his conversion. Part of it reads:

> *Amazing grace! how sweet the sound,*
> *That saved a wretch like me!*
> *I once was lost, but now am found—*
> *Was blind, but now I see. . . .*
>
> *Through many dangers, toils, and snares*
> *I have already come;*
> *'Tis grace hath brought me safe thus far,*
> *And grace will lead me home.*

What do we mean by grace? What keeps you from opening yourself to God's grace more fully than you are now doing? Describe a time when you seemed to feel God's grace at work in your life.

4. Explain the meaning of each of the following statements:

- "I have never discarded beliefs deliberately. I have left them in the drawer, and, after a while when I opened it, there was nothing there at all." (William Graham Sumner)
- "If you wish to be convinced of eternal truths, do not augment your arguments but weed out your passions." (Blaise Pascal)
- "Faith is not belief. Belief is passive. Faith is active. It is vision which passes inevitably into action." (Edith Hamilton)

Personal Reflection

A journalist gave this advice to a young friend who was having faith problems:

> *The darkness you are encountering is in itself a rich experience. If it be that you really want to meet our Lord, then it is by moonlight that you must seek him under an olive tree. You will find him flat on the ground, and you will have to lie down on your face with him if you are to catch his words.*

What event in Jesus' life is being referred to when the journalist says "it is by moonlight that you must seek him under an olive tree . . . flat on the ground"? What is the connection between this event and the young person's faith problems? Compose a short prayer to Jesus about some of the questions or problems that you are currently experiencing with regard to your own personal faith.

Bible Reading

Pick a passage. After reading it prayerfully, write out a brief prayer to God that reflects your personal feelings about it.

1. Opening to grace   John 1:35–51
2. Closing to grace   Matthew 19:16–26
3. Trusting in God   Genesis 22:1–19
4. Trusting in Jesus   Luke 5:1–11
5. Moments of darkness   Luke 24:13–35

2 Tradition and Scripture

A sailor was assigned to an artillery gun crew. He was given a pair of heat-resistant gloves and told to catch the foot-long shell casings that ejected from the huge gun after each firing.

The reason for the gloves was that the casings were hot. The reason for catching them was to keep them from rolling around the gun pit and bothering the gun crew.

Suppose we saw someone with heat-resistant gloves holding a shell casing. What are three ways we could learn whether or not the casing was hot?

Finding God

There are three ways of learning whether the shell casing is hot. First, we could touch it and experience the heat ourselves. Second, we could spit on it and, if it sizzled, reason that it was hot. Finally, we could ask the sailor holding the casing. Presumably he knows and will tell us the truth.

Can we find God in nature?

This raises a question. To what extent can we apply these same three *ways of knowing* to God? In other words, to what extent can we know God—

■ by experience,
■ by reason, or
■ by believing another?

Experience Points to God

The famous British author Bede Griffiths recalls this childhood experience.

One summer evening, Griffiths was walking alone outside. Suddenly, he noticed how beautiful everything was. He wondered why he hadn't noticed this beauty before. Griffiths writes:

> *Everything then grew still*
> *as the sunset faded. . . . I remember now*
> *the feeling of awe which came over me.*
> *I felt inclined to kneel on the ground. . . .*
> *Now I was suddenly made aware*
> *of another world of beauty and mystery*
> *such as I had never imagined existed.*
> THE GOLDEN STRING

Griffiths says that it was as if God reached out and touched him at that moment. It was an *experience* he would never forget. "Now that I look back on it," he says, "it seems to me to have been one of the decisive events of my life."

Because this experience had such a decisive impact on his life, Griffiths believes that it was, indeed, an *experience* of God.

Like Griffiths, other people have had similar experiences. And like Griffiths, they too believe they experienced God.

This brings us to the second way of knowing.

Reason Points to God

Whittaker Chambers was a famous American Communist and a staunch atheist. One day something happened that changed all this. He writes:

> *I was sitting in our apartment. . . .*
> *My daughter was in her high chair.*
> *I was watching her eat.*
> *She was the most miraculous thing*
> *that ever happened in my life.*

> *I liked to watch her*
> *even when she smeared porridge on her face*
> *or dropped it meditatively on the floor.*
> *My eye came to rest*
> *on the delicate convolutions of her ear—*
> *those intricate perfect ears.*
> THE WITNESS

Suddenly, the thought occurred to Chambers that those ears could never be the product of chance. They had to be the product of design.

The thought was "involuntary and unwanted." He tried to crowd it out of his mind. For if he completed it, he would have to conclude that design presupposed a designer. Chambers said later, "I did not know it then but, at that moment, the finger of God was laid on my forehead."

Eventually, Chambers reasoned that the beauty and order in our universe demanded the existence of a God. Chance could never explain it.

It was this same order and beauty in the universe that convinced Saint Paul that we could know God from reason alone (Romans 1:20).

This brings us to the third and final way of knowing.

Faith Opens to God

Although many people are convinced that they have experienced God, others are not so sure.

Likewise, many people are convinced that we can reason to God and God's nature from the beauty and order in the universe. But others are not so sure. They say, "Perhaps science will someday find an explanation—other than God—for this beauty and order."

For such people, the only way to know anything for sure about God is to open themselves to what God has revealed through divine *revelation*.

Revelation

The term *revelation* comes from the Latin word meaning "to unveil." By divine revelation we mean God's own "unveiling" of God and God's plan for us.

Divine revelation is a *gift* from God. It gives us a share in God's *divine knowledge*. Its goal is to prepare us for an even greater gift: a share in God's *divine life*. Divine revelation, therefore, is the first step of a larger plan.

Revelation Took Place Gradually

Divine revelation began with God's call to Abraham. It continued with God's self-revelation to Israel by loving deeds: God freed the Israelites, forgave them, and taught them. God inspired people like Moses, Miriam, Deborah, and David to interpret these deeds for the community. God also inspired people like the prophets to record these deeds and their interpretations for future generations.

Divine revelation continued in New Testament times, reaching its ultimate expression in Jesus Christ. The Apostles were the privileged witnesses of this revelation. By the coming of the Holy Spirit, they were enlightened and commissioned to share this revelation with others. Their *apostolic witness* is the *basis* and *norm* for our own Catholic faith.

It is this divine revelation that the Apostles entrusted to the bishops, their successors (Titus 1:7–9). It is this revelation that the Church, guided by the Spirit, never ceases to ponder, develop, and formulate in words that speak more clearly to each new generation. It is this revelation that Saint Paul spoke of when he wrote:

> *God spoke to our ancestors*
> *many times and in many ways*
> *through the prophets,*
> *but in these last days*
> *he has spoken to us*
> *through his Son.*
> HEBREWS 1:1–2

God spoke to our ancestors through the prophets.

We Respond to Revelation

This brings us to our great privilege and responsibility as human beings. It is to open ourselves to God's self-revelation and, with the help of the Holy Spirit, to respond to it. It is to enter into a relationship of love with Jesus and to receive from him the most incredible gift of all: a share in God's own divine life.

We may view divine revelation, therefore, as taking two forms: *immediate* revelation and *mediate* revelation. By *immediate* revelation we mean the "unveiling" of God and God's plan to the community of God's people in biblical times. By *mediate* revelation we mean the "handing on" of that divine revelation to future generations. A more popular name that we give this *mediate* revelation is *tradition*.

Tradition

The word *tradition* comes from the Latin word meaning to "hand on." By tradition, we mean two things: the *content* of revelation that is "handed on," and the *process* by which it is "handed on." First, consider the *content*.

When we speak of the *content* of tradition, we mean both teachings and practices. These teachings and practices may be either essential to the faith (can't be changed) or nonessential to the faith (can be changed for a good reason).

An example of *essential* tradition is the teaching that Jesus is *really present* in the Eucharist. Concerning this teaching, Saint John writes:

> *Jesus said . . . "I am the living bread*
> *that came down from heaven.*
> *If anyone eats this bread, he will live forever.*
>
> *"The bread that I will give him is my flesh,*
> *which I give so that the world may live. . . .*
> *For my flesh is the real food;*
> *my blood is the real drink.*
>
> *"Whoever eats my flesh and drinks my blood*
> *lives in me, and I live in him."*
>
> JOHN 6:32, 51, 55–56

This teaching can never be changed. We sometimes refer to *essential tradition* as tradition with a capital *T*.

An example of *nonessential* tradition is the practice that priests don't marry. This tradition can be changed for a good reason. We sometimes refer to *nonessential* tradition as tradition with a small *t*.

Ultimately the Church, guided by the Holy Spirit, decides which traditions are *essential* and which are *nonessential*.

This brings us to the *process* of tradition. When we speak of tradition as being a *process,* we mean the way in which revelation is "handed on." This *process* takes two forms: spoken word and written word. Thus we speak of—

- *oral* tradition: handing on revelation by the spoken word, and
- *written* tradition: handing on revelation by the written word.

At first, God's revelation to the people of biblical times was "handed on" almost entirely by the spoken word, or *oral* tradition. Only later was it written down. The most important form that *written* tradition takes is Scripture.

"I am the living bread that came down from heaven. If anyone eats this bread, he will live forever."

Scripture

Some people are surprised to learn that large parts of Scripture were *not* written down immediately. Rather, they were passed on orally for a considerable length of time. Scripture itself makes this clear.

For example, Saint Matthew says that after Jesus rose from the dead, the guards were paid to say that the disciples stole Jesus' body while they slept. He then adds, "That is the report spread around by the Jews to this very day" (Matthew 28:15).

The words "to this very day" indicate that a considerable length of time elapsed between the actual event and Matthew's recording of it.

This brings us to a very important point.

Not All Revelation Is Recorded

Sometimes people are surprised to learn that the Gospels do not contain all the *oral* traditions about Jesus. But the Gospel writers make this quite clear. For example, the concluding sentence in Saint John's Gospel reads:

> *Now, there are many other things
> that Jesus did.
> If they were all written down one by one,
> I suppose that the whole world
> could not hold the books.*
> JOHN 21:25

This means that not all the *oral* traditions about Jesus were recorded in Scripture. Rather, many of them continued to be "handed on" by word of mouth. Saint Paul alludes to this when he writes:

> *Hold on to those truths [traditions]
> which we taught you,
> both in our preaching
> and in our letter.*
> 2 THESSALONIANS 2:15

An example of an oral tradition that was not written down in Scripture is the teaching that Mary, the mother of Jesus, remained a virgin all

This fifteenth-century Italian wood carving portrays Saint Matthew composing his Gospel. Unaware that books did not appear until about a hundred and fifty years after Matthew lived, the artist has the evangelist write in a book, not on a scroll.

her life. There are many references to this teaching in early Christian writings, but it was never explicitly recorded in Scripture.

This brings us to another important point.

Scripture Is Inspired

We often speak of written tradition as being *inspired.* Thus Saint Paul writes, "All Scripture is inspired by God" (2 Timothy 3:16). To understand what we mean when we speak of Scripture as being inspired, we need to recall something that Jesus said. Speaking to his disciples about the coming of the Holy Spirit, Jesus said:

> *"When . . . the Spirit comes,
> who reveals the truth about God,
> he will lead you into all the truth."*
> JOHN 16:13

By these words, Jesus assured his disciples that the Holy Spirit would assist them in understanding and in communicating God's revelation to them.

And so by the word *inspiration* we mean that the Holy Spirit enlightened and assisted the biblical writers in such a way that they wrote all and only what the Spirit intended them to write.

Because the Bible is inspired, we may draw this important conclusion: The Bible is free from error *in matters that relate to our salvation.* This does not mean that the Spirit also protected the biblical writers from historical and scientific error. God never intended them to compose books on science and history.

Nor is the Bible free from scientific and historical error. For example, Deuteronomy 14:7 lists the hare among those animals that chew cud, a fact that is scientifically inaccurate. Nor is it free from historical error. For example, 1 Samuel 31:4 says that Saul killed himself, while 2 Samuel 1:9–10 says someone else killed him.

What Books Belong to Scripture?

The Bible is divided into two main parts: the Hebrew Scriptures (Old Testament) and the Christian Scriptures (New Testament). Each of these two parts is further divided into books.

There is disagreement between Catholics and Protestants on the *canon* of Hebrew Scriptures. The word *canon* derives from the Greek word for "measuring stick." As used of the Bible, it means the *official list* of books inspired by God and, therefore, serving as the "measuring stick," or norm, for faith.

Catholics include seven books that Protestants do not. These books are:

1 and 2 Maccabees
Judith
Tobit
Baruch
Sirach
Wisdom

The disagreement stems from early times when Jews themselves could not agree on these books. Many Jews who converted to Christianity had been using a larger collection of religious writings, called the *Septuagint.*

Inspiration and the Bible

The Last Temptation of Jesus is a controversial novel by Nikos Kazantzakis. One episode in the novel describes Jesus discovering Matthew writing in a book. Matthew stopped and said to Jesus: "Here I recount your life and works for men of the future." Then he handed the book to Jesus. After reading a few paragraphs, Jesus looked puzzled and asked Matthew where he got his information. Matthew answered, "The angel revealed it to me. . . . The one who comes each night . . . and dictates what I write."

Two extreme theories are proposed as to *how* the Holy Spirit inspired the biblical writers.

The first is that the Holy Spirit dictated to them similar to the way the angel dictated to Matthew in Kazantzakis's novel. It is sometimes called the "divine dictation" theory. It reduces the biblical writers to robots who simply record what the Holy Spirit, in some unknown way, dictates to them.

The second theory is that the biblical writers were inspired in a "religious" way, much as songwriters are inspired in a "musical" way. According to this theory, the Holy Spirit simply intervened when the biblical writers were on the verge of making an error. This second theory is sometimes called the "negative assistance" theory. It reduces the Holy Spirit to a "divine watchdog" who keeps the biblical writers from making any mistakes.

The Church rejects both of these extremes. It holds that the first theory goes too far and that the second theory doesn't go far enough. In other words, the first theory has the Holy Spirit doing too much; the second theory has the Holy Spirit doing too little.

The Church's understanding of the mystery of inspiration is sometimes called the "positive assistance" theory. It holds that the Holy Spirit enlightened and assisted the biblical writers in a positive, divine way. What the exact nature of the Spirit's contribution was, they don't try to say. For like everything divine, it partakes of mystery. This much can be said, however. Whatever the Holy Spirit's positive contribution was, it left the biblical writers free to use their own talents and resources in the process. Because of this, we can rightly say that the Bible is "the word of God in the words of men."

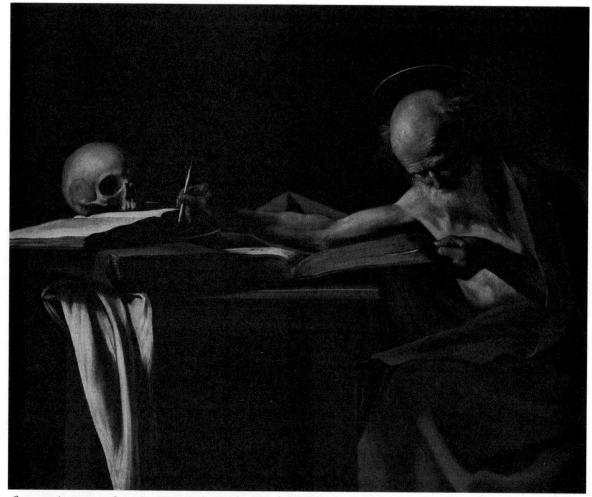

Caravaggio portrays Saint Jerome translating the Bible from Hebrew and Greek into Latin some four hundred years after Jesus' birth.

This collection was translated from Hebrew into Greek about two hundred fifty years before Jesus' birth. It was this *larger* collection that Matthew, Mark, Luke, John, and the other New Testament authors quoted over three hundred times in composing the Christian Scriptures.

When Jews finally defined their canon, about a century after Jesus' birth, they dropped the seven books of the larger collection. Sixteenth-century Protestants followed the later Hebrew canon. Today many Protestants include the seven disputed books in their Bible, but in a separate section apart from the others.

Although Catholics and Protestants disagree on the canon of the Hebrew Scriptures, they agree on the canon of the Christian Scriptures.

Recap

Divine revelation is God's own "unveiling" of God and God's plan for us. *Tradition* is the "handing on" of God's revelation from one generation to another, either by the *spoken* or the *written* word. The *Scriptures* are the most important form that written tradition takes.

The Scriptures include forty-six books called the *Hebrew Scriptures* (Old Testament) and twenty-seven books called the *Christian Scriptures* (New Testament).

When we say the Scriptures are *inspired,* we mean that the Holy Spirit assisted the biblical writers so that what they wrote is free from error in matters that relate to salvation.

Books of the Bible

Many books of the Bible are in a class by themselves. Trying to classify them is difficult. Nevertheless, at the risk of oversimplification, we may list and classify the seventy-three books of the Bible as follows.

HEBREW SCRIPTURES
(46 books)

PENTATEUCH
(5 books)

Genesis
Exodus
Leviticus
Numbers
Deuteronomy

WISDOM BOOKS
(7 books)

Job
Psalms
Proverbs
Ecclesiastes
Song of Songs
Wisdom
Sirach

HISTORICAL BOOKS
(16 books)

Joshua
Judges
1-2 Samuel
1-2 Kings
1-2 Chronicles
Ezra
Nehemiah
1-2 Maccabees

PROPHETIC BOOKS
(18 books)

Major Prophets

Isaiah
Jeremiah
Lamentations
Baruch
Ezekiel
Daniel

Special

Ruth
Tobit
Judith
Esther

Minor Prophets

Hosea	Haggai
Amos	Zechariah
Micah	Obadiah
Nahum	Joel
Habbakkuk	Jonah
Zephaniah	Malachi

CHRISTIAN SCRIPTURES
(27 books)

GOSPELS
(4 books)

Matthew	Luke
Mark	John

ACTS OF THE APOSTLES
(1 book)

LETTERS
(21 books)

Paul's Letters

Early	*Great*
1-2 Thessalonians	Galatians
	1-2 Corinthians
	Romans

Prison	*Pastoral*
Philippians	1-2 Timothy
Colossians	Titus
Ephesians	
Philemon	

Other Letters

General	*Special*
1-2-3 John	Hebrews
1-2 Peter	
James	
Jude	

BOOK OF REVELATION
(1 book)

Understanding Tradition and Scripture

Review

Finding God

1. List and explain the three ways we can know things.

2. What convinced Bede Griffiths that he had, indeed, experienced God?

3. What convinced Whittaker Chambers that reason demanded the existence of God?

4. Why is "believing" the only certain way for some people to learn about God?

Revelation

5. What do we mean by divine revelation?

6. List and explain the two stages of divine revelation.

Tradition

7. Explain the following: (a) tradition as *process,* (b) tradition as *content,* (c) oral tradition, (d) written tradition, (e) essential tradition, (f) nonessential tradition.

8. What is the most important form that written tradition takes?

9. Give an example of each of the following: (a) essential tradition, (b) nonessential tradition.

Scripture

10. Give an example to show how a considerable length of time often elapsed between an event described in Scripture and the recording of it.

11. Explain how Saint Paul makes it clear that an oral tradition continued along with written tradition.

12. Give an example of the following: (a) an important revelation that is not recorded in the Gospel but is preserved by oral tradition, (b) a historical error in the Bible, (c) a scientific error in the Bible.

13. Explain what we mean by the following: (a) inspiration, (b) canon of the Bible.

14. Because the Bible is inspired, what important conclusion can we draw concerning it?

15. What is the *Septuagint* and how does it help to explain why Catholics and Protestants differ regarding the canon of the Hebrew Scriptures?

16. List the seven books that Catholics accept as inspired, but which Protestants do not.

Inspiration and the Bible

17. List and explain two theories that people have proposed concerning *how* God inspired the biblical writers, and tell why modern scholars reject these theories?

18. Explain (a) how modern scholars think God inspired the biblical writers and (b) in what sense we may say that the Bible is truly "the word of God in the words of men."

Books of the Bible

19. List the four major groups into which the books of the Hebrew Scriptures are divided and the number of books in each group.

20. List the four major groups into which the books of the Christian Scriptures are divided and the number of books in each.

Exercises

1. A. Cressy Morrison is a former president of the New York Academy of Sciences. His book *Man Does Not Stand Alone* lists seven reasons why he believes in God. The first reason is the incredible complexity of the universe. He suggests this experiment to illustrate that this complexity cannot be the product of chance. Take ten pennies and mark them 1 to 10. Put them in your pocket and give them a shake. Then try to draw them out in sequence from 1 to 10, putting each coin back after each draw.

What are the odds that you will draw (a) 1 on the first try, (b) 1 and 2 in a row, (c) 1, 2, and 3 in a row, (d) all ten in a row? How does this experiment illustrate that the complexity of the universe cannot be explained by chance?

2. Suppose a TV camera crew got into a time machine and flew back into history to Jesus' time. Suppose the crew filmed Jesus' entire life, fed it into a computer, and programmed it. By typing the name of any event, you could bring it up on a screen and see and hear exactly what the Apostles did and said.

Now suppose you are given a choice. You could trade the four printed Gospels (that we now have) for the computerized film. If you traded, the human race would lose the four printed Gospels forever. They would be replaced by the computerized film.

Why would/wouldn't you make that trade? List some of the advantages and disadvantages that a film of Jesus' life would have.

3. Bob Richards, an Olympic gold medal pole vaulter, says that he will always remember two "expressions of faith in God" from his Olympic experiences. The first is the sight of United States basketball star Bill Bradley giving a Russian athlete a Bible, saying, "It's the most important thing I own." The second is the sight of United States pole vaulter Fred Hansen reading a letter from his father, in between vaults. In the letter, Fred's father reminded him of these words of the prophet Isaiah:

> *Those who trust in the LORD for help*
> *will find their strength renewed.*
> *They will rise on wings like eagles;*
> *they will run and not get weary;*
> *they will walk and not grow weak.*
> ISAIAH 40:31

Describe an "expression of faith in God" by a family member or a friend that you will probably "always remember."

Personal Reflection

A high school girl writes:

> *I woke up Sunday morning feeling unusually depressed. I don't know why, because this was the day of the big outdoor rock concert at Hawthorne Racetrack. While waiting in the long line to enter the track, my depression began to leave. Once inside the track, we sprawled out on the grass with thousands of others.*
>
> *After the second band finished playing, I looked around, seeing what looked like a million people. (In truth there were about 70,000.) Wow! What a sight! Now I was really starting to feel good. The sound system was awesome, and everyone was like best friends, sharing whatever they had. When it came time for the last band, my friends and I moved closer to the stage. The band opened with a rock classic that energized everyone. As far as you could see, everybody was on their feet, clapping their hands over their heads, and swaying with the music. It was fantastic. Then right in the midst of these supersensational vibrations, a strange thought popped into my head. I thought to myself: "God has got to be right here with us."*
>
> *While eating supper later at a restaurant, I shared this thought with my friends, and they all felt the same way.*

Describe in writing one of the following: (a) one of the best times you ever enjoyed with some close friends, as the girl enjoyed with her friends at the rock concert, (b) a time when you felt God's presence, as the girl did at the concert.

Bible Reading

Pick a passage. After reading it prayerfully, write out a brief prayer to God that reflects your feelings or thoughts about it.

1. Reasoning to God   Romans 1:20–25
2. Experiencing God   Genesis 3:1–17
3. Believing in God   John 20:24–29
4. Written stage   Luke 1:1–4
5. Scripture is inspired   2 Timothy 3:14–4:5

3 Hebrew Scriptures

The Book of Genesis is the first book of the Hebrew Scriptures. The first chapter of Genesis says that God created people last. But the second chapter says that God created people first. The first chapter also says that God created light on the first day, but didn't create the sun until the fourth day.

Contradictory statements like these led one woman to say, "The Bible is responsible for more atheism and agnosticism than any other book ever written."

This raises two important questions. First, when these statements were recorded, wasn't the biblical writer aware of the apparent contradictions in them? And second, if so, why did the writer record them anyway?

Interpreting the Bible

The question of "apparent contradictions" in the Bible brings us to the important subject of biblical interpretation.

Bible readers may be divided into two groups: literalists and contextualists.

Literalists interpret the Bible rigidly, saying, "It means exactly what it says." In other words, literalists (also called *fundamentalists*) concern themselves with only the *text* of the Bible.

Contextualists interpet the Bible more broadly, saying, "We must consider not only the *text* but also the *context* of the Bible. In other words, we must also consider such things as the historical and cultural situation in which the Bible was written."

To see how contextualists interpret the Bible, consider the creation story in the Book of Genesis. You may wish to reread it at this point (Genesis 1:1–2:4).

The Creation Story

The Book of Genesis describes creation as taking place in six days. The description of each day follows a *somewhat similar* poetic pattern:

- introduction: "Then God commanded,"
- command: "Let the water . . . ,"
- execution: "It was done,"
- rejoicing: "God was pleased,"
- identification: "the third day."

What is true of each *day* of creation is true also of the week of creation. It too follows a poetic pattern:

- three days of separation (light from dark, water from water, water from land),
- three days of population (sky, air and sea, land), and
- one day of celebration (God blessed and rested).

The literary patterns of the creation story suggest that we are dealing with a special kind of writing. It is not the kind of writing found in a science book or a newspaper report. Rather, it is the kind of writing found in children's books. It is a kind of *poetic* writing. Authors of children's books often use simple poetic stories to teach children about life.

The Genesis writer used a similar approach in composing the creation story. The writer used simple poetic stories to teach people about God and creation. (Recall that most ancient peoples could not read or write. They learned by listening.) Poetic stories were enjoyable to listen to and easy to remember.

God was pleased with all that was created.

What about Angels? And Satan?

Christian tradition teaches that angels are a part of God's *unseen* creation. We refer to this belief in the Creed at Mass, when we profess our faith in God, the "maker" of "all that is seen and *unseen.*"

The word *angel* comes from the Greek word *angelos,* which translates the Hebrew word *mal'ak* ("messenger"). The Hebrew Scriptures portray angels as being messengers of God. For example, the Book of Genesis says an "angel of the LORD" kept Abraham from sacrificing Isaac (Genesis 22:11).

The Christian Scriptures portray angels in a similar way. For example, an angel announces to Mary that she is to be the mother of Jesus (Luke 1:26).

Jesus referred to angels on a number of occasions. For example, he said of a group of children, "Their angels in heaven . . . are always in the presence of my Father" (Matthew 18:10).

Christian tradition holds that after the angels were created by God, they underwent a "test," as Adam and Eve did. Like Adam and Eve, a vast number failed.

This leads to a second question: What about Satan and the other evil spirits that Scripture speaks of? Christian tradition identifies these beings with "fallen angels," who failed the test given them by God (Revelation 12:9-10).

The Gospels portray Satan and the other evil spirits as opposing Jesus at every stage of his ministry. They portray Jesus as engaged in an all-out battle to overthrow "Satan's kingdom" and establish in its place the "Kingdom of God" (Luke 11:14-23).

It is that same struggle that the Christian community is involved in today—both at a *personal* level and at a *social* level. This struggle with evil will continue in every human heart and in every nation until the end of the world.

Creation Story Teaching

A study of the creation story reveals that it teaches four new religious truths. These truths may be summarized as follows:

- There is only one God;
- God planned creation;
- God created everything good;
- God made the Sabbath holy.

Let's take a closer look at each of these four religious truths.

There Is Only One God

To understand the first religious truth that the creation story teaches, we need to consider the *context* in which the story was written. The biblical author composed it at a time when people worshiped every kind of god imaginable. Deuteronomy 4:15–19 refers to this when it warns its readers not to worship things like other humans, animals, birds, or heavenly bodies.

It is against this background that the biblical writer portrays God creating all the "gods" that other people worshiped. The biblical writer's point is this: If God created these gods, they cannot be God. Rather, there is only one God, the one who created them.

And so the first new teaching of the creation story may be summarized this way:

- Old teaching: There are many gods.
- New teaching: There is only one God.
- How taught: The one God creates other "gods."

God Planned Creation

To understand the second religious truth that the creation story teaches, we need to consider its *context* again. The biblical writer composed the creation story at a time when people believed that the world came into being by chance. (Even today, some people still believe this.)

It is against this background that the biblical writer portrays God creating the world in an orderly way and according to a plan—much as

God created everything good.

ancient carpenters built ancient structures. The biblical writer's point is this: God planned the world; it did not happen by chance.

And so the second new teaching of the creation story may be summarized this way:

- Old teaching: Creation happened by chance.
- New teaching: Creation was planned by God.
- How taught: God creates in an orderly way.

God Created Everything Good

To understand the third religious truth that the creation story teaches, we again need to look at the *context* in which it was written. Many ancient peoples believed that parts of creation were evil. For example, they believed the human body was evil, because it seemed to war against the spirit.

Against this background the biblical writer has God affirm that everything is good, including the human body.

And so the third new teaching of the creation story may be summarized this way:

- Old teaching: Creation is partially good.
- New teaching: Creation is totally good.
- How taught: God affirms the goodness of creation.

God Made the Sabbath Holy

This brings us to the final religious truth that the creation story teaches. To understand this truth, we must remember that in ancient times the Sabbath day was considered to be like any other day.

Against this background the biblical writer portrays God as blessing the Sabbath day and resting on it. The biblical writer's point is this: God made the Sabbath to be a holy day of rest and prayer.

And so the final new teaching of the creation story may be summarized this way:

- Old teaching: The Sabbath is like other days.
- New teaching: The Sabbath is a holy day.
- How taught: God blesses the Sabbath and rests on it.

In brief, the contextualist interprets the creation story as teaching four important truths—truths that were new and revolutionary in the context of their time:

- There is only one God;
- God planned creation;
- God made everything good;
- God made the Sabbath holy.

The De-creation Story

In his book *Our Plundered Planet,* Fairfield Osborne warns, "Another century like the last and our civilization will be facing its final crisis." What Osborne warns us about is the subject of an anonymous satirical poem called "De-creation":

In the beginning was the earth,
and the earth was beautiful.
But the people living on the earth said,
"Let us build skyscrapers
and expressways."
So they paved the earth with concrete
and said, "It is good!"

On the second day,
the people looked at the rivers and said,
"Let us dump our sewage into the waters."
So they filled the waters with sludge
and said, "It is good!"

On the third day,
the people looked at the forest and said,
"Let us cut down the trees
and build things."
So they leveled the forests
and said, "It is good!"

On the fourth day,
the people saw the animals and said,
"Let us kill them for sport and money."
So they destroyed the animals
and said, "It is good!"

On the fifth day,
the people felt the cool breeze and said,
"Let us burn our garbage
and let the breeze blow it away."
So they filled the air with carbon
and said, "It is good!"

On the sixth day,
the people saw other nations on earth
and said,
"Let us build missiles
in case misunderstandings arise."
So they filled the land with missile sites
and said, "It is good!"

On the seventh day,
the earth was quiet and deathly silent,
for the people were no more.
And it was good!

The poem "De-creation" dramatizes the fact that industrial wastes are pouring into the earth's atmosphere to the point that clouds are producing acid rain. Acid rain, in turn, is slowly polluting the lakes and destroying the forests. Similar industrial wastes are pouring into the upper atmosphere to the point that the earth's ozone layer is eroding. This erosion, in turn, is threatening the future of the planet.

The ruthless devastation of the environment caused by pollution is sometimes referred to as "de-creation": the *physical* destruction of God's creation.

As tragic as the *physical* de-creation is, however, there is an even worse de-creation taking place. It is *spiritual* de-creation: the *spiritual* destruction of God's creation.

Spiritual de-creation has its origin in the human heart. It consists in misusing the free will that God gave us. Catholic tradition calls spiritual de-creation *sin.*

Sin

Sin is an unpopular topic today. People are reluctant to talk about it. They are even more reluctant to admit that they sin. This reluctance has a lot of people worried.

For example, you wouldn't expect the dean of American psychiatry to start talking about sin. But that's exactly what Dr. Karl Menninger does in his book *Whatever Became of Sin?* He is disturbed by the fact that so many people today refuse to admit that they sin.

We will discuss sin in detail later. For our purposes here, we may describe sin as a fracture or a total break in our love relationship with God and God's people.

We may divide sin into two categories: *personal* and *social.*

Personal Sin Involves Individuals

The first category of sin is called *personal* because it concerns the free act of a single individual. It takes two forms: *commission* and *omission.*

A personal sin of *commission* consists in doing something we should not do. For example, we lie or steal. A personal sin of *omission,* on the other hand, consists in *not* doing something we should do. For example, we see people in need but look the other way to avoid the inconvenience of helping them.

Social Sin Involves Groups

The second category of sin is called *social* because it involves the collective behavior of a group of people, like a community or a nation. It also takes two forms: *commission* and *omission.* For example, a social sin of *commission* occurs when a group of people discriminates against a minority group in its midst. A social sin of *omission* occurs when a community ignores its poor and homeless or lets industry pollute the environment.

Social sin is especially destructive because no single individual feels responsible for it. Social sin is something "society" does, not "me."

Social evil is tolerated for many reasons. For example, people excuse themselves, saying that their isolated opposition is too tiny to make

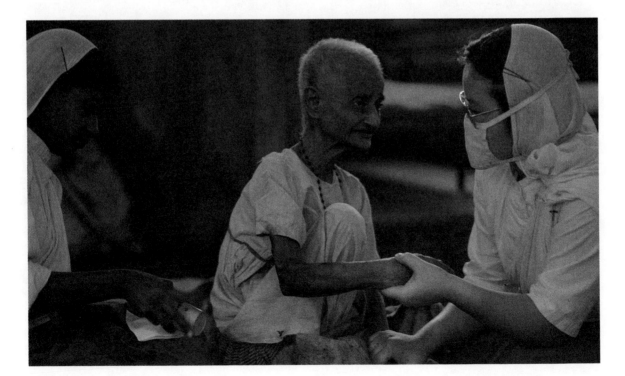

a difference. But regardless of their reasons or excuses, the bottom line on social sin is this: The responsibility to oppose it rests with individuals. Individuals who shirk this responsibility are guilty of a *personal* sin of *omission*. For as Martin Luther King noted: "Whoever accepts evil without protesting against it is really cooperating with it."

De-creation Raises a Question

The widespread presence of evil in our world poses a vexing question: If God created everything good, where did evil come from?

The biblical writer responds to this question right after the creation story. The writer's response may be called the "de-creation story."

This story begins with a snake entering the garden into which God placed the first couple. The snake then addresses the woman:

"Did God really tell you
not to eat fruit
from any tree in the garden?"

"We may eat the fruit
of any tree in the garden,"
the woman answered,
"except the tree in the middle of it.
God told us
not to eat the fruit of that tree
or even touch it; if we do, we will die."

The snake replied,
"That's not true; you will not die.
God said that because he knows
that when you eat it,
you will be like God
and know what is good and what is bad."

The woman saw how beautiful the tree was
and how good its fruit would be to eat,
and she thought how wonderful it would be
to become wise.
So she took some of the fruit and ate it.
Then she gave some to her husband,
and he also ate it.

As soon as they had eaten it,
they were given understanding
and realized that they were naked;
so they sewed fig leaves together
and covered themselves.
GENESIS 3:1–7

De-creation Teaching

Contextualists interpret the de-creation story the same way they interpret the creation story. It is somewhat like the parables that Jesus told. It is a *symbol* story, created by the biblical writer to answer the question, If God created everything good, how did evil enter the world?

The key to understanding the biblical writer's answer lies in two sets of symbols used in the creation story. The first set precedes the first sin; the second set follows it. They are—

- the *snake* and
- the *eating* of the fruit,

- the *awareness* of nakedness and
- the couple's *expulsion* from the garden.

Let's begin with the first set of symbols and see how they provide the answer to the question, If God created everything good, how did evil enter the world?

Sin Brings Evil

The key symbol is the snake. To understand it, we must keep in mind the *historical* context in which the de-creation story was composed.

Archaeology reveals that snakes played a bizarre role in the worship ceremony of the Canaanites, the ancient enemy of the Hebrew people. Thus the snake became a symbol of evil to the Hebrews, who regarded Canaanite worship as an abomination. And so the snake symbolizes the *devil* in the de-creation story.

This brings us to the second symbol: the *eating* of the fruit. Recall that the snake told the woman that if she *ate* the fruit, she would *know* good from bad. The snake makes a connection between *eating* and *knowing.* To understand this connection, we must, again, keep in mind the historical *context* in which the de-creation story was composed.

Because most ancient peoples could not read, *experience* became a major source of *knowledge* for them. This explains the connection between

This stained-glass window portrays the re-creation story. The top panel portrays salvation. God says to the snake (Satan): "Her offspring [Jesus] will crush your head" (Genesis 3:15). The middle panel portrays salvation begun. The cloth-draped cross symbolizes Jesus' death and resurrection. The boat symbolizes the Church, which Jesus founded. The bottom panel portrays salvation continuing. The net symbolizes the Church continuing the work of Jesus, who said to Peter, the former fisherman, "Come with me, and I will teach you to catch men" (Matthew 4:19).

eating and *knowing. To eat* means *to know* by *experience.* It is a symbolic way of saying that the first couple *learned* about evil by *experiencing* it. They "tasted" evil. They became evil. They sinned.

And so the biblical writer's answer to the question about how evil entered the world is this: It entered the world through the first sin of the first couple.

This brings us to the second set of symbols: *awareness* of nakedness and *expulsion* from the garden. Let's now investigate their meaning.

Sin Dooms the Human Race

After the first couple sinned, the Bible says they were *aware* that they were naked (Genesis 3:7). To understand this strange statement, we need to go back to the creation story. There we read, "The man and the woman were both naked, but they were not embarrassed" (Genesis 2:25).

The couple's *awareness* of nakedness *after* they sinned symbolizes that sin did something to them. They were no longer at ease with themselves. Something went wrong inside them. Sin "flawed" them.

The couple's *expulsion* from the garden brings down the curtain on the de-creation story. The point of the expulsion is obvious. It symbolizes that because of sin the first couple is now separated from God.

And so the first sin not only introduced evil into the world but also "flawed" the first couple and "separated" them from God. The first sin did even more. It opened the floodgates of sin. Soon sin engulfed the world (Genesis 11:1–9). The human race was *doomed.*

The tragic situation or state that the first sin produced in the world is sometimes referred to as the *state of original sin.* This means that the first sin of the first couple—

- introduced evil into the world,
- flawed the human race, and
- doomed it to destruction.

And so the biblical writer's answer to the question about how evil entered the world is as follows: Evil entered the world through the first sin of the first couple, which flawed and doomed their offspring.

The Re-creation Story

After the first sin, the only hope of the human race was that God would intervene and rescue it from destruction. And that is exactly what God decided to do. God decided to re-create the human race.

God's rescue and re-creation of the human race began with a man named Abram.

God Covenants with Abram

> [One day] the LORD said to Abram,
> "Leave your country,
> your relatives, and your father's home,
> and go to a land
> that I am going to show you. . . .
>
> "I make this covenant with you:
> I promise that you will be the ancestor
> of many nations.
> Your name will no longer be Abram,
> but Abraham,
> because I am making you the ancestor
> of many nations. . . .
>
> "You must no longer
> call your wife Sarai;
> from now on her name is Sarah.
> I will bless her,
> and I will give you a son by her. . . .
> You will name him Isaac."
> GENESIS 12:1; 17:4–5, 15–16, 19

And so God's covenant with Abram and Sarai changes their life in a remarkable way. It gives Abraham a—

- new identity: God's chosen person, and a
- new destiny: father of many nations.

Eventually, Sarah gave birth to Isaac. He grew up, married Rebecca, and they had two sons: Esau and Jacob.

One night while Jacob was sleeping under the stars, God said to him: "Your name is Jacob, but from now on it will be Israel" (Genesis 35:10).

Israel became the father of twelve sons, forerunners of the twelve tribes of Israel, who became known as Israelites.

Jacob's favorite son was Joseph. One day, in a fit of jealousy, Joseph's brothers sold him into slavery in Egypt. There he rose to prominence by foretelling a famine and preparing Egypt for it.

Joseph invited his family to come to Egypt. They came, prospered, and grew into a great people. After Joseph died, however, they fell into disfavor and were enslaved by the Egyptians. Eventually, a leader named Moses arose to lead them out of Egypt to freedom.

God Covenants with Israel

Moses led the Israelites out of Egypt to the foot of Mount Sinai. There God covenanted with them, giving them a—

- new identity: God's Chosen People, and a
- new destiny: leaven of nations.

The Israelites became God's *Chosen* People in the sense that God chose them to be a leaven (or instrument) to prepare the other nations of the world for the re-creation of the human race.

After covenanting with the Israelites, God schooled them in the desert and, eventually, led them into the land promised to Abraham, their father.

In the "promised land," God formed the Israelites into a powerful nation. God also raised up a great leader to shepherd them. That leader was David.

God Covenants with David

David made Jerusalem the capital of his nation. Then came a remarkable moment. God promised David:

> "You will always have descendants,
> and I will make your kingdom last forever.
> Your dynasty will never end."
> 2 SAMUEL 7:16

Ancient cathedrals have been called "Bibles in stone." This was because ancient artists retold the main Bible stories in sculptured stone. The five Old Testament figures shown here are part of France's 700-year-old Cathedral of Chartres. Each holds a symbol that says something about his role in the Bible: Melchizedek holds a chalice (Genesis 14:18); Abraham holds Isaac (Genesis 22:1–12); Moses holds a stone tablet (Deuteronomy 5:22); Samuel holds a lamb (1 Samuel 7:9); David holds a crown (2 Samuel 5:4).

This promise is one of the most important in the Bible, for it begins a series of promises called the "messianic prophecies." They point to the coming of a king (Messiah) from David's line, whose kingdom (God's Kingdom) will "stand firm forever." And so God covenants with David, giving him a—

- new identity: God's chosen king, and a
- new destiny: ancestor of the Messiah.

Times of Trial Come

After David's death, a civil war split the nation in two: Israel (north) and Judah (south).

With the passage of the centuries, Israel was conquered and destroyed. Centuries later, Judah was conquered and condemned to forced labor in Babylon. For fifty years the people of Judah lived in a foreign land. But, because of prophets like Ezekiel, they kept their faith alive. Finally, the day came when the people of Judah were able to return to their homeland and rebuild it.

In the centuries following Judah's return from exile, the tiny nation went through one trial after another. These trials tested Judah's faith in God. They asked themselves, "Whatever happened to God's covenant with us? Whatever happened to the promised Messiah? Whatever happened to the promised kingdom?"

The People Wait and Pray

The Hebrew Scriptures end without their final chapter being written. They end with the people waiting for God to act. They end with devout Jews praying for the coming of the promised Messiah and promised Kingdom of God.

And so the people gathered each Sabbath in synagogues to read the Scriptures and to wait for God to resume the work of "re-creating" the world. They never lost hope.

Recap

To interpret the forty-six books of the *Hebrew Scriptures* correctly, we need to consider not only their *text* but also their *context*.

The *content* of the Hebrew Scriptures may be divided into three parts: the *creation* story (God makes us), the *de-creation* story (we sin), and the *re-creation* story (God saves us).

The *re-creation* story involves covenants with Abram, Israel, and David. God's covenant with David began a series of prophecies called the *messianic* prophecies. They point to a king (Messiah) from David's line, whose kingdom (God's Kingdom) will never end.

Understanding Hebrew Scriptures

Review

Interpreting the Bible

1. List and explain the two major groups into which Bible readers fall.

The Creation Story

2. List and illustrate the general pattern used to describe each day of creation.

3. List and illustrate the general pattern used to describe the week of creation.

4. What do these patterns suggest about the kind of writing used in the creation story? Why did the biblical writer use this kind of writing?

Creation Story Teaching

5. List and explain (a) the *new teachings* contained in the creation story, (b) the *old beliefs* these teachings replace, (c) how the biblical writer communicates each new teaching.

The De-creation Story

6. Explain the two ways our world is being de-created. Give an example of each.

Sin

7. Explain the following kinds of sin: (a) personal, (b) social, (c) commission, (d) omission. Give an example of each.

8. Explain the following points concerning *social* sin: (a) why it is especially bad, (b) one reason why we tolerate it, (c) the bottom line on where the responsibility to oppose it rests.

9. What serious question does the widespread presence of evil in the world pose?

De-creation Teaching

10. Explain the meaning of the following symbols in the de-creation story: (a) snake, (b) eating of fruit, (c) awareness of nakedness, (d) expulsion from the garden.

11. Describe what is meant by original sin, listing the threefold impact it had on the human race.

The Re-creation Story

12. Explain the new *identity* and the new *destiny* that God's covenants gave to (a) Abram, (b) Israel, (c) David.

13. Explain why God's covenant promise to David is one of the most important in the Bible.

14. Into what two groups did a civil war split God's Chosen People after David's death, and what happened to each group?

15. How do the Hebrew Scriptures end?

What about Angels? And Satan?

16. Explain the origin and role of (a) good spirits and (b) evil spirits.

Exercises

1. The movie *Lili* is a delightful fantasy about a girl who is a member of a traveling carnival in France. She becomes depressed one day because she thinks no one cares about her, especially the carnival's young, bashful puppeteer. Her only friends are the puppets of the young puppeteer. She decides to run away. Before leaving, however, Lili says good-bye to the puppets. As they hug her and weep, Lili suddenly feels them trembling. Only then does she make the connection between the puppets and the puppeteer.

How is this sequence in the movie a kind of parable of God and the human race? In other words, what do the following stand for: Lili, the young puppeteer, the puppets? Describe a time when you felt like leaving home.

2. *Greenpeace* magazine (July/August 1990) contains these alarming facts concerning the de-creation of our planet:

- The automobile is the biggest single source of "greenhouse gases," which threaten our planet. Even clean-burning cars produce twenty pounds of carbon dioxide for every gallon of gas they burn.
- Do-it-yourself mechanics in the world (who change their own car oil) dump more oil down sewers in two and one half weeks than the *Exxon Valdez* dumped in the big Alaskan spill.
- India and China have 40 percent of the planet's population but less than 1 percent of its cars. Yet they are also victims of the destructive impact that cars have on the planet.
- Los Angeles drivers waste one out of four gallons of gas simply by idling their cars in traffic jams.

Which of these facts disturbs you most? If you could recommend one thing to begin reversing this situation, what would it be?

Greenpeace *enviromentalists monitor pollution.*

3. Years ago there was a TV program called "The Mork and Mindy Show." Mork was an alien from another planet. He had remarkable powers, which he used only to help others, never himself. In one episode of the show, Mork decides to share some of his powers with his "earth friends." Touching his fingertips to theirs, he transfers to them some of his powers. Right away they begin using it to make people do silly things like turn cartwheels and jump around. When Mork sees this, he cries out in anguish, "Stop! Stop!"

Why does Mork cry out *in anguish*? How is this episode of "The Mork and Mindy Show" a kind of parable of God and the human race?

4. The cartoon strip "Calvin and Hobbes" occasionally deals with environmental problems. One day Hobbes gets fed up with the way people are wrecking our planet. He tells Calvin, "One reason why I think there's *intelligent* life on other planets is that the inhabitants of those planets are avoiding contact with us."

Explain (a) Hobbes's point, (b) the biggest reason why our planet is in such sad shape, (c) some action that young people (who will inherit this mess) can take to get citizens, industry, and government to stop destroying the planet.

5. When Jacob saw his son Joseph in Egypt, "Joseph threw his arms around his father's neck and cried for a long time" (Genesis 46:29). This touching scene stands in stark contrast to the way many modern parents and children greet one another. For example, one parent wrote to Ann Landers: "The greatest regret of my life is that I kept my son at arm's length. I believed it was unmanly for males to show affection for one another. I treated my son the way my father treated me, and I realize now what a terrible mistake it was."

On an unsigned slip of paper, answer the following: (a) When was the last time you hugged your parents? (b) Would you like to have a more affectionate relationship with your parents than you now have? (c) What might you do to improve your relationship with them? Tally the results on the chalkboard and discuss them.

Personal Reflection

In a joint statement on *Justice,* the bishops of the world said something that jarred many complacent Catholics. They said it was not enough to preach the Gospel to the world; Catholics must also work for justice in the world. Then the bishops spelled out the kind of justice Catholics must work for. It's not just making sure that people get a fair shake in everyday life. It's far more demanding than that. It's combating those structures in society that contradict the Gospel of Jesus Christ. It's declaring outright war on attitudes, structures, and procedures that exploit the poor, oppress minorities, and allow powerful special-interest groups to impose their will on the majority of citizens.

List three examples of injustice that bother you very much. Select one of these examples and suggest what people like yourself might do about it.

Bible Reading

Pick a passage. After reading it prayerfully, write out a brief prayer to God that reflects your personal feelings about it.

1. God creates the world	Genesis 1:1–2:4
2. God covenants with Abram	Genesis 15
3. God covenants with Israel	Exodus 19–20
4. God covenants with David	2 Samuel 7–8
5. God re-creates the world	Revelation 21:1–8

4 Christian Scriptures

Three high school students set out for a four-day climb up Mount Hood in Oregon. About nine thousand feet up, a blinding blizzard struck. Unable to move up or down the mountain, they tunneled into a snowbank to wait out the storm.

A week passed and the blizzard raged on.

The students passed the time reading from a pocket Bible that one of them had. There was barely enough light to read by. It was an eerie sight: one student lying in a sleeping bag reading, the other two listening. Periodically, they paused to pray, sometimes together, sometimes alone in silence.

As the blizzard raged into the second week, the daily ration of food dwindled to two spoonfuls of pancake batter a day for each.

Now the waiting became unbearable. The three were losing strength; they were losing faith; they were losing hope.

Finally, on the sixteenth day, the weather cleared. The students crawled out of the cave, barely able to stand. It was then that they saw a rescue team coming up the mountain.

Birth of Jesus

The situation of the students, as they waited and waited, gives us an insight into the situation of the Jewish people before the birth of Jesus. They, too, were beginning to lose hope as they waited and waited for the Messiah. Some of them, too, were beginning to lose faith as they waited for the one of whom the prophets said:

> *The LORD says, "The time is coming*
> *when I will choose as king*
> *a righteous descendant of David. . . .*
> *He will be called*
> *'The LORD Our Salvation.' "*
> JEREMIAH 23:5–6

It is against this background that we pick up the Christian Scriptures and begin reading the Gospel according to Matthew. Matthew takes great pains to situate Jesus' birth against the background of the Old Testament prophecies. He writes:

> *This is how*
> *the birth of Jesus Christ took place.*
> *His mother Mary was engaged to Joseph,*
> *but before they were married,*
> *she found out*
> *that she was going to have a baby*
> *by the Holy Spirit.*
> MATTHEW 1:18

Matthew then goes on to say that Mary's unusual pregnancy was a stumbling block for Joseph, until an angel appeared to him in a dream and said:

> *"Joseph, descendant of David,*
> *do not be afraid to take Mary*
> *to be your wife.*
> *For it is by the Holy Spirit*
> *that she has conceived.*
> *She will have a son,*
> *and you will name him Jesus—*
> *because he will save his people*
> *from their sins."*
> MATTHEW 1:20–21

Matthew concludes, saying:

> *Now all this happened*
> *in order to make come true*
> *what the Lord had said through the prophet,*
> *"A virgin will become pregnant*
> *and have a son,*
> *and he will be called Immanuel"*
> *(which means, "God is with us").*
> MATTHEW 1:23

Magi Visit Jesus

Matthew then narrates a story connected with Jesus' birth. He describes how Magi (students of the stars) "from the East" arrived in Jerusalem, searching for "the baby born to be the king of the Jews" (Matthew 2:2). When they found Jesus, they presented him with gifts of gold, frankincense, and myrrh (Matthew 2:11).

Christians have always considered these gifts to be highly symbolic. Gold is the "king of metals" and, therefore, is an ideal symbol of Jesus' *kingship*. Frankincense is used in religious worship and, therefore, is an ideal symbol of Jesus' *divinity*. Finally, myrrh is used to prepare people for burial and, therefore, is an ideal symbol of Jesus' *humanity*.

Commenting on the Magi story and its symbolism, an early Christian writer said:

> *The Magi gaze in deep wonder at what they see:*
> *heaven on earth, earth in heaven,*
> *man in God, God in man. . . .*
> *As they look they believe and do not question,*
> *as their symbolic gifts bear witness:*
> *gold for a king, incense for God,*
> *and myrrh for one who is to die.*
> Peter Chrysologus

And so Matthew's story of Jesus' birth serves as a kind of preface to his Gospel. It paves the way for his presentation of Jesus as the Messiah foretold by the prophets.

Baptism of Jesus

Matthew begins his presentation of Jesus as the Messiah with an event that took place on the banks of the Jordan River. One day a holy man named John came out of the desert and began preaching to the people. " 'Turn away from sin,' he said, 'because the Kingdom of heaven is near!' " (Matthew 3:2).

People came to him from Jerusalem,
from the whole province of Judea,
and from all over the country
near the Jordan River.
They confessed their sins,
and he baptized them in the Jordan.
MATTHEW 3:5–6

You can imagine John's surprise when, suddenly, he saw Jesus wade into the water to be baptized. He said to Jesus:

"I ought to be baptized by you. . . ."
But Jesus answered him,
"Let it be so for now.
For in this way
we shall do all that God requires."
MATTHEW 3:14–15

After Jesus was baptized, a remarkable thing happened.

While he was praying,
heaven was opened,
and the Holy Spirit
came down upon him
in bodily form like a dove.
And a voice came from heaven,
"You are my own dear Son.
I am pleased with you."
LUKE 3:21–22

Three striking images stand out in this brief description:

- the sky opens above Jesus,
- a dovelike form descends upon Jesus,
- a heavenly voice identifies Jesus.

To understand these three images, we need to consider them within the *context* of the times.

The Sky Opens above Jesus

To understand this first image, we need to understand how ancient Jews viewed the universe. They perceived it as being made up of three worlds stacked one upon the other, like pancakes:

- the world of God   (top world),
- the world of the living   (middle world),
- the world of the dead   (bottom world).

After the first sin of the first couple, a tidal wave of sin engulfed the *world of the living.* Holy people prayed to God to come down from God's world and do something about the evil in their world.

Thus the prophet Isaiah prayed to God, saying, "Why don't you tear the sky open and come down?" (Isaiah 64:1). And the psalmist prayed, "O LORD, tear the sky open and come down" (Psalm 144:5).

It is within this context that we must interpret the image of the sky opening above Jesus. It signifies that God has heard the prayer of the Jewish people and is entering their world (in the person of Jesus) to do something about the evil in it.

And so the opening of the sky symbolizes that a *new era* is beginning in human history.

A "Dove" Descends upon Jesus

This brings us to the next image. Again, the *context* is important. We must view the dove image against the background of the Book of Genesis. There, the biblical writer describes the spirit or "power of God ... moving over the water" at the dawn of creation (Genesis 1:2). Ancient rabbis compared this "power of God ... moving over the water" to a dove hovering over its newborn.

Given this context, we may interpret the dovelike form hovering over Jesus in the water as a *new creation* ("re-creation") that is taking place. What the prophet Isaiah had foretold is now coming to pass:

> The LORD *says,*
> *"I am making a new earth. . . .*
> *Be glad and rejoice forever in what I create."*
> ISAIAH 65:17–18

A Voice Identifies Jesus

This brings us to the last image: the voice from heaven saying of Jesus, "You are my own dear Son."

Again, the *context* is important. The creation story in the Book of Genesis portrays God creating Adam as the first person of the human family. He is, as it were, God's firstborn son. It is against this background that we must interpret the final image.

Given this context, Jesus is portrayed as being the *new Adam*. He is God's firstborn son of the "new creation." Commenting on the parallel between the first Adam and the last Adam (Jesus), Saint Paul says:

> *"The first man, Adam,*
> *was created a living being";*
> *but the last Adam [Jesus]*
> *is the life-giving Spirit. . . .*

> *The first Adam, made of earth,*
> *came from the earth;*
> *the second Adam [Jesus]*
> *came from heaven. . . .*
> *Just as we wear the likeness*
> *of the man made of earth,*
> *so we will wear the likeness*
> *of the Man from heaven.*
> 1 CORINTHIANS 15:45, 47, 49

The Long-Awaited Moment Comes

In brief, then, the three events that take place after Jesus' baptism signify the following:

- open sky: *new era* begins,
- dovelike form: *new creation* begins,
- heavenly voice: *new Adam* appears.

And so the long-awaited moment has arrived. The final phase of the "re-creation" of the world is at hand. The promised Messiah has come to inaugurate the promised Kingdom of God.

Miracles of Jesus

Shortly after his baptism, Jesus began the process of inaugurating the Kingdom of God on earth. One of the striking features of this process was the miracles Jesus worked.

The Gospel writers use three different words to refer to them: *teras, dynamis, semeion.* Each of these Greek words (the Gospels were written in Greek) gives us a different insight into what a miracle is.

Teras means "marvel." A miracle is something marvelous. It amazes us. We don't know what to make of it.

Dynamis means "power" (the word *dynamite* comes from this Greek word). A miracle is something explosive and powerful. It can restore hearing to a deaf person.

Semeion means "sign." A miracle is like a flashing red light. The important thing is not the flashing light but what it *signifies.* Similarly, the important thing about Jesus' miracles was not the miracles themselves but what they *signified.*

Miracles Are Signs

Saint John's favorite word for a miracle was *semeion.* He chose this word because it underscored the two important points about miracles. They are *signs* that—

- Jesus is the Messiah, and that
- Jesus is inaugurating God's Kingdom.

Miracles Point to the Messiah

To understand how Jesus' miracles pointed to the Messiah, we need to keep in mind the *context* in which the miracles occurred.

The prophet Isaiah had foretold that certain signs would identify the arrival of the Messiah.

> *The blind will be able to see,*
> *and the deaf will hear.*
> *The lame will leap and dance,*
> *and those who cannot speak*
> *will shout for joy.*
> ISAIAH 35:5–6

One day some people asked Jesus, "Are you the one John said was going to come, or should we expect someone else?" Jesus replied:

> *"The blind can see,*
> *the lame can walk,*
> *those who suffer from dreaded skin diseases*
> *are made clean,*
> *the deaf can hear, the dead are raised to life."*
> LUKE 7:19, 22

By his reply, Jesus is saying that the *signs* foretold by Isaiah are now happening. In other words, Jesus is telling the people, "I am the promised *Messiah.*"

Miracles Point to God's Kingdom

Once again, to understand how Jesus' miracles signified the coming of God's Kingdom, we need to recall their *context.*

The first sin of the first couple opened the floodgates of sin, and a tidal wave of evil engulfed the world. The human race fell under the influence of sin. The "kingdom of Satan" held sway on earth.

It is against this background that we must read the Gospel accounts of Jesus' miraculous power over demons. For example, one day Jesus was teaching in the synagogue at Capernaum.

> *In the synagogue was a man*
> *who had the spirit*
> *of an evil demon in him;*
> *he screamed out in a loud voice,*
> *"Ah! What do you want with us,*
> *Jesus of Nazareth?*
> *Are you here to destroy us?*
> *I know who you are:*
> *you are God's holy messenger!"*
>
> *Jesus ordered the spirit,*
> *"Be quiet and come out of the man!"*
> *The demon threw the man down . . .*
> *and went out of him. . . .*
> *The people were all amazed. . . .*
> *And the report about Jesus*
> *spread everywhere in that region.*
> LUKE 4:33–37

By this action, Jesus makes it clear that Satan's power in the world is now being destroyed. The "kingdom of Satan," which had held sway over the human race for so many centuries, is now being replaced by the "Kingdom of God" (Luke 11:20).

In other words, Jesus' miraculous power over demons is a sign that the long-awaited "Kingdom of God" is being inaugurated on earth.

Jesus compared the Kingdom of God to the planting of a seed. After the seed is planted, it takes time for it to grow and bear fruit (Mark 4:26–29). It is the same way with God's Kingdom. It is "planted," but it will take time to bear fruit. Moreover, the kingdom of Satan will not collapse without a struggle.

And so the miracles of the Gospel are dramatic signs that—

- Jesus is the Messiah, and that
- Jesus is inaugurating the Kingdom of God.

Sufferings of Jesus

After the Last Supper, Jesus went to the Mount of Olives to a small orchard called Gethsemane. There he began the first of four sufferings that marked his final hours on earth.

First, Jesus endured sufferings of the *mind*. He suffered *mentally*. He was tortured by thoughts of the painful ordeal that lay ahead of him. Luke says that Jesus' suffering became so great that "his sweat was like drops of blood falling to the ground" (Luke 22:44).

Second, Jesus endured sufferings of the *heart*. He suffered *emotionally*. He was betrayed by Judas, denied by Peter, and deserted by the other disciples. This treatment by his closest friends crushed his heart.

Third, Jesus endured sufferings of the *body*. He suffered *physically*. He was whipped, crowned with thorns, nailed to a cross, and left hanging there until he died. One ancient document says that the pain of crucifixion was so great that victims sometimes went insane.

Fourth, Jesus endured sufferings of the *soul*. He suffered *spiritually*. One of the greatest pains a person can endure is the feeling of having been abandoned by God. Jesus experienced this feeling just before he died (Mark 15:34). The words, which Jesus prayed on the cross, describe it:

> *My God, my God,*
> *why have you abandoned me? . . .*

> *My strength is gone,*
> *gone like water spilled on the ground.*
> *All my bones are out of joint. . . .*
> *My throat is as dry as dust. . . .*
> *They tear at my hands and feet. . . .*
> *They gamble for my clothes*
> *and divide them among themselves.*
> *O Lord, don't stay away from me!*
> *Come quickly to my rescue!*
> PSALM 22:1, 14-19

What did Jesus want his suffering to teach us? What did he want it to say to us?

First, Jesus wanted his suffering to be a *sign* of his love for us. He wanted his crucifixion to say in a visual way what he had so often said in a verbal way: "The greatest love a person can have for his friends is to give his life for them" (John 15:13).

Second, Jesus wanted his suffering to be a *revelation* about love. He wanted his crucifixion to say that true love always entails suffering. Again, he wanted to say in a visual way what he had said so often in a verbal way: "If anyone wants to come with me, he must forget himself, take up his cross every day, and follow me" (Luke 9:23).

Finally, Jesus wanted his suffering to be an *invitation* to love. He wanted his crucifixion to say in a visual way what he had said so often in a verbal way: "Love one another, just as I love you" (John 15:12).

Rising of Jesus

An Associated Press reporter might have described Jesus' death on Good Friday this way:

> JERUSALEM (AP)—
> *Jesus of Nazareth was executed today*
> *outside the walls of this ancient city.*
> *Death came at about three o'clock.*
> *A freak thunderstorm*
> *scattered the crowd of curious onlookers*
> *and served as a fitting climax*
> *to the brief but stormy career*
> *of the controversial preacher*
> *from the hill country of Galilee.*
> *Burial took place immediately.*
> *A police guard was posted at the grave site*
> *as a precautionary measure.*
> *The Galilean is survived by his mother.*

The events of Good Friday left Jesus' followers in a state of shock. Their faith was shaken to the foundation. Weren't Jesus' miracles *signs* that he was the Messiah? Weren't they *signs* that he was inaugurating the Kingdom of God? How, then, could all this be reconciled with what had just taken place? Suddenly, all their hopes and dreams seemed buried with Jesus.

But then came Easter Sunday.

Jesus Is Risen

Some women went to visit the tomb on the Sunday after Good Friday. They were not prepared for what they found. It was empty!

As they stood there totally bewildered, two men in white appeared and said:

> *"Why are you looking among the dead*
> *for one who is alive?*
> *He is not here;*
> *he has been raised."*
> LUKE 24:5–6

The women were beside themselves, not knowing what to make of this. So they ran back to tell the Apostles what they had found.

Peter got up and ran to the tomb;
he bent down and saw the grave cloths
but nothing else.
Then he went back home
amazed at what had happened.
LUKE 24:12

Jesus was alive! He had done what no one had ever done before. He had resurrected from the dead.

Jesus Is Totally Transformed

The word *resurrection* does not mean a restoration to one's previous life, such as happened to Lazarus, the widow of Nain, or Jairus' daughter. It is not *resuscitation*. It is something infinitely more.

The word *resurrection* designates a quantum leap forward into a totally new life. It is something that no human being had yet experienced. In other words, the body of Jesus that rose on Easter Sunday was radically different from the body that was buried on Good Friday.

Saint Paul compares the body "planted" in the grave to a seed planted in the earth.

When the body is buried, it is mortal;
when raised, it will be immortal.
When buried, it is ugly and weak;
when raised, it will be beautiful and strong.
When buried, it is a physical body;
when raised, it will be a spiritual body.
1 CORINTHIANS 15:42–44

Sending the Spirit

The resurrection gave Jesus a totally new relationship with his followers. As a result, he was now able to send the Holy Spirit upon them, just as he had promised he would (John 14:16–17).

After the Holy Spirit came upon Jesus' followers, they went forth to tell the good news of Jesus to all the world.

"Jesus of Nazareth was a man
whose divine authority was clearly proven . . .
by all the miracles and wonders
which God performed through him. . . .

"He has been raised
to the right side of God, his Father,
and has received from him the Holy Spirit,
as he had promised.
What you now see and hear is his gift
that he has poured out on us. . . .

"Each one of you must turn away from his sins
and be baptized in the name of Jesus Christ,
so that your sins will be forgiven;
and you will receive God's gift,
the Holy Spirit."
ACTS 2:22, 33, 38

Recap

The twenty-seven books of the *Christian Scriptures* grow out of the Hebrew Scriptures and complete them.

Jesus' baptism, teachings, and miracles identify him as the *promised Messiah,* who inaugurates God's *promised kingdom* on earth.

By his death and resurrection, Jesus sets up a new relationship with his followers. That is, he is able to send the *promised Holy Spirit* upon them. The coming of the Holy Spirit empowers Jesus' followers to complete God's Kingdom on earth (the re-creation of the world).

Understanding Christian Scriptures

Review

Birth of Jesus

1. Against what background does Matthew situate Jesus' birth?

2. What name is Joseph told to give Mary's child by the Holy Spirit? Why is this name given?

3. What gifts did the Magi present to Jesus? Why do Christians consider these gifts to be highly symbolic?

Baptism of Jesus

4. List the three images contained in Luke's description of Jesus' baptism, and explain *what* each symbolized and *how* it did this.

Miracles of Jesus

5. What three Greek words did the Gospel writers use to refer to Jesus' miracles? How does each word contribute to our understanding of a miracle?

6. Explain how Jesus' miracles signified the coming of (a) the Messiah, (b) God's Kingdom.

Rising of Jesus

7. Explain the difference between *resurrection* and *resuscitation*.

8. Explain the comparison Paul uses to show how the human body after resurrection differs from the body before resurrection.

Sending the Spirit

9. What did the risen Jesus' new relationship with his followers enable him to do?

10. How did the Spirit's coming affect Jesus' followers? What is our role as modern followers of Jesus?

Sufferings of Jesus

11. Explain and give examples to illustrate what we mean when we say Jesus endured sufferings of the body, mind, heart, and soul.

12. Explain in what sense Jesus intended his crucifixion to be (a) a *sign*, (b) a *revelation*, and (c) an *invitation*.

Exercises

1. One day Jesus told this parable:

> "There was once a landowner who planted a vineyard, put a fence around it, dug a hole for the wine press, and built a watchtower. Then he rented the vineyard to tenants and left home on a trip. When the time came to gather the grapes, he sent his slaves to the tenants to receive his share of the harvest. The tenants grabbed his slaves, beat one, killed another, and stoned another. Again the man sent other slaves, more than the first time, and the tenants treated them the same way. Last of all he sent his son to them. 'Surely they will respect my son,' he said. But when the tenants saw the son, they said to themselves, 'This is the owner's son. Come on, let's kill him, and we will get his property!' They grabbed him, threw him out of the vineyard, and killed him.
>
> "Now, when the owner of the vineyard comes, what will he do to those tenants?" Jesus asked.
>
> "He will certainly kill those evil men," they answered, "and rent the vineyard out to other tenants, who will give him his share of the harvest at the right time." . . .
>
> The chief priests and the Pharisees heard Jesus' parables and knew that he was talking about them.
>
> MATTHEW 21:33–45

Explain how this parable summarizes the "story of re-creation." In other words, how do the following details of the story match up with people and events in the "story of re-creation": (a) landowner, (b) vineyard, (c) first rental, (d) tenants, (e) slaves, (f) other slaves, (g) son, (h) second rental, (i) other tenants?

2. An atheist, Pat, and her Christian friend, Sharon, came upon a gang of hoodlums as they walked down the street. Pat pointed to the toughs and said, "Look, Sharon, it's been two thousand years since your Jesus came into the world, and it's still full of sinners." Five minutes later, Pat and Sharon came upon a group of dirty-faced children. Now it was Sharon's turn. She pointed to the kids and said, "Look, Pat, it's been two thousand years since soap was discovered, and the world is still full of dirty faces."

What is Sharon's point? How do you think Jesus might handle the gang problem, if he were living today?

3. Normally, only men appeared in Jewish family trees. It is surprising, therefore, to find women listed in Jesus' family tree (Matthew 1:5). Even more surprising is that one of the women was Rahab, a prostitute (Joshua 2:1), and another was Ruth, a Gentile, or

G. van den Eeckbout's Ruth and Boaz.

non-Jew (Ruth 1:4). There's something beautiful here. Already on the first page of the Gospel, we find a preview of how Jesus will make walls tumble down between male and female, Jew and Gentile, and outcast and "in-group" (Mark 2:13–17).

Why are these walls so slow in tumbling down, nearly two thousand years after Jesus? What would you suggest to make them tumble faster? What are other walls that divide groups in your school or community? What might be done to make them tumble down?

4. One day an adventuresome fish wandered far away from its "village" in the ocean. Suddenly, it came upon divers using snorkels to explore the ocean's floor. As it watched from behind a rock, the fish noticed that the divers had apparently come from "outer water." The fish hurried back to the village to warn the fish "leaders" about these strange "aliens from outer water." But the leaders simply laughed and laughed, saying, "There can't be life in outer water. Too much oxygen! Not enough water! Nothing can live in conditions like that. You were simply tripped out on too much seaweed."

How does this story illustrate one of the problems Jesus ran into when he tried to teach the people about the Kingdom of God? Why do you think Jesus used parables to teach the people about the Kingdom of God?

5. An ancient Islamic parable concerns a traveler who strayed into the "Land of the Fools." As the traveler walked along, a group of people approached, shouting hysterically, "There's a monster in our field!" With that, they led the traveler to a field and pointed to a watermelon—something they'd never seen before. The traveler saw the chance to play the hero. Drawing a sword, the traveler plunged it into the melon, sliced it up, and ate it. Now, the people became even more hysterical, shouting, "This traveler is even worse than the monster!" And they drove the traveler out of their land. Months later the scene repeated itself with another traveler. This time the traveler didn't play the hero. Rather, the traveler took up residence among the fools, won their trust, and taught them to overcome their fear of watermelons. Before the traveler left, the villagers were even eating watermelons.

List some of the points the parable makes. In what sense was the second traveler like Jesus? Give one example to show how you might apply one of the points of the parable to your life.

Personal Reflection

An unknown author wrote:

> One day Jesus began to teach his disciples, saying: "Happy are those who know they are spiritually poor; the Kingdom of heaven belongs to them! . . . Happy are those whose greatest desire is to be what God requires. . . . Happy are those who are merciful" (Matthew 5:3–9). Peter said, "Do you want us to write this in our notebooks?" And Andrew said, "Will this be on the test?" And Judas said, "What does this have to do with life, anyway?" And Jesus wept.

What did the author have in mind, and why does the author have Jesus weep? What was the most enjoyable course you ever took, and what made it special?

Bible Reading

Pick a passage. After reading it prayerfully, write out a brief prayer to God that reflects your personal feelings or thoughts about it.

1. Birth of Jesus   Luke 2:1–20
2. Temptations of Jesus   Luke 4:1–15
3. Two major miracles   Luke 8:40–56
4. Jesus' final hours   John 18–19
5. Seeds and stars   1 Corinthians 15:35–58

5 God

The movie called *Laura* is about a young woman who is mysteriously killed in her apartment. A young detective named Mark MacPherson is assigned to the case. He spends the next few days in Laura's apartment, searching for clues. He dusts for fingerprints, goes through Laura's belongings, and even reads her diary. He leaves no stone unturned.

After a while, something strange begins to happen. The more Mark learns about Laura, the more he is fascinated by her. He finds himself attracted to her. He finds himself wishing with all of his heart that she were still alive.

Late one night Mark is seated in Laura's apartment, thinking about her. The lights are low, and he is tired. Soon he nods and falls asleep.

Suddenly, something awakens Mark. He opens his eyes; and there, standing in the doorway, is a beautiful young woman. He can hardly believe what he sees. It's Laura!

Then an amazing story unfolds. Laura had gone to the country for a weekend of quiet. In all that time, she had not read a newspaper. She had not listened to a radio. She had not heard the reports of her own death.

It turns out that the murdered woman was one of Laura's acquaintances, who had used the apartment while Laura was away.

How does the movie end? You guessed it. Laura and Mark start dating, fall in love, marry, and live happily ever after.

Commenting on the movie, a theology teacher said, "*Laura* makes a good parable of God, ourselves, and God's plan for us." Assuming that the teacher is right, we might ask ourselves, How is this so?

God in Scripture

Like Mark, we find ourselves in an "apartment" (God's apartment: the universe). And like Mark, we get an insight into God from the universe, just as Mark got an insight into Laura from her apartment. And just as Mark found himself attracted to Laura, so we find ourselves attracted to God. Finally, as Mark fell in love with Laura and lived happily ever after, so God intends our story to have the same ending.

But the created universe can give us only an insight into who God is. It can give us only a *glimpse* of what God is like. It can't paint a detailed portrait of God. Dr. Mortimer Adler, a modern philosopher, made this point in an interview with TV's Bill Moyers, saying:

> *If reason enabled me*
> *to know everything about God,*
> *God would not have to reveal himself. . . .*
> *Reason alone can't bridge*
> *from an infinite supreme being . . .*
> *to a being that is just, merciful . . .*
> *[and] caring.*

That gap must be bridged by God's own self-revelation in the Scriptures.

When we read the Scriptures, we need to keep in mind that they were originally written for people who lived a simple way of life close to nature. As a result, God's self-revelation is described in simple images, often drawn from nature. Consider just a few.

- God is a mother eagle, who nurtures her young and teaches them to fly (Deuteronomy 32:11).
- God is a shepherd, who leads the flock to "fields of green grass" (Psalm 23:2), seeks them out when they are lost, and nurses them when they are sick (Ezekiel 34:16).
- God is a mother bird, who gathers her young under her wings and protects them in time of danger (Matthew 23:37).
- God is a gracious host, who seats guests at table and feeds them generously and joyfully (Psalm 23:5).

- God is a great king, who is strong and mighty (Psalm 24:8, 10).
- God is the Holy One, before whom the angels bow and cry out, "Holy, holy, holy!" (Isaiah 6:3).
- God is the Creator, who "set the earth firmly on its foundations" and decorated it with seas and mountains (Psalm 104: 5–8).
- God is a father, who embraces his children and presses them lovingly to his cheek (Hosea 11:1–4).
- God is a mother, who gives birth to and loves her child with an everlasting love (Isaiah 49:15).

These metaphors are just some of the images that the Scriptures use to "paint a portrait" of God.

Let's look more closely at two of these images: God as Creator and God as Father or parent.

Three God-Views

People tend to fall into three groups when it comes to the way they view God.

The first group stresses the *transcendence* of God. That is, they tend to stress God as being "beyond" the world. They focus on God's *otherness:* God's distance and difference from the world. Judaism and Islam tend to fall into this group.

Pushed to the extreme, this "God-view" results in *deism,* picturing God as being totally detached from human affairs. We find such a view of God in F. Scott Fitzgerald's *The Great Gatsby.* Although this novel's main concern is not God, it does compare God to a big billboard overlooking New York City. Like the billboard, God has been around for as long as people can remember. Like the billboard, God looks down on the world in a totally detached way. God sees all, knows all, and cares less.

The second group of people stresses the *immanence* of God. This means they tend to stress God as being "within" the world. They focus on God's

relatedness: God's closeness and involvement in the world. Hinduism and Buddhism tend to fall into this group.

Pushed to the extreme, this God-view results in *pantheism.* That is, it equates God with the world. God and the world are one and the same thing.

The third group views God as being a delicate *balance* between the transcendent and the immanent. That is, this group pictures God as being transcendent ("beyond our world") but yet immanent ("within our world"). God is totally different from the world but not totally separated from it. God is, paradoxically, the "beyond within." Christianity falls into this group. Nowhere is its vision of God more clearly stated than in the *incarnation:* the mystery of God taking flesh and living among us.

Each of the above groups has developed its own *creed* (what it believes), *code* (how it behaves), and *cult* (how it worships). The combination of creed, code, and cult gives each religion its particular spirit.

God as Creator

Four days before Christmas 1968, *Apollo 8* lifted off from Cape Kennedy. On board the spaceship were astronauts Frank Borman, Bill Anders, and Jim Lovell.

Three days later, on Christmas Eve, *Apollo 8* lost all contact with earth as it disappeared behind the moon. Millions of people sat glued to their television sets, waiting and praying for the spaceship to emerge safely.

Then came a spectacular moment. As the spaceship rounded the moon and came into view, the crew took turns reading the story of creation from the Book of Genesis.

The story of *Apollo 8* and the reading of the story of creation from the Scriptures make a good introduction to "God as Creator."

God Created All Things

The Scriptures portray God planning the world, creating it, and pronouncing it good. The high point of creation is the fashioning of the first human beings. The Bible says:

> Then the LORD God
> took some soil from the ground
> and formed a man out of it;
> he breathed life-giving breath into his nostrils
> and the man began to live. . . .
>
> Then the LORD God
> made the man fall into a deep sleep,
> and while he was sleeping,
> he took out one of the man's ribs
> and closed up the flesh.
> He formed a woman out of the rib.
> GENESIS 2:7, 21–22

God's creation of the first human beings reveals the closeness or intimacy between God and them. It shows God sharing a part of God's own being: the "breath of life."

To appreciate how revolutionary this idea was, recall that the Genesis writer penned the creation story at a time when other religions were stressing the distance between their gods and humans. In contrast to this, the Genesis writer portrays God as being closer to humans than a mother is to her own baby. This explains why God says through the prophet Isaiah:

> *"Can a woman forget her own baby*
> *and not love the child she bore?*
> *Even if a mother should forget her child,*
> *I will never forget you. . . .*
> *I have written your name*
> *on the palms of my hands."*
> ISAIAH 49:15–16

In brief, then, the first thing that the image of God as Creator reveals is that God created *all* that exists. Creation may be compared to images on a movie screen, and God may be compared to the projector that puts them on the screen. Just as the images would not exist were it not for the projector, so creation would not exist were it not for God.

God Sustains All Things

But God does more than create. God also *holds* creation in existence. Without God, creation could not remain in existence. In other words, creation depends upon God to stay in existence.

Again, consider the example of the images on the movie screen. The projector not only *gives* the images existence but also *holds* them in existence. If the projector withdrew its light, the images would cease to be. They would dissolve into nothingness.

It is the same with creation. If God stopped holding creation in existence, all would dissolve into nothingness.

God Resides in All Things

Besides *creating* and *sustaining* everything, God *resides* in creation, especially in humans, who are made in the image and likeness of God. In other words, God becomes present in the world through creation.

Again, consider the example of the movie projector. The projector not only *casts* the images on the screen but also *resides* in them. In other words, the light from the projector (which generates the images) gives the projector a real presence on the screen.

It is the same with God. In a true sense, God is present in the world through creation.

God's presence in creation leads us to an important point. God resides in the world in different ways and degrees:

- through creation, which God made;
- through Scripture, which God inspired;
- through Jesus, the Son of God become one of us.

An example may help to illustrate. A child can be present to its mother in different ways and degrees:

- through a drawing made for her;
- through a letter sent to her;
- in person, by sitting beside her.

The child's presence through the drawing corresponds to God's presence through creation. The child's presence through the letter corresponds to God's presence through Scripture. And the child's presence in person corresponds to God's presence in Jesus.

The different ways that God is present in the world prompted the psalmist to say of God:

Where could I go to escape from you?
Where could I get away from your presence?
If I went up to heaven, you would be there. . . .
If I flew away beyond the east
or lived in the farthest place in the west,
you would be there to lead me,
you would be there to help me.
PSALM 139:7–10

God as Father

Years ago, Lois Olson contracted polio at the age of ten. The entire lower half of her body was in a cast. One night a tornado struck. A feeling of utter helplessness swept over her. Just then her father appeared at the door and carried her down the steps to the basement.

As he struggled under the weight of the cast, Lois could see beads of sweat breaking out on his forehead and blood vessels bulging from his temples.

God is like that. God is a caring father, a loving parent. Jesus uses this image no less than 177 times to describe God. In fact, his first and last recorded words refer to God as Father. When Jesus was twelve, he said to his parents, "Didn't you know that I had to be in my Father's house?" (Luke 2:49). And just before he died, Jesus said, "Father! In your hands I place my spirit!" (Luke 23:46).

A word for Father that Jesus used is *Abba.* Palestinian children still use this word to refer to their father. Literally, it means "Daddy." Thus Jesus taught us to have the same trust in God as a child has in his or her parent.

But God's love is not limited, as is the love of human fathers and mothers. God is all-loving. Peter van Breeman explains the difference between God and ordinary parents this way:

> *We are divided in our love.*
> *We like a person very much (90%)*
> *or in an ordinary way (50%)*
> *or very little (20%).*
> *God does not measure love.*
> *God cannot but love totally—100%.*
> *If we think God is a person*
> *who can divide his love,*
> *then we are thinking not of God*
> *but of ourselves. . . .*
> *We* have *love, but God* is *love.*
> AS BREAD THAT IS BROKEN

The point is this: God loves us with an infinite love. God loves us infinitely more than even our parents love us and infinitely more than we can ever love ourselves.

Recap

Reason alone cannot give us a "portrait" of God. Only Scripture can do that. Scripture uses a variety of images to "paint a portrait" of God. Among these are *Creator* and *Father.*

The image of *God as Creator* reveals that God created all that exists, sustains creation, and is present in our world through creation.

The image of *God as Father* reveals that God loves us as a devoted parent loves a child. God loves us even more. God loves us with an *infinite* love.

Greatest Discovery

Late one afternoon, archaeologist Gene Savoy and a companion became lost in a jungle in Peru. A sickening feeling came over them. They knew that if they did not reach camp by sundown, they would never reach it alive.

In a state of near panic, they began to run about feverishly, searching for the trail they had used to enter the jungle. Suddenly they realized that this frenzied running was only making matters worse. Then they stopped and stood perfectly still. As they did, a strange thought flashed across Savoy's mind.

God is in the jungle. It is God's house. Gene had been introduced to the beauties of nature when he was a boy in Oregon. His parents taught him that God had created the universe, sustains it, and resides in it. Why had he closed his eyes to God's presence in the jungles of Peru? Didn't God create them, also? Doesn't God sustain them, also? Doesn't God reside in them, also?

Instantly, Gene relaxed and put all his trust in God, in whose house he was. He said later, "I looked up into the beautiful emerald world of wild orchids, and fragrant blossoms where hummingbirds hovered. Yes, God was here, too. My heart quieted."

At that moment, something deep down within Gene seemed to say, "Walk a few paces to the left." He did. And there was the tiny trail! Gene said later, "I am proud of my archaeological discoveries. But my greatest discovery, I believe, was in recognizing God's presence everywhere."

Understanding God

Review

God in Scripture

1. Briefly explain how the movie *Laura* might serve as a kind of parable of God and us.

2. Why must we supplement our knowledge of God from reason and experience with God's self-revelation in Scripture?

3. List and briefly describe four images that the Scriptures use to try to "paint a portrait" of God.

God as Creator

4. List and briefly explain the three truths that the image of God as Creator reveals.

5. Explain one important way the creation story portrayed God as differing from the way other ancient religions portrayed God.

6. Using the example of a movie projector, explain what we mean when we say that God creates, sustains, and resides in creation.

7. Briefly explain three ways God has become present to us in the course of history and how they parallel three ways a child can be present to its mother.

God as Father

8. Roughly, how many times does Jesus refer to the image of "God as Father" in Scripture?

9. Scripture portrays Jesus referring to the image of "God as Father" in the first and the last recorded words of his earthly life. What was the setting or occasion for the first reference? The last?

10. Describe how Peter van Breemen illustrates the difference between God's love and human love.

Three God-Views

11. List and briefly describe the three groups into which people tend to fall when it comes to picturing God.

12. Into which of the above three groups do the following tend to fall: Hinduism, Judaism, Christianity, Islam, Buddhism?

13. Explain what we mean when we speak of the creed, the code, and the cult of a religion.

Exercises

1. Explain the point contained in each of the following statements:

    a. "God is the Dancer . . . Creation the Dance. . . . Be silent and look at the Dance. Just look: a star, a flower, a fading leaf. . . . And hopefully it won't be long before you see . . . the Dancer." (Anthony DeMello)

    b. "I fear God, but I am not afraid of [God]." (Thomas Browne)

2. An Islamic legend says that one night Ibrahim ibn Adham was taking his usual walk under the stars around the sacred Kaaba, an Islamic shrine in Mecca. Since no one was in sight, Ibrahim walked close to the Kaaba's door and whispered, "My God, keep me from ever disobeying you." No sooner had he said this than a voice said, "Ibrahim, if I granted your prayer, how would you ever learn about the special love that I have for you?"

    What did the voice mean? How does that legend shed light on the meaning of this saying: "God loves us not so much because of who we are but because of who God is"?

3. Jean Webster's story *Daddy Long Legs* concerns an orphan girl who received many gifts from a person she never knew and never met. As a result, she grew up blessed with remarkable opportunities that she would never have otherwise had. Often she tried to imagine what the mysterious stranger was like, but she had no way of knowing if her image was correct. Then one day the magic moment came: she met the stranger. She was delighted. He exceeded her wildest dream. All she could do was thank him. And that was enough, because he understood.

How is the orphan girl in *Daddy Long Legs* similar to every person who has ever lived? Why is there so much ingratitude in the world? What are three things you are extremely grateful for?

4. The great nineteenth-century British poet Elizabeth Barrett Browning wrote:

Earth's crammed with heaven,
And every common bush afire with God.
But only he who sees takes off his shoes;
the rest sit round it and pluck blackberries.

What is Browning's point? Why do so many people today fail to take off their shoes and just sit around plucking blackberries? Where do you find God most easily in today's world?

5. Sunday morning, May 18, 1980, Mount Saint Helens, an active volcano, exploded in Washington state. The eruption blasted 1,300 feet of earth, molten rock, and

Mount Saint Helens erupting.

volcanic ash from the top of the 10,000-foot mountain, reducing its height to 8,700 feet. Photographer David Crocket of KOMO-TV, Seattle, was caught at the foot of the volcano when it blew. He was nearly buried by the flying debris (which included thousands of trees, millions of rocks, and tons of suffocating volcanic ash). David remained motionless for the next several hours to conserve air amidst the dust and ash that engulfed the site like a huge cloud. Then a miraculous thing happened. A Coast Guard helicopter spotted David, picked him up, and rushed him to a hospital. After his ordeal, Crocket wrote in *Guideposts* (January 1981): "During those ten hours I saw a mountain fall apart. I saw a forest disappear. It wiped away many of my set beliefs. I saw that God is the only one who is unmovable, unshakable, infallible. . . . I feel somehow that I'm being allowed to start over . . . whatever is in his master plan for me."

To what extent do you agree with David that God has a "master plan" for the human race and each of us has a part to play in it? Describe the closest you have ever come to death. To what extent did it affect your life or your faith, as David's brush with death did?

Personal Reflection

A woman dove into a raging river to rescue a drowning boy. Miraculously, she succeeded. After the boy had recovered from temporary shock, he threw his arms around the woman and thanked her. The woman held the boy tight and whispered in the boy's ear, "That's okay, son! Just make sure your life was worth saving."

How is this story a parable of every person who ever lived? List three possibilities that you are considering doing with your life. After each possibility, write at least one pro and one con. Which of the three possibilities are you leaning toward and why?

Bible Reading

Pick a passage. After reading it prayerfully, write out a brief "note to God" that reflects your personal feelings or thoughts about it.

1. Loving Father   Hosea 11:1–4
2. Loving Host   Psalm 23
3. Loving Creator   Psalm 8
4. Forgiving Father   Luke 15:11–32
5. Forgiving Jesus   John 8:1–11

6 Jesus

A *Peanuts* cartoon shows Linus saying to Charlie Brown, "That's ridiculous!" Charlie says, "Maybe so! But come and see for yourself." With that, they go into the living room where Snoopy is sitting on the television set. His ears are pointed up and out like an antenna. Charlie says, "See! It does make the picture better." An amazed Linus says to Charlie, "You're right!"

A college girl said of this particular *Peanuts* cartoon, "If Jesus were on earth today, he might use it as a kind of *parable* to teach people about himself and God."

Assuming the girl is right, what or who in the cartoon stands for God? Jesus? The human race? What point about God, Jesus, and the human race does the cartoon "parable" make?

ICHTHYS

A seminarian pulled into a parking lot in Dallas, Texas. On the rear of his car were the letters *ICHTHYS,* in the shape of a fish. A woman asked him what the fish-shaped letters meant. He said they were the first letters of the Greek expression that is translated "Jesus Christ, Son of God, Savior."

The seminarian also said that the letters *ICHTHYS* spell the Greek word *fish.* This explains why early Christians made the fish a symbol for Jesus.

The four expressions—"Jesus," "Christ," "Son of God," "Savior"—sum up four important truths about Jesus. Let's now take a closer look at each truth.

Jesus

The most personal thing we possess is our name. It identifies us as belonging to the *human* family—having a *human nature.* It identifies us as being a *human* person, someone totally unique. It is the way our friends address us, and it is the way people speak about us.

Jesus' name did the same thing for him. It identified Jesus as belonging to the *human* family—having a *human nature.* It identified him as being a totally unique person. It was the way his friends addressed him and spoke about him.

But in biblical times, names sometimes went a step further. They often revealed something special about the person.

Jesus' name was like that. It revealed something special about him. The name *Jesus* means "God saves." It was given to Jesus before he was born. An angel told Joseph in a dream:

"You will name him Jesus—because he will save his people from their sins."
MATTHEW 1:21

And so the name *Jesus* identifies Jesus having a human nature and, also, a special mission from God.

Tabernacle door.

Site of Capernaum synagogue in which Jesus preached.

Christical*

Thistical* brings us to the second expression: "Christ." To understand this title of Jesus, recall one of the critical moments in the Gospel. It occurs when Jesus asks Peter, "Who do you say I am?" Peter replies, "You are the Messiah" (Mark 8:29).

The word *Messiah* is a Hebrew word, which means "Anointed One." It is translated into Greek as *Christos,* from which we get our English word *Christ.* Thus, the words *Messiah* (Hebrew), *Christos* (Greek), and *Christ* (English) are simply different ways to refer to the same person: the long-awaited descendant of David, promised by God through the Hebrew prophets.

Jesus first referred to himself as being "anointed" in the synagogue in Nazareth. He did it after reading this passage from the prophet Isaiah:

> *"The Spirit of the Lord is upon me,*
> *because he has chosen [anointed] me*
> *to bring good news to the poor . . .*
> *to proclaim liberty to the captives*
> *and recovery of sight to the blind . . .*
> *and [to] announce that the time has come*
> *when the Lord will save his people."*
> LUKE 4:18–19

Then Jesus uttered these memorable words: "This passage of scripture has come true today, as you heard it being read" (Luke 4:21).

Thus Jesus identifies himself as having been "anointed" by the "Spirit of the Lord" to carry out a special mission from God. The title *Christ* designates Jesus as being the long-awaited descendant of David, whose reign will extend to all peoples and never end.

Word of God

Recall the cartoon of Snoopy sitting on the television set. The college girl said of it, "If Jesus were on earth today, he might use it as a kind of parable to teach people about himself and God." Her point is this: As Snoopy gave Charlie Brown and Linus a clearer picture of the image on the television screen, so Jesus gives the human race a clearer picture of God.

> *Jesus reflects the brightness of God's glory and is the exact likeness of God's own being.*
> HEBREWS 1:3

Because Jesus tells us about God, Saint John calls him the "Word of God." John writes:

> *Before the world was created, the Word already existed; he was with God, and he was the same as God. . . . The Word became a human being and . . . lived among us.*
> JOHN 1:1, 14

But Jesus is the "Word of God" in yet another sense. Jesus also *tells us about ourselves.* He tells us what we are capable of becoming. He *tells us what God made us to be.* A story will illustrate.

One day a missionary began her class on Jesus, saying to the children: "Today I want to tell you about someone you must meet. He is a person who loves you and cares for you even more than your own family and friends. He is a person who is kinder than the kindest person you know."

The missionary noticed that a little girl was getting more and more excited as she talked. Suddenly the girl blurted out, "I know that man! He lives on our street."

That story illustrates the second way that we may call Jesus the "Word of God." He tells us about ourselves. By his own human life on earth, Jesus tells us what we are capable of becoming—if we open ourselves to his Spirit. We are capable of loving enemies, forgiving sinners, bringing to completion the re-creation of ourselves and our world.

Son of God

A woman was seated in front of her fireplace, thinking about the birth of Jesus. The more she thought about it, the more incredible it seemed. Why would the Creator of the universe decide to be born on earth and live among us? The whole thing seemed absurd.

Just then she heard a strange sound outside. Going to the window, she saw a half dozen geese staggering about in the snow. They had apparently wandered off from a warm barn and were now cold and confused.

The woman went outside, opened the door to her garage, and tried to herd the geese into it. But the more she tried to help them, the more frightened they became and the more they scattered across the lawn.

Finally, after twenty minutes, she gave up. She realized that the geese had no idea that she was trying to help them.

A strange thought came to her: "If just for one minute I could become one of them—an ordinary goose—I could talk to them in their own language and explain to them what I am trying to do!"

Then it struck her. That was what the birth of Jesus was all about! It was about the Creator of the universe deciding to be born on earth, live among us, speak our own language, and tell us what was for our happiness.

Jesus Is the Son of God

We now come to the most important title of all: "Son of God." The Hebrew Scriptures use this title in a *figurative* sense. That is, they call someone the "son of God" somewhat the way we call a good person an "angel" or a bad person a "devil." For example, they give the title "son of God" to Israel's kings (2 Samuel 7:14) and to Israel itself (Hosea 11:1).

The Christian Scriptures, on the other hand, use the title in a totally unique way. They use it in the *literal* sense. Moreover, they use it only of Jesus. And they give Jesus this title nearly a

*Artist's
conception
of the
Jerusalem Temple.*

hundred times. For example, Saint Mark opens his Gospel, saying:

> *This is the Good News
> about Jesus Christ, the Son of God.*
> MARK 1:1

Jesus Is Unique

The Christian Scriptures apply the title "Son of God" to Jesus in the *literal* sense because this is precisely who they believe Jesus is, God's only Son. For example, take this passage from John:

> *The Festival
> of the Dedication of the Temple
> was being celebrated in Jerusalem.
> Jesus was walking . . . in the Temple,
> when the people gathered around him
> and asked . . . "Tell us the plain truth:
> are you the Messiah?"*
>
> *Jesus answered,
> "I have already told you,
> but you would not believe me.
> The deeds I do by my Father's authority
> speak on my behalf. . . .
> The Father and I are one."*

> *Then the people . . .
> picked up stones to throw at him.
> Jesus said to them,
> "I have done many good deeds . . . ;
> for which one of these
> do you want to stone me?"*
>
> *They answered,
> "We do not want to stone you
> because of any good deeds,
> but because of your blasphemy!
> You are only a man,
> but you are trying to make yourself God!"*
> JOHN 10:22–25, 30–33

Thus by calling Jesus the "Son of God," the Christian Scriptures identify him as having a *divine nature* in addition to a *human nature.* Jesus joins together all that is divine with all that is human. This makes him unique among all the people who ever lived.

In an effort to express this great mystery of God become human, the poet Richard Crashaw said of Jesus:

> *Welcome all wonders in one sight!
> Eternity shut in a span!
> Summer in Winter! Day in Night!
> Heaven on Earth, and God in Man.*

Jesus the Man

Artist Murray De Pillars says in *Ebony* magazine, "If we are to believe the life Jesus lived, the pictures that were painted of him just didn't fit the man." De Pillars's observation raises two interesting questions: What kind of a body did Jesus have? What kind of a personality did Jesus have?

Although the Bible is silent on both of these questions, it does offer some interesting clues. First, consider Jesus' body. The Bible suggests that Jesus—

- walked miles at a stretch (John 4:3-4),
- spent whole nights in prayer (Luke 6:12),
- often slept out under the stars (Luke 9:58).

Second, consider these clues that relate to Jesus' personality. Descriptions of Jesus in the Bible suggest that he—

- held crowds spellbound (Mark 6:34-36),
- liked children (Luke 18:15-16),
- developed deep personal friendships (John 11:1-6, 21:7).

The above clues lead some biblical experts to conclude that Jesus had a strong body and a warm personality. The important thing, however, is not what kind of body and personality Jesus had, but who he was.

Sea of Galilee on whose shores Jesus spent hours in prayer.

Savior

One day Jesus met a woman at a well outside a village. She was so impressed with Jesus that she hurried back to her village. Describing Jesus to the villagers, she said, "Could he be the Messiah?" (John 4:29). The villagers went to Jesus and invited him to teach them. After listening to him for two days, they said to one another, "He really is the *Savior of the world*" (John 4:42).

Jesus impacted other people in the same way. For example, Saint John writes in a letter to early Christians:

> *What we have seen and heard*
> *we announce to you also . . .*
> *that the Father sent his Son*
> *to be the* Savior of the world.
> 1 JOHN 1:3, 4:14

To appreciate in what sense Jesus is the "Savior of the world," recall the first sin. As a result of this sin, evil began to spread across the world, and the human race was doomed to destruction.

Saint Paul describes the first sin and its effect on the human race this way:

> *Sin came into the world*
> *through one man,*
> *and his sin brought death with it.*
> *As a result,*
> *death has spread to the whole human race*
> *because everyone has sinned.*
> ROMANS 5:12

Paul then goes on to describe how Jesus' death and resurrection *saved*, or *redeemed*, the human race. He writes:

> *So then,*
> *as the one sin condemned all mankind,*
> *in the same way*
> *the one righteous act [of Jesus]*
> *sets all mankind free and gives them life.*
> ROMANS 5:18

And so the title "Savior of the world" (or Redeemer) designates Jesus as being the one who will save the human race, which was doomed to destruction as a result of the first sin.

This church door in Germany contrasts the "tree of forbidden fruit" (de-creation) with the "tree of the cross" (re-creation). The first Adam and the first Eve are contrasted with Jesus (the new Adam) and Mary (the new Eve).

Recap

The Greek word *ICHTHYS*, which means "fish," was used by early Christian communities to symbolize the person who stands at the center of the Christian faith. He is—

- Jesus,   who has a *human* nature;
- Christ,   who is the *promised Messiah;*
- Son of God, who has a *divine* nature;
- Savior,   who *saved the world* from sin.

Understanding Jesus

Review

ICHTHYS

1. Explain why early Christians used a fish as a symbol of Jesus.

Jesus

2. How did Jesus get his name, and what does it mean?

Christ

3. Explain the relationship between the following: (a) Messiah, (b) Christos (Christ), and (c) the Anointed One.

4. By whom did Jesus say he was "anointed" and for what purpose?

5. On what occasion did Jesus make this announcement?

Son of God

6. Explain how the Hebrew Scriptures and the Christian Scriptures differ in the way they use the title "Son of God."

7. Describe one occasion on which Jesus clearly identified himself with God.

8. Explain what makes Jesus unique among all the people who ever lived.

Savior

9. Cite two occasions when the Christian Scriptures call Jesus the "Savior of the world."

Word of God

10. Explain the twofold sense in which Jesus may be called the "Word of God."

Jesus the Man

11. List three clues from Scripture that suggest Jesus was physically fit and three clues that suggest he had an attractive and warm personality.

Exercises

1. Albert Schweitzer gave up a musical career on the concert stages of Europe to become a missionary doctor in Africa. Toward the end of his life, he was awarded the Nobel Peace Prize and voted the "Man of the Century" by an international committee. When someone asked him what starting point he used to introduce Africans to Jesus, Schweitzer said: "When I speak to them of the difference between a restless heart and a peaceful heart, they know what I mean. And when I tell them that Jesus brings peace to the restless heart, they understand who Jesus is and why he came to live among us."

What is Schweitzer's point? What are some things that cause your heart to be restless at this time in your life?

2. A woman said that if we accept the Gospels as being faithful to Jesus' claim, the following three options are open to us:

- *Jesus was a liar.* He knew that he was not one with God the Father and deliberately deceived the people into thinking that he was.
- *Jesus was a lunatic.* He was a sick person, who was under the false illusion that he was one with the Father.
- *Jesus was the Lord.* He was the "living bread that came down from heaven" (John 6:51). He was the only "Son of God," of whom John said, "For God loved the world so much that he gave his only Son, so that everyone who believes in him may not die but have eternal life" (John 3:16).

Explain why you agree/disagree that Jesus was (a) a liar, (b) a lunatic, (c) the Lord.

3. Leonard LeSourd wrote an article called "The Five Christs I Have Known." It describes how his personal relationship with Jesus developed as he grew up.

- *First,* there was the *fanciful* Christ of his childhood. This Christ was like Santa Claus and the Easter Bunny—pretty much a figment of his imagination.
- *Second,* there was the *historical* Jesus of his student years. This Christ was like Abraham Lincoln or George Washington: an admirable person.
- *Third,* there was the *teacher* Christ of his early adult life. This Christ was like Aristotle: a wise person whose teaching was still valid.
- *Fourth,* there was the *savior* Christ. This Christ was different from any other person who ever lived. He was the Son of God, the Savior of the world. After discovering this Christ, LeSourd fell on his knees and asked Jesus to take control of his life.
- *Finally,* there was the *indwelling* Christ, who began to live in Jesus' followers after Pentecost. This Christ formed them into one body and empowered them to go forth and transform their world. It was this same Jesus who now took control of LeSourd's life.

Using LeSourd's "five Christs" as a guide, describe how your own relationship with Jesus has changed as you have grown older. How would you describe your present relationship with Jesus: declining, growing, in a holding pattern? Explain.

4. There was once a handsome prince who had a crooked back. This defect kept him from being the kind of prince he was meant to be. One day the king had the best sculptor in the kingdom make a statue of the prince. It portrayed him, however, not with a crooked back but with a straight back. The king placed the statue in the prince's private garden. When the prince saw it, his heart beat faster. For some reason it gave him hope. He began to dream that somehow he might become like the statue. In the days ahead, the prince found himself sitting in front of the statue daily, studying it, and desiring with all his heart to be like it. Months passed, and the people began to say to one

another, "Have you noticed? The prince's back doesn't seem as crooked as it once was." When the prince heard this, his heart beat even faster. Now he began to spend hours studying the statue and meditating on it. Then one day a remarkable thing happened. The prince found himself standing as straight as the statue.

Who/what do the following stand for in the parable: the king, the prince, the prince's crooked back, the garden, the statue, the prince's studying the statue? Explain how you might apply this parable to your own personal life.

5. A woman commented that the "Emmaus episode" (Luke 24:13–32) illustrates three ways that people still encounter the Risen Christ in today's world: in the broken person (15–19), the broken word (25–27, 32), and the broken bread (30–31).

Read the Emmaus episode and explain what the woman means by (a) broken person, (b) broken word, (c) broken bread. In which of the three ways do you find that you encounter Jesus most convincingly today?

Personal Reflection

Here is an imaginary dialogue between a wayfarer and Jesus.

WAYFARER: *I am traveling an unknown land to an unknown city. The sky is dark and misty. Soaring mountains and turbulent seas obscure my path. I have no map or person to guide me. My heart trembles.*

JESUS: *Fear not. I'll be your guide. I'll light up your darkness, move mountains from your path, help you walk on water, calm your heart and teach it to sing.*

What point does the dialogue make? Compose a dialogue that might take place between a modern high school student and Jesus.

Bible Reading

Pick a passage. After reading it prayerfully, write out a brief prayer to God that reflects your feelings or thoughts about it.

1. Lord and God	John 20:24–28
2. Son of God	Mark 15:22–39
3. Word of God	John 1:1–18
4. The Anointed One	Luke 4:16–22
5. Savior of the World	1 John 4:13–18

7 Holy Spirit

A missionary in Africa returned to England for a vacation. One day he saw a colorful sundial for sale. He thought, "That would be ideal for my villagers in Africa. I could teach them to tell time." So he bought the sundial, crated it up, and took it back with him.

When the chief saw how beautiful the sundial was, he insisted on putting it in the center of the village. The villagers were thrilled. And, of course, the missionary was delighted. He was therefore unprepared for what happened next. The villagers built a roof over the beautiful sundial to protect it from the rain and the sun.

After recovering from shock, the missionary thought to himself, "That beautiful sundial and the roof the villagers built over it are like the beautiful mystery of the Trinity and our Christian response to it."

What do you think the missionary had in mind?

God as Trinity

The central revelation of Christianity is God's self-revelation as Trinity. We Christians have correctly made this mystery the cornerstone of our faith. We stand in awe of it.

But instead of applying the teaching on the Trinity to our daily lives, we have "built a roof over it." For many of us God's self-revelation as Trinity has little practical impact on our daily lives. We treat the Trinity more like an "ornament" of our faith.

Put simply, the mystery of the Trinity says that in God there are three distinct persons: Father, Son, and Spirit. The Father is God, the Son is God, and the Holy Spirit is God. Yet there are not three Gods, but only one God.

Creation Reflects the Trinity

To give ancient Christians an idea of the Trinity, Saint Patrick used the image of a shamrock. It has one leaf that is made up of three petals. Saint Ignatius of Loyola used the image of three musical notes played simultaneously. The notes are totally different from one another, but they blend together to form only one sound. John Wesley used the image of three lighted candles. They are distinct from one another, but they blend together to form one light.

A modern theologian used the image of H_2O. This single chemical compound exists in three distinct forms: liquid (water), solid (ice), and vapor (steam). Finally, another modern theologian used the image of a woman. She is one person but relates to people in three different ways: as mother, as wife, and as friend.

These are feeble comparisons, but they may help us to better appreciate the incredible mystery of the Trinity.

Scripture Reveals the Trinity

The most dramatic reference to the Trinity occurs after the baptism of Jesus. Then the Holy Spirit "came down upon Jesus in bodily form like a dove." And a voice from heaven said, "You are my own dear Son" (Luke 3:22). The voice (Father), the dovelike form (Spirit), and Jesus (Son)—these three images create a graphic image of God as Trinity.

The clearest reference to the Trinity occurs just prior to Jesus' ascension into heaven, when he instructs his disciples:

> *Go . . . to all peoples everywhere*
> *and make them my disciples:*
> *baptize them*
> *in the name of the Father,*
> *the Son, and the Holy Spirit.*
>
> MATTHEW 28:19

References to the Trinity occur most frequently in John's Gospel. There Jesus mentions either the Father or the Spirit over a hundred different times. For example, he says:

> *"The Helper, the Holy Spirit,*
> *whom the Father will send in my name,*
> *will teach you everything*
> *and make you remember*
> *all that I have told you."*
>
> JOHN 14:25

The most intriguing references to the Trinity occur in Luke's Gospel and in his companion book to it, the Acts of the Apostles. Although Luke does not say so explicitly, a study of his two books shows that his vision of salvation history is trinitarian:

- Old Testament times: era of the Father,
- Gospel times: era of the Son, and
- post-Gospel times: era of the Spirit.

And so the idea of God as Father, Son, and Holy Spirit is reflected in creation and revealed in Scripture.

The Maestro and the Boy

A mother bought a ticket to a concert by Ignace Paderewski, the famous pianist. She took her five-year-old son, Jason, with her, hoping the experience would encourage his own musical efforts.

The mother was delighted to see how close to the stage their seats were. Then she met an old friend sitting nearby. She got so involved talking with her friend that she didn't notice Jason slip away to do some exploring.

At eight o'clock the auditorium lights dimmed, the audience hushed, and a spotlight fell on the piano on stage. Only then did the audience notice a tiny boy sitting on the piano bench, innocently picking out "Twinkle, Twinkle, Little Star." It was Jason. His mother gasped in total disbelief. But before she could do anything, Paderewski appeared on stage.

Walking over to Jason, the maestro whispered, "Keep playing!" Then, leaning over Jason, he reached out his left hand and began playing. A few seconds later, he reached around the other side of the boy, encircling him, and added a running obbligato. When they finished, the audience broke out in cheers.

The image of the great maestro transforming the boy's tiny contribution into something beautiful is a good image of how the Holy Spirit is at work in our lives. The Holy Spirit can take our talent, which may seem tiny in the eyes of the world, and turn it into something beautiful.

God as Spirit

I n his book *Meditations,* Anthony Bloom quotes a Japanese as saying to him: "In the Christian religion I think I understand about the Father and the Son, but I can never discover the significance of the honorable bird."

That Japanese is not alone. Many people find it hard to grasp the significance of the Holy Spirit.

Whenever we think of the Holy Spirit, we usually think of Pentecost: the coming of the Spirit upon the Apostles.

In a certain sense, however, it is dangerous to speak of the "coming of the Spirit." It can create the impression that the Holy Spirit did not exist before Pentecost. That is not true. The Holy Spirit has always existed. The Holy Spirit is as eternal as the Father and the Son.

The Acts of the Apostles makes it clear that the Spirit always existed. It portrays the Holy Spirit acting in the world long before Pentecost. For example, it says the Holy Spirit inspired David (Acts 1:16) and inspired Isaiah (Acts 28:25).

The Gospels also make it clear that the Holy Spirit acted in the life of Jesus. For example, the Holy Spirit—

- anointed Jesus   (Acts 10:38),
- empowered Jesus   (Luke 4:14), and
- guided Jesus   (Luke 4:1).

Even though the Holy Spirit acted in Old Testament times and in Gospel times, something unique and monumental *did* happen with the coming of the Spirit on Pentecost.

Morazzone's Pentecost.

The Spirit and Pentecost

A small boy got a toy sailboat for his birthday. He was so excited he could not sit still. He ran around the house, showing it to everybody. Finally, he ran to the window, looked at the sky, and said, "O God! Have you seen my boat?"

A long pause followed, as if the boy were waiting for God to answer. Then the boy turned and asked his mother, "What is God like?" But before his mother could answer, he shouted, "I know! He's like the wind!"

Ancient Jews would have applauded the boy's insight. They, too, saw a parallel between the wind and God. (The Hebrew word *ruah* ["wind"] may also be translated as "spirit" of God.) The unseen wind's breathlike touch and its stormlike power spoke to Jews of God's own unseen touch and power.

Another biblical image of God was fire. This probably grew out of Moses' experience of God in the burning bush (Exodus 3:3–6) and the people's experience of God coming down on Mount Sinai in firelike form (Exodus 19:16–18).

It is against this background of wind and fire that we should read the Pentecost story. Recall it. The disciples were gathered together in a house in Jerusalem.

The Spirit Begins a New Era

The first thing that amazed the crowd (many of whom were foreigners) was that they heard the Apostles speaking in their own languages (Acts 2:6). They asked:

> *"How is it . . . that all of us hear them speaking in our own native languages?"*
> ACTS 2:8

To answer this question, we need to recall the Old Testament story of the Tower of Babel. Prior to the building of the tower, the Bible says that all people spoke "one language" (Genesis 11:6).

The thing that motivated the people to build the tower was pride (Genesis 11:4). Because of their pride, God mixed up their language, and they could not go on building the tower. The story ends by saying that people scattered "all over the earth."

It is against this background that we must interpret the remark that people from "every country in the world" understood the Apostles in their "own native languages" (Acts 2:5–6).

It means that what happened at the Tower of Babel is now being reversed. What sin split apart, the Holy Spirit is now joining back together.

The coming of the Holy Spirit marks a quantum leap forward in God's plan to re-create the world.

Suddenly there was a noise from the sky
which sounded like a strong wind blowing,
and it filled the whole house
where they were sitting.
Then they saw
what looked like tongues of fire
which spread out
and touched each person there.
They were all filled with the Holy Spirit
and began to talk in other languages,
as the Spirit enabled them to speak.
ACTS 2:2–4

The "noise from the sky" was so loud that it was heard throughout the city and attracted a crowd to the house. Hearing the crowd gathering, Peter and the other Apostles went out to speak to them.

Brueghel's Tower of Babel.

The Spirit Makes Us One in Christ

When the excited crowd quieted down, Peter explained that what had happened was what God had foretold through the prophet Joel:

> *"I will pour out my Spirit on everyone.*
> *Your sons and daughters*
> *will proclaim my message."*
> ACTS 2:17

Peter's words moved the people. Nearly three thousand asked to be baptized that very day. And from that moment on, the people shared not only the same belief but also the same life in the Spirit (1 Corinthians 12:12–27).

And so the unique and monumental thing that happened on Pentecost is this: The Holy Spirit came upon the disciples and, from that moment on, they began to experience what Jesus had foretold:

> *"that I am in my Father*
> *and that you are in me,*
> *just as I am in you."*
> JOHN 14:20

In other words, the disciples began to experience that the Holy Spirit had come upon them and formed them into "Christ's body," the Church.

We may draw this breathtaking comparison:

- Jesus' coming on Christmas made God present on earth in a special way: *in the person* of Jesus.
- The Spirit's coming on Pentecost made God present on earth in a special way: *in the community* of Jesus' followers.

As a result, we may draw this breathtaking conclusion: What Jesus was for his world, the Church (the community of his followers) is for our world:

- a *sign* of God's presence on earth, and
- an *instrument* of God's activity on earth.

Our Mission

The famous Italian composer Puccini wrote a number of operas. His last one was *Turandot* (Tour-en-doe). Many people consider it his best. While writing it, he was stricken with cancer. When his cancer worsened, he said to his students, "If I don't finish this opera, I want you to finish it for me."

Then came the fateful day. Puccini was taken to Brussels for an operation and died two days after surgery. In the months that followed, his students completed his final opera.

The world premiere was performed in Milan. It was directed by Puccini's favorite student, Toscanini.

Everything went well until the opera reached the place where Puccini finished writing. Tears ran down Toscanini's cheeks. He stopped the music, put down his baton, turned to the audience, and cried out, "Thus far the Master wrote, but he died." Then there was silence throughout the Milan opera house. No one moved; no one spoke.

After a minute, Toscanini picked up the baton again, smiled through his tears, and cried out, "But the disciples finished his work." When the opera ended, the audience broke into a thunderous applause.

The story of *Turandot* bears a striking resemblance to the story of Christianity. Before Jesus could complete his Father's work on earth, he died. But before he did, he asked his disciples to complete it.

It is now up to us, the disciples of Jesus, to finish the work he began, just as Puccini's disciples finished his work.

Spirit as Sanctifier

One day Jesus was in Jerusalem, celebrating the Feast of the Tabernacles. Part of the celebration involved drawing water from the Pool of Siloam and carrying it in procession to the Temple. At this point in the celebration, Jesus turned to his disciples and said:

*"As the scripture says,
'Whoever believes in me,
streams of life-giving water
will pour out from his heart.' "*

*Jesus said this about the Spirit,
which those who believed in him
were going to receive.*

JOHN 7:38-39

Some people ask, "Why did Jesus choose the image of water to refer to the Holy Spirit?" One early Christian writer, Cyril of Jerusalem, answered this way: "Because all *physical* life depends on water." He went on to say:

*Water descends from heaven as rain.
Although it is always the same in itself,
it produces different effects
in different things: one in the palm tree,
another in the vine, and so on. . . .
Rain adapts itself to every creature.*

It is the same with the Holy Spirit. All *spiritual* life depends on the Holy Spirit. And the Holy Spirit produces different effects in different people: one effect in one person, another effect in another person, and so on. The Holy Spirit adapts to each person. That is, the Holy Spirit gives different gifts to different persons. Saint Paul writes:

*The Spirit's presence
is shown in some way in each person
for the good of all.*

*The Spirit
gives one person a message full of wisdom,
while to another person . . .
he gives the power to heal.*

*The Spirit gives one person
the power to work miracles;*

*to another,
the gift of speaking God's message;
and to yet another,
the ability to tell the difference
between gifts that come from the Spirit
and those that do not.*

1 CORINTHIANS 12:7-10

The end purpose of these gifts is "to build up the body of Christ" (Ephesians 4:12). Or to put it another way, it is to sanctify (*make holy*) the community of Jesus' followers—just as Jesus was holy. Saint Augustine had this in mind when he wrote:

*Breathe in me, Spirit of God,
that I may think what is holy.*

*Drive me, Spirit of God,
that I may do what is holy.*

*Draw me, Spirit of God,
that I may love what is holy.*

*Strengthen me, Spirit of God,
that I may preserve what is holy.*

*Guide me, Spirit of God,
that I may never lose what is holy.*

Recap

The central mystery of Christianity is the revelation of *God as Trinity*. This mystery is "imaged" in creation and revealed in Scripture.

The third person of the Trinity is the Holy Spirit. With the Father and the Son, the Spirit is eternal: without beginning or end. The Holy Spirit acted in Old Testament times and in Jesus' life.

The coming of the Holy Spirit upon Jesus' followers marks a quantum leap forward in the *re-creation* of the world. It forms the disciples into Christ's Body and makes them the *sign* and the *instrument* of God's presence in our world— just as Jesus was in his world.

Understanding Holy Spirit

Review

God as Trinity

1. Explain how the following serve as an image of the Trinity: (a) three musical notes sounded simultaneously, (b) the chemical compound H_2O, (c) a woman.

2. Explain the following references to the Trinity in Scripture: (a) the most dramatic, (b) the clearest.

3. Where do references to the Trinity occur most frequently? Give an example.

4. How does Luke present a trinitarian view of salvation history?

God as Spirit

5. Give two examples of the Spirit's action during each of the following: (a) Old Testament times, (b) Gospel times (Jesus' life).

The Spirit and Pentecost

6. What was the first thing that amazed the crowd on Pentecost when the Apostles spoke to them? What is the meaning of this experience in the light of the Old Testament story of the Tower of Babel?

7. What breathtaking comparison and what breathtaking conclusion may we draw as a result of the Spirit's coming on Pentecost?

Spirit as Sanctifier

8. Explain why water is a good image of the Holy Spirit.

9. List three examples of different gifts that Saint Paul says God gives to people.

10. For what end purpose does the Holy Spirit give different gifts to different persons?

Exercises

1. The Olympic flame was flown from its home in Olympia, Greece, to New York in 1984. From there, runners carried it across the country to the 1984 Summer Games in Los Angeles. As the journey progressed, something beautiful began to happen. Towns greeted the runners by ringing church bells and blowing sirens. Tears flowed down the cheeks of spectators, and spontaneous singing broke out. An elderly woman spoke for many when she said to one runner, "Thank you, son, for making me feel like this again." When the torch reached the site of the games in Los Angeles Colosseum, 93,000 people stood up and cheered. It was the climax of a patriotic experience of unity that temporarily transformed our nation into a family. At that moment the president might have said to Americans what Saint Paul said to early Christians after Pentecost: "Do your best to preserve the unity which the Spirit gives" (Ephesians 4:3).

How do you account for the impact that the Olympic torch ritual had on our nation? Describe a time when you felt a special sense of unity with those around you (for example, a rock concert, a retreat experience, a march or walk for a good cause, a team victory). Be specific about some of the things that happened to make it an experience of unity.

2. A Tennessee mountaineer read an advertisement about a power saw. The ad said a person could cut six times more wood with it than with a plain saw. He bought one. But to his dismay, he found it no better than a plain saw. So he returned it to the store. "I don't understand," said the salesman. "It's our best saw. Here, let me check it." He pulled the cord, and a burst of noise and blue smoke came from the saw. The mountaineer jumped back and said, "What's that?" The salesman said, "That's the *power*. That's what enables you to cut six times more wood with it than with a plain saw."

A woman said, "That story could be used to illustrate the difference between Jesus' disciples before and after Pentecost."

Explain the woman's point. How are many people today like the Tennessee mountaineer?

3. Kathryn Koob was one of 52 Americans held hostage for 444 days by Iran in 1980–81. She remembers how angry students used to parade outside the embassy and shout, almost around the clock. She was terrified. One night she dozed off momentarily. Then she was awakened by what seemed to be someone sitting on the edge of her bed. She says, "I turned over quickly. . . . But no one was there. Instantly, I was reminded of the Holy Spirit the Comforter. And with the sense of [the Spirit's] presence came a real knowledge that I had a source of strength that the students and mobs didn't have." From that moment forward, Kathryn's fear vanished. She even found herself trying to appreciate the perspective of her captors, so that she could respond to it with understanding rather than with resentment.

What suggests to you that Kathryn's experience was a true experience and not an imaginary one? Recall a frightening experience you had and the role that prayer played (if it did) in helping you cope with it. Be specific.

4. Connie Charette says, "The Holy Spirit is at the heart of feminist *spirituality*. We go beyond the male image of God when we speak of the Spirit." In fact, she says, "The Spirit is spoken of as a woman" in the ninth, tenth, and eleventh chapters of the Book of Wisdom. For example, Solomon asks God to send the "holy spirit" (Wisdom 9:17) upon him, saying:

"Send her from the holy heavens,
down from your glorious throne,
so that she may work at my side. . . .
She knows and understands everything."
WISDOM 9:10–11

Someone described *spirituality* as "the way we approach and relate to God, especially in prayer and worship." Keeping this description in mind, explain how the following might differ in the way they "approach and relate to God": (a) male vs. female, (b) young vs. old, (c) rich vs. poor. Give one example to illustrate how one *spirituality* can enrich another.

5. Malcolm Muggeridge, the British television celebrity, was one of the first media people to interview Mother Teresa of Calcutta. The technical evaluation of his taped interview was that it was hardly usable. Mother Teresa had a thick accent that made for tedious listening and viewing. Nevertheless, one high-ranking television official felt the interview possessed a mysterious power. He scheduled it during prime time on a Sunday night. The viewer response was dynamite—both in terms of mail to the TV station and contributions to Mother Teresa's work. Muggeridge's explanation of the interview was this: What came through was not Mother Teresa's eloquence, but the Holy Spirit speaking through her.

Concretely, what did Muggeridge mean? Describe an occasion (a test, a confrontation, a dangerous situation) when you felt helped by the Holy Spirit. Be as detailed as you can.

Personal Reflection

A man wrote:

Of the three persons of the Trinity, I relate to God the Father best. The reason is that I too am a father. I know how God must feel when he sees his children (the human race) ignore his advice, refuse his help, and disobey him. And I'm sure God knows how I feel when I see my children doing the same thing. I'm also sure that God worries about his children the way I sometimes worry about mine. On the other hand, I'm sure that God also gets tears in his eyes when he sees his children act out of love and generosity, rather than out of personal gain and selfishness. The Father and I have a lot in common. He's my model and my inspiration. Not a day goes by that I don't turn to him for some kind of guidance.

Write a similar paragraph concerning which person of the Trinity you relate and pray to best.

Bible Reading

Pick a passage. After reading it prayerfully, write out a brief prayer to God that reflects your personal feelings about it.

1. Jesus and the Spirit	Luke 4:14–22
2. Wait for the Spirit	Acts 1:1–8
3. Outpouring of the Spirit	Acts 2:14–18
4. Fruits of the Spirit	Galatians 5:16–26
5. Life in the Spirit	Romans 8:1–17

8 Church

There's a poem about six blind men from Indostan. They are standing around an elephant, wondering what it looks like. One blind man feels its side and says the elephant looks like a wall. Another feels its tail and says it looks like a rope. A third feels its trunk and says it looks like a snake. A fourth feels its ear and says it looks like a fan. A fifth feels its tusk and says it looks like a spear. A sixth feels its leg and says it looks like a tree. The poem ends:

And so these men of Indostan
Disputed loud and long,
Each in his own opinion
Exceeding stiff and strong.
Though each was partly in the right,
They all were in the wrong.
John Godfrey Saxe

A theology teacher used this poem in a talk to explain the different views that people have of the Catholic Church. Then she asked her audience two questions: "First, how do we get our view of the Church? Second, how can we keep from making the same mistake that the blind men did?"

How would you answer her questions?

A tiny seed grows into a great tree.

Models of the Church

Like the elephant in the poem, the Catholic Church is a many-sided reality. And like the blind men in the poem, some people see only one side of it at a time. As a result, they often end up making the error that the blind men did.

Because the Church is a many-sided reality, it can't be described in simple terms. This explains why theologians today also use *models* to describe the Church. A *model* is an *image* that helps us better understand a complex reality.

Theologians are not the only ones who use models. Scientists also use them. For example, no scientist has ever seen the complex reality known as the electron. The word *electron* is simply a name they give to a consistent set of events that happen in certain circumstances.

In dealing with the electron, scientists sometimes use a *wave* as their model, and sometimes a *particle*. What they can't explain by one model, they can usually explain by the other.

Jesus Used Models

Jesus also used models to help people get an idea of the Kingdom of God. For example, Jesus compared it to—

- a tiny seed that grows into a great tree (Matthew 13:31–32),
- a tiny bit of yeast that makes a large batch of dough rise (Matthew 13:33),
- a pearl that a merchant finds and then he sells all he has in order to buy it (Matthew 13:45–46).

Jesus' use of many images to describe the Kingdom of God illustrates an important point about models. They must be used in *clusters,* never alone. A single model, used alone, distorts reality rather than clarifies it. This is evident in the case of the blind men and the elephant.

Six Church Models Are Used

Before we discuss some of the models that are used to describe the Church, we should clarify three points.

First, the Church is a "mystery" (Ephesians 5:32, NAB). It is so complex that we will never fully understand it in this life. This is why the Christian Scriptures use so many images to explore the mystery of the Church.

Second, the Church is a "sign" and "servant" of God's Kingdom, which is already in our midst but not yet fully realized. In other words, the Church is called to "point to" and "work for" the *completion* of the Kingdom of God that Jesus will hand over to his Father at the end of time—

an eternal and universal kingdom:
a kingdom of truth and life,
a kingdom of holiness and grace,
a kingdom of justice, love, and peace.
PREFACE OF THE MASS FOR CHRIST THE KING

Finally, the Church is a "community." When the Christian Scriptures use the word *church* (which they do about a hundred times), they do not mean a *building,* as we often do. They mean a *community.* Early Christians never thought of "going to church." They "were the church." And so theologians also use the word *church* to refer to a *community.*

This brings us to some of the *models* that theologians use to describe the Church and the kind of community each focuses on.

Model	Kind of Community
Disciples	faith
Body	life-sharing
Basic sacrament	sacramental
People of God	witnessing
Institution	hierarchical
Servant	ministering

Disciples Model

In 1980 a religious persecution left large parts of Guatemala without priests. But this has not kept Guatemalan Catholics from meeting each Sunday. Since they have no priests, they rely on the Holy Spirit to guide them in their worship. Describing the form their worship takes, Fernando Bermudez writes in *Death and Resurrection in Guatemala*: "All confess their sins together, aloud, kneeling, everyone at once, then singing a song asking God's forgiveness."

Next, a lay leader reads a Bible passage and explains it. Finally, others are invited to share what meaning the passage holds for them.

Once a month the communities send a representative to a part of Guatemala where priests are still allowed to function. Traveling as much as eighteen hours on foot, these representatives take part in the celebration of Mass in the name of their parish.

Before Mass, they put baskets of bread on the altar to become the Eucharist. After Mass, they carry the Eucharist back to their parishes.

These loosely structured communities, relying on the Holy Spirit to guide them, bring to mind the first Church communities described in the Acts of the Apostles. They give us an insight into what theologians mean by the *disciples* model of the Church.

Focus and Message

The disciples model focuses on the fact that the Church is a *faith community* of Jesus' disciples guided by the Holy Spirit. The Church is a group of people who believe in Jesus and try to follow his teaching. Jesus promised this faith community of his disciples:

"The Helper, the Holy Spirit,
whom the Father will send in my name,
will teach you everything
and make you remember
all that I have told you . . .
[and] lead you into all the truth."
JOHN 14:26, 16:13

This promise underscores the fact that the Church is still learning. (The word *disciples* means "learners.") In other words, the Church does not have ready-made answers to all the problems of modern life. But the Church is guided by the Holy Spirit in our times, just as Jesus was guided by the Holy Spirit in Gospel times (Luke 4:1).

And so the disciples model contains this important message:

> As the Spirit *guided Jesus in Gospel times,*
> so the Spirit *guides the Church in modern times.*

Fire is a biblical symbol of God.

Strength and Weakness

A *strength* of the disciples model is its stress on the need for the Church to be open to the Holy Spirit's guidance.

A *weakness* is that we can focus so strongly on the need to be open to the Spirit that we can forget that the Spirit acts in a unique way through Church leaders. Therefore, openness to the Spirit also means openness to the guidance of those commissioned to shepherd the Church (Matthew 18:19).

Four Marks of the Church

Father Walter Ciszek was arrested in Russia during World War II. He spent twenty-three years in prison. In his book *He Leadeth Me,* he describes how a tiny community of Catholic prisoners used to gather in secret to celebrate the Eucharist "in drafty storage shacks, or huddled together in mud and slush in the corner of a building site foundation."

At these Masses, the prisoners prayed together the same Creed that we pray at each Sunday Eucharist. A portion of it reads: "We believe in one holy catholic and apostolic Church."

Let's take a brief look at what we mean when we say "one," "holy," "catholic," and "apostolic." Called the *four marks* of the Church, they simultaneously describe the Church and identify its mission.

First, the Church is *one*. At the Last Supper, Jesus prayed for his followers, saying:

> *"I pray that they may all be one.*
> *Father! May they be in us,*
> *just as you are in me and I am in you."*
> JOHN 17:21

On Pentecost, the Holy Spirit gave to Jesus' disciples a special unity, forming them into the Body of Christ. The Church's mission is not only to preserve that unity but also to deepen it.

Second, the Church is *holy* in the sense that it is the Body of Christ and shares the holiness of Christ himself. Again, this holiness is in "seed" form and must be cultivated by prayer and service.

Third, the Church is *catholic*. The word *catholic* (Greek, *katholike*) means "universal." The Christian Scriptures show that Jesus intended his Church to carry the Gospel to *all* nations and *all* cultures. Moreover, the Church is catholic in the sense that it has the potential to embrace forms of religious expression as diverse as the cultures in which it finds itself. Again, this is a *potential* that is present in the Church but not yet completely realized.

Finally, the Church is *apostolic* in the sense that it not only traces its origin back to the Apostles but also continues to preserve and proclaim their original faith vision and teaching.

Body Model

Many people are surprised to learn that Saint Paul began his life as an enemy of Christianity. One day while on his way to Damascus to persecute Christians, Paul had a remarkable experience.

> *Suddenly a light from the sky*
> *flashed around him.*
> *He fell to the ground*
> *and heard a voice saying to him,*
> *"Saul, Saul! Why do you persecute me?"*
>
> *"Who are you, Lord?" he asked.*
> *"I am Jesus, whom you persecute,"*
> *the voice said.*
> ACTS 9:3-5

This experience led Paul to an incredible realization: Jesus and his followers form one body. To persecute the followers of Jesus is to persecute Jesus himself.

Caravaggio's portrayal of Paul's Damascus experience.

This brings us to what theologians call the *body* model of the Church.

Focus and Message

The body model focuses on the fact that the Church is a *life-sharing community.* The members of the Church form a single body with Jesus as their head (Colossians 1:18). As head of the Church, Jesus is the source of its life (Ephesians 4:15-16). Jesus stressed this point when he said:

> *"I am the vine, and you are the branches.*
> *Whoever remains in me, and I in him,*
> *will bear much fruit. . . .*
> *Whoever does not remain in me*
> *is thrown out like a branch and dries up."*
> JOHN 15:5-6

In other words, just as a branch cannot live apart from a vine, so we cannot live apart from the Body of Christ.

And so the body model contains this important message:

> As Jesus *shared his Father's life,*
> so the Church *shares Jesus' life.*

Strength and Weakness

A *strength* of the body model is its stress on the fact that the Church is not an organization but an *organism,* the living body of the Risen Christ.

A *weakness* is that we can focus so strongly on Jesus' role as *head* of the body that we forget our responsibility as *members* of the body. Just as the human body counts on each cell to do its part, so the Body of Christ counts on each of us to do our part. As Saint Paul said, "If one part of the body suffers, all the other parts suffer with it" (1 Corinthians 12:26).

Basic Sacrament Model

One day Jesus said, "Whoever has seen me has seen the Father" (John 14:9). These words explain why theologians sometimes call Jesus the *sacrament* of God's presence.

The word *sacrament,* applied to Jesus, means that Jesus is the sign and source of our intimate union with God, and of unity of the whole human race.

This gives us an insight into what theologians mean by the *basic sacrament* model of the Church.

Focus and Message

The basic sacrament model focuses on the fact that the Church is a *sacramental community.* The Church is Jesus, the Body of Christ, present and active in the world in a tangible way—in a way that we can see, hear, and feel. In other words, just as Jesus could say, "Whoever has seen me has seen the Father," so the Church can say, "Whoever has seen me has seen Jesus."

Theologians call the Church the *basic* sacrament to distinguish it from the *individual* seven sacraments (Baptism, and so forth), which are actions of Christ himself continued in the Church.

And so the basic sacrament model contains this important message:

> As the Father
> is *present and works in Jesus,*
> so Jesus
> is *present and works in the Church.*

Strength and Weakness

A *strength* of the basic sacrament model is its stress on the fact that through the Church (especially the seven sacraments) we encounter the risen Jesus in a tangible way.

A *weakness* is that through ignorance of what the sacraments are, or through routine celebration of them, we treat them as "dead" rituals rather than as "living" encounters with the risen Jesus.

The Christ of the Andes in South America.

People of God Model

The Scottish theologian William Barclay tells a beautiful story of an old African chief taking part in the celebration of the Eucharist one Sunday morning. Tears came to the chief's eyes as he watched members of the Ngoni, Senga, and Tumbuka tribes worshiping side by side.

Suddenly his mind flashed back to his boyhood. The chief recalled watching Ngoni warriors, after a day's fighting, washing Senga and Tumbuka blood from their spears and bodies. The contrast between what he saw then and now was the difference between night and day.

That morning at the Eucharist the old chief understood, as never before, what Christianity is all about. It is God calling all people, in and through Jesus, to put an end to all hostility and live together as one family.

The story of the African chief gives us an insight into what is meant by the *People of God* model of the Church.

Focus and Message

The *People of God* model focuses on the fact that the Church is a *witnessing community.* The Church proclaims, not only by *word* but also by *worship,* what Jesus proclaimed: the good news of God's Kingdom. The Church proclaims that the "kingdom of Satan" that held sway over the human race for so many centuries is now being replaced by the "Kingdom of God" (Luke 11:20).

Like the community of the African warriors, worshiping side by side, the community of the Church *witnesses* to the good news that, in and through Jesus, God is bringing to completion the *re-creation* of the world. The First Letter of Peter refers to this *witness,* saying to newly baptized Christians:

> *You are the chosen race,*
> *the King's priests, the holy nation,*
> *God's own people,*
> *chosen to proclaim the wonderful acts of God,*
> *who called you out of darkness*
> *into his own marvelous light.*
> *At one time you were not God's people,*
> *but now you are his people;*
> *at one time you did not know God's mercy,*
> *but now you have received his mercy.*
> 1 PETER 2:9-10

These stirring words affirm that *all* baptized Christians share not only in Jesus' *prophet* ministry (witness by *word*) but also in his *priestly* ministry (witness by *worship*). We have been consecrated a priestly people, not in the *ordained* sense of priesthood, but in a related sense: different in degree and essence.

And so the *People of God* model of the Church focuses on the fact that the Church is a *witnessing* community. This means that just as the Father could say of Jesus, "This is my Son, whom I have chosen—listen to him!" (Luke 9:35), so Jesus could say of his Church, "Whoever listens to you listens to me" (Luke 10:16). The *People of God* model contains this important message:

> As Jesus *spoke in his Father's name*,
> so the Church *speaks in Jesus' name*.

Strength and Weakness

A *strength* of this model is its stress on the Church proclaiming the good news of salvation, namely, that through Jesus, God is *re-creating* the world.

A *weakness* is that we can focus so strongly on "speaking" the good news that we can forget that actions speak louder than words. We can forget that one of the most effective ways to "speak" is by worship and work. Referring to this, Jesus said to his followers:

> *"You are like light for the whole world. . . .*
> *Your light must shine before people,*
> *so that they will see the good things you do*
> *and praise your Father in heaven."*
> MATTHEW 5:14, 16

Institution Model

One day Jesus was teaching the Apostles. After a while, he turned to Peter and said:

> *"You are a rock,*
> *and on this rock foundation*
> *I will build my church. . . .*
> *I will give you*
> *the keys of the Kingdom of heaven;*
> *what you prohibit on earth*
> *will be prohibited in heaven,*
> *and what you permit on earth*
> *will be permitted in heaven."*
> MATTHEW 16:18–19

This is one of the most amazing passages in the Christian Scriptures. It shows Jesus sharing his power and authority with Peter. In other words, Jesus gives Peter a special leadership role in the Church, the community of Jesus' followers.

Peter's special responsibility explains why he is always first on the list of Apostles (Luke 6:14–16). It also explains why Peter exercises a special leadership in the community of the Church (Acts 1:15).

Jesus' conferral of power and authority on Peter brings us to the *institution* model of the Church.

Focus and Message

The institution model focuses on the fact that the Church is a *hierarchical community*. In other words, not all members of the Church have the same authority and responsibilities. To put it in another way, Jesus gave certain members of the Church the special responsibility and authority to speak and act in his name.

This means that we must take seriously Jesus' words to his Apostles:

> *"Whoever listens to you listens to me;*
> *whoever rejects you rejects me;*
> *and whoever rejects me*
> *rejects the one who sent me."*
> LUKE 10:16

And so the institution model contains this important message:

> As Jesus *shared his Father's authority,*
> so the Church *shares Jesus' authority.*

Strength and Weakness

A *strength* of this model is its stress on the fact that Jesus gave the leaders of his Church definite authority.

A *weakness* of this model is that the Church's leaders (humans like ourselves) can abuse their authority. They can use it in a dictatorial or bureaucratic way.

Servant Model

Cardinal Richard Cushing was a popular archbishop of Boston. He was also a close friend of President John F. Kennedy. In a beautiful letter to the people of his diocese, the cardinal wrote:

> *Jesus came*
> *not only to proclaim*
> *the coming of the Kingdom,*
> *but also to give himself for its realization.*
> *He came to serve, to heal,*
> *to reconcile, to bind up wounds.*
> *Jesus, we may say,*
> *is in an exceptional way the Good Samaritan.*
> *He is the one who comes alongside of us*
> *in our need and in our sorrow;*
> *he extends himself for our sake.*
> *He truly dies that we might live*
> *and he ministers to us that we might be healed.*

Cardinal Cushing's description of Jesus gives us an insight into what theologians mean by the *servant* model of the Church.

Focus and Message

The servant model focuses on the fact that the Church is called to be a *ministering community*. All members of the Church are called to follow Jesus himself, who said:

> *"The Son of Man did not come to be served;*
> *he came to serve."*
> MARK 10:45

And so the servant model contains this important message:

> As Jesus was a *person for others,*
> so the Church is a *community for others.*

Strength and Weakness

A *strength* of this model is its stress on the fact that the Church is called to render special service to society's needy: the poor, the exploited, the powerless.

A *weakness* is the obvious risk this involves. Members of the Church can champion the cause of society's needy in a way that abandons the teachings of the Gospel. They can begin to operate only for political gain and resort to purely political strategies and tactics to achieve their goals.

Light and Darkness

The Church is unlike any other community on earth. It has two dimensions that make it unique:

- a *divine* dimension and
- a *human* dimension.

The *divine* dimension is the invisible dimension of the Church. This dimension is Christ himself, who is the head of the body of the Church, and whose own life makes the body live.

The *human* dimension is the visible dimension of the Church. This dimension is the members of the body of the Church. They make Christ tangibly present and active in the world by their witness and worship. Because this dimension of the Church is human, it is like anything else that is human. It is flawed.

Because the Church on earth is flawed, it does not always show to the world the "face of Christ." All members—and even its divinely commissioned leaders—fall victim to human weakness. This means that we often see the Church community as being like ourselves: sinful and still struggling to become what God called it to be.

As a result, the pilgrim Church on earth will always be a mixture of light and darkness. There will always be enough light for those who wish to see, and enough darkness for those whose disposition is otherwise.

And that is how it should be. The light should never overpower us; it only invites us. That is, it never takes away our freedom.

Or to put it another way: When it comes to Jesus' presence in the Church, he never manifests himself so clearly as to leave us without questions. And he never *conceals* himself so completely as to mislead the sincere searcher. He leaves open both possibilities. Jesus respects each individual's freedom to accept or reject him, the Light of the World.

Recap

The Church is a mystery. Like a diamond, it has many facets and can't be viewed all at once. A study of some of the Church's facets (called *models*) reveals these parallels between Jesus and the Church:

Disciples	As Jesus was guided by the Spirit, the Church is guided by the Spirit.
Body	As Jesus shared his Father's life, the Church shares Jesus' life.
Sacrament	As the Father is present and works in Jesus, so Jesus is present and works in the Church.
People of God	As Jesus spoke in his Father's name, the Church speaks in Jesus' name.
Institution	As Jesus shared his Father's authority, the Church shares Jesus' authority.
Servant	As Jesus was a person for others, the Church is a community for others.

Understanding Church

Review

Models of the Church

1. What is a model and why are models used? Give three models, or images, that Jesus used to describe the Kingdom of heaven.

2. Why must we use models in clusters rather than alone?

3. Explain (a) what we mean when we speak of the Church as a mystery and (b) what the Scriptures mean when they speak about "the Church."

4. Explain (a) what we mean by the Kingdom of God and (b) the threefold relationship of the Kingdom of God to the Church.

Disciples Model

5. List and briefly explain the (a) focus, (b) message, (c) strength, and (d) weakness of the disciples model.

Body Model

6. List and briefly explain the (a) focus, (b) message, (c) strength, and (d) weakness of the body model.

Basic Sacrament Model

7. List and briefly explain the (a) focus, (b) message, (c) strength, and (d) weakness of the basic sacrament model.

People of God Model

8. List and briefly explain the (a) focus, (b) message, (c) strength, and (d) weakness of the People of God model.

Institution Model

9. List and briefly explain the (a) focus, (b) message, (c) strength, and (d) weakness of the institution model.

Servant Model

10. List and briefly explain the (a) focus, (b) message, (c) strength, and (d) weakness of the servant model.

Light and Darkness

11. Explain the following: (a) the divine dimension of the Church, (b) the human dimension of the Church, (c) the statement that the Church "will always be a mixture of light and darkness," (d) why it is fitting that the Church should be this kind of mixture.

Four Marks of the Church

12. List and briefly explain the four marks of the Church.

Exercises

1. When eighty-four-year-old Dorothy Day died in 1980, the *New York Times* praised her as one of the heroines of our time. She became a Catholic in her adult years and worked among New York's poor. In her autobiography, *The Long Loneliness,* she makes this candid statement: "I loved the Church for Christ made visible. Not itself, because it was so often a scandal to me." She compared the human dimension of the Church to the cross on which Christ was crucified, saying that you cannot "separate Christ from his cross." And so, even though the Church was often a scandal to her, she still became a Catholic and remained one until she died.

What is Dorothy's point when she says she loves the Church because it makes Christ "visible"? To what Church *model* is she referring? How does Jesus' parable in Matthew 13:24–30 help us to understand evil (scandal) in the Church? What point does Jesus make in this parable? What is one thing about the Church that you find to be a scandal? How do you cope with it?

2. Martin Luther King wrote a famous letter while confined in the Birmingham City Jail. He explained how early Christians rejoiced that they were able to suffer for their faith. "In those days," he wrote, "the Church was not merely a thermometer that recorded ideas and principles of popular belief; it was a thermostat that transformed the mores of society." He continued: "If the Church of today does not recapture the sacrificial spirit of the early Church, it will lose its authentic ring, forfeit the loyalty of millions, and be dismissed as an irrelevant social fan club with no meaning for the twentieth century."

Explain the difference between a thermostat and a thermometer. In what sense did Jesus intend his Church to be a thermostat?

3. An old Jew, named Samuel, stopped going to the synagogue because someone there had publicly humiliated him. One day an old rabbi from the synagogue visited Samuel. He asked to come in and sit with Samuel in front of his fireplace. And so the two men sat together in complete silence, watching the fire burn. After twenty minutes, the old rabbi picked up a pair of tongs, took a glowing coal from the fireplace, and set it on Samuel's hearth. As they watched, the coal slowly lost its glow. Then it died completely. A few minutes later, Samuel turned to the old rabbi and said, "I understand. I'll come back to the synagogue."

What did Samuel understand? Interview someone who has stopped practicing the faith. *After reading the story of Samuel to them,* ask them the following four questions:

- Why did you stop practicing the faith?
- What keeps you from returning?
- What do you miss most?
- What have you put in place of church attendance to keep your faith alive?

Write a brief report, covering the following three points:

- the age and profession of the person you interviewed,
- the responses the person gave to the four questions,
- your evaluation of the interview, in general, and the responses to the questions, in particular.

4. A survey shows that 40 percent of Catholics between the ages of fifteen and twenty-nine stop practicing their faith for a period of two years or more. Seventy percent of these return to the Church. Sixty percent of those who return do so because of the positive influence of a friend, relative, or neighbor.

On a scale of one (rarely) to ten (regularly), how would you grade the frequency of your own participation in the celebration of Sunday Mass? On a scale of one to ten, how would you grade your involvement in youth activities in your parish? Give a brief explanation for both of your answers.

5. A young pastor took over his new parish. He found the services poorly attended and the spirit of the parish dead. He went door-to-door to talk to the people. All agreed that the parish was dead, and no one knew how to revive it. The young pastor then announced that since the parish was dead, he would hold a funeral service for it the following Sunday. People's curiosity was aroused and the church was filled. In front of the pulpit was a casket. After the pastor had preached a moving eulogy, he invited all to come forward to view the corpse. The people filed up to the casket, looked in, and saw a mirror that reflected back to them their own faces. Many were indignant, but many more got the point.

What was the point? If the young pastor asked you to be a part of a team to breathe life back into the parish, how would respond and why? If the young pastor asked you for one suggestion to get young people more involved in your parish, what would it be?

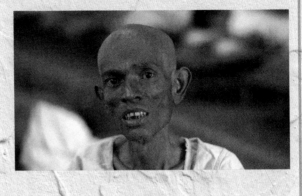

Personal Reflection

During his visit to Peru in 1985, Pope John Paul II visited the economically and socially deprived. At one stop, a spokesperson for the poor read this statement to him:

We are hungry,
we live in misery,
we are sick and out of work.
Our women give birth in tuberculosis,
our infants die,
our children grow weak. . . .
But despite this
we believe in the God of life. . . .
We have walked
with the Church and in the Church,
and it has helped us . . .
to live in dignity
as children of God
and brothers and sisters of Christ.

What was the spokesperson's point? Imagine the Holy Father visited your community and you acted as spokesperson for its youth. Write out what you would say to the pope concerning youth and the Church.

Bible Reading

Pick a passage. After reading it prayerfully, write out a brief prayer to God that reflects your feelings or thoughts about it.

1. Community of disciples   Acts 2:43–47
2. Body of Christ   Romans 12:4–8
3. Basic sacrament   John 14:8–14
4. People of God   Acts 4:1–20
5. Institution   Matthew 16:13–19
6. Servant   Romans 12:6–21

9 Afterlife

Imagine you are a television script writer for NBC-TV. You have been commissioned to create a script about the end of the world. You go to the Bible and read:

*On that Day
the heavens will disappear
with a shrill noise,
the heavenly bodies will burn up
and be destroyed,
and the earth with everything in it
will vanish. . . .*

*And so, my friends,
as you wait for that Day,*

*do your best
to be pure and faultless in God's sight
and to be at peace with him.*
2 PETER 3:10, 14

After reflecting on this passage, you decide that there are three possible ways for you to begin your script. You can begin it—

- before the end of the world takes place,
- while it is taking place,
- just after it takes place.

Which of these times would you choose? Why would you choose this time?

End of the World

Author Thomas Blackburn began his script about the world's end just after it takes place. He had someone in heaven interview four people about what they were doing when the world ended. His script begins:

A San Francisco housewife said,
"I had just put the coffee on . . .
when I felt the whole house start to shake.
Then there was this terrific flash
of lightning and the whole sky lit up.
And I thought, my heavens!
The children are going to get soaking wet!"

A St. Louis schoolgirl had this to say,
"I was in history class.
Mr. Fenkle's our teacher.
I leaned over to Sally—she's my girlfriend—
and whispered, 'Fenkle's awfully cute'—
I mean Mr. Fenkle—and anyhow
I had just said that to Sally
when the whole place went dead still.
And I noticed something funny
about the sky."

A sailor from New York had another version.
"I was in a bar on West 25th.
I was in a booth
drinking beer with this blonde. . . .
Things were just getting interesting
when all of a sudden the whole joint
started coming apart at the seams.
There was a real weird light in the sky."

Finally,
a real-estate man from Florida said,
"You know when you come right down to it,
the whole thing happened
just like they said it would."*

The Return of Jesus

Regardless of how we imagine the end of the world, our scenario must include the *glorious return* of Jesus. Jesus' return in majesty and glory will bring history to its appointed end and mark the culmination of God's re-creation of ourselves and our world.

Just before ascending to heaven, Jesus told his disciples: "I am going to prepare a place for you. . . . And . . . I will come back and take you to myself" (John 14:2–3). And just after Jesus ascended to heaven, the disciples were told, "This Jesus, who was taken from you into heaven, will come back in the same way that you saw him go to heaven" (Acts 1:11).

Concerning the exact time of his return, Jesus said it will take place when people least expect it. Jesus dramatized this point in his Parable of the Ten Young Women (Matthew 25:1–13). To better appreciate this parable, consider the following story.

Years ago, Dr. Alexander Findlay was approaching a village in the Holy Land. Suddenly, he saw ten festively clad young women going down the street, dancing and singing. He was told that they were going to a wedding.

Ancient weddings began with a bridal party of ten young women keeping the bride company until the groom arrived for the wedding. When he was seen coming, the bridal party went out to meet him and escort him to the bride's house.

Findlay was also told that it was a custom for the groom to try to catch the bridal party by surprise. Some grooms even waited until the middle of the night to do this.

---

* *Sense and Incense* by Thomas Blackburn © 1960. Reprinted by permission of Loyola University Press, Chicago.

Escorting a groom to a bride's house in the middle of the night was a dramatic sight. Each member of the bridal party carried an oil lamp.

It is against this background that we must read Jesus' Parable of the Ten Young Women.

The parable portrays the bridal party at the home of the bride. They are awaiting the arrival of the groom. Each has an oil lamp in case the groom comes at night. Five of the young women are "wise" and have an extra supply of oil, in case of an emergency. The other five are "foolish" and have no extra supply.

As luck would have it, the groom delayed his arrival, and the ten became drowsy and fell asleep. At midnight someone woke the bridal party, shouting, "The bridegroom is coming!"

When the foolish ones saw that their lamps were about to go out, they went to get more oil. While they were gone, the groom arrived. The five wise members escorted him to the bride's house. When the five foolish members returned, they were too late. The door was closed and locked for the night.

The point of Jesus' Parable of the Ten Young Women is this: Jesus' return at the end of the time will surprise everyone and catch many people unprepared—just as the groom's midnight arrival surprised the bridal party and caught half of them unprepared.

Judgment

There's an ancient play called *Everyman*. In it God sends Death to the hero to tell him that his life is over. When the hero recovers from the shock, the hero asks Death to give him a few minutes to ask his friends—Money, Fame, Power, and Good Works—to accompany him into the afterlife. Death obliges. To the hero's surprise, however, the only person who agrees to accompany him is Good Works. All the rest refuse.

The play *Everyman* makes an important point. As we pass through death, filled with hope in the risen Jesus' promises, there is only one thing that matters: the good we tried to do while we lived on earth.

The research of Dr. Elisabeth Kubler-Ross of the University of Chicago confirms this. She has interviewed hundreds of people who have been declared clinically dead and then revived. These people commonly report experiencing a kind of instant replay of their lives—a kind of "judgment after death." Dr. Kubler-Ross quotes these people as saying:

> *When you come to this point,*
> *you see there are only two things*
> *that are relevant:*
> *the service you rendered to others, and love.*
> *All those things we think are important,*
> *like fame, money, prestige, and power,*
> *are insignificant.*
> DEATH AND DYING

The play *Everyman* and the research of Dr. Kubler-Ross lead us to a major theme of Scripture: judgment after death. Commenting on the *purpose* of this judgment, Saint Paul says:

> *All of us must appear before Christ,*
> *to be judged by him.*
> *Each one will receive what he deserves,*
> *according to everything he has done,*
> *good or bad, in his bodily life.*
> 2 CORINTHIANS 5:10

The Scriptures speak of two kinds of judgment after death:

■ *last,* at the end of the world, and
■ *individual,* at the end of life on earth.

This sculptured scene above the main doorway of the Cathedral of Notre Dame in France portrays the Last Judgment. The top *panel shows Jesus seated on the judgment throne surrounded by angels and saints. The* middle *panel shows the* damned *on the left being led off to hell and the* saved *on the right being led off to heaven. The* bottom *panel shows people rising from the dead to be judged.*

Last Judgment

One day Jesus talked to his disciples about the end of the world. He described it this way:

*"When the Son of Man comes as King
and all the angels with him,
he will sit on his royal throne,
and the people of all the nations
will be gathered before him.
Then he will divide them into two groups,
just as a shepherd separates
the sheep from the goats. . . .*

*"Then the King will say
to the people on his right,
'Come, you that are blessed by my Father!
Come and possess the kingdom
which has been prepared for you
ever since the creation of the world.*

*" 'I was hungry and you fed me,
thirsty and you gave me a drink;
I was a stranger
and you received me in your homes,
naked and you clothed me;
I was sick and you took care of me,
in prison and you visited me.'. . .*

*"Then he will say to those on his left,
'Away from me,
you that are under God's curse!
Away to the eternal fire
which has been prepared
for the Devil and his angels! . . .
I tell you, whenever you refused to help
one of these least important ones,
you refused to help me.' "*
MATTHEW 25:31–32, 34–36, 41, 45

Jesus' dramatic description indicates that the entire human race will face a *last* (general) judgment. This judgment—

■ will take place at the end of the world, and
■ will mark the culmination of God's re-creation of ourselves and our world.

Individual Judgment

Besides the *last* (general) judgment, each person will experience an *individual* (personal) judgment as she or he passes through death into eternal life. Jesus referred to the *individual* judgment in a parable about two men who lived in the same town: a rich man and a poor man. The rich man lived in a fine home and feasted on fine foods. The poor man, named Lazarus, lived in a shack and had barely enough to eat. But the rich man ignored Lazarus.

Eventually both men died. The rich man ended up in a place of torment. Lazarus ended up in a place of comfort: the bosom of Abraham. The rich man pleaded with Abraham:

> *"Take pity on me, and send Lazarus*
> *to dip his finger in some water*
> *and cool off my tongue,*
> *because I am in great pain in this fire!"*
> LUKE 16:24

Abraham explained that a "deep pit" prevented anyone from crossing to "where you are." Then the rich man pleaded with Abraham to send Lazarus back to earth to warn his family, lest they end up as he did. Abraham replied:

> *"If they will not listen to Moses*
> *and the prophets,*
> *they will not be convinced*
> *even if someone were to rise from death."*
> LUKE 16:31

Jesus' Parable of the Rich Man and Lazarus indicates that immediately after death, each person will face an *individual* (personal) judgment. This judgment leads to an eternal life *with* God or eternal separation *from* God. Thus when the rich man and Lazarus died, they were separated and placed in opposite situations of torment and comfort.

And so we may conclude that the *individual* (personal) judgment—

■ will take place at the end of life on earth, and
■ will be followed by eternal union with God or eternal separation from God.

Scripture and tradition teach that one's individual (personal) judgment ends in one of the following destinies:

■ hell,
■ purgatory, or
■ heaven.

Hell

Some American tourists were viewing an active volcano in Italy. Struck by the fiery lava spewing from it, a young New Yorker exclaimed, "Wow, it's just like hell." An Italian villager, standing nearby, turned to her friend and said, "My goodness, these American tourists have been everywhere!"

That story illustrates the popular notion that hell is a "place of fire." Jesus himself often used the image of fire in talking about hell. For example, one day Jesus told this parable:

> *"A man sowed good seed in his field.*
> *One night, when everyone was asleep,*
> *an enemy came*
> *and sowed weeds among the wheat*
> *and went away.*
> *When the plants grew*
> *and the heads of grain began to form,*
> *then the weeds showed up.*
>
> *"The man's servants came to him. . . .*
> *'Do you want us to go*
> *and pull up the weeds?' they asked him.*
> *'No,' he answered,*
> *'because as you gather the weeds*
> *you might pull up some of the wheat*
> *along with them.*
> *Let the wheat and the weeds*
> *both grow together until harvest.*
> *Then I will tell the harvest workers*
> *to pull up the weeds first,*
> *tie them in bundles and burn them,*
> *and then to gather in the wheat*
> *and put it in my barn.' "*
> MATTHEW 13:24–30

Later, when the disciples asked Jesus to explain the parable, he said—

■ the field is the world;
■ the sower of the wheat is Jesus;
■ the good seed are the children of God;
■ the sower of the weeds is the devil;
■ the weeds are the children of the devil;
■ the harvest is the end of the world;
■ the harvesters are God's angels (Matthew 13:38–39).

Jesus ended his Parable of the Weeds and the Wheat, saying that just as the weeds were thrown into a fire, so evildoers will be thrown into a "fiery furnace" (Matthew 13:50).

Weeds and Wheat.

What about Hell?

The Parable of the Weeds and the Wheat raises two questions. First, what did Jesus intend to say about hell? Second, how did Jesus intend us to understand the image of hell fire?

Bible interpreters respond to the first question in one of three ways: Hell is—

- a place,
- a condition,
- a state.

Literal interpreters hold that Jesus teaches that hell is an actual *place*. An imaginative portrayal of hell as a place is found in Dante's *Divine Comedy*. Dante portrays hell as consisting of a series of levels, each with its own punishment, corresponding to the nature of one's sinfulness.

Contextual interpreters hold that Jesus had no intention of saying that hell was a real place. His primary intention, they say, was to teach that human freedom includes the terrifying option of rejecting God.

Some contextualists hold that hell is best understood as a *condition*. They say that to reject God is to reject Being itself. It is to opt for nonbeing, or nothingness. In other words, hell is simply the condition of no longer existing.

Other contextualists hold that hell is best understood as a *state*. They say that the essence of hell is living in a state of eternal separation from God—and experiencing eternally whatever suffering this involves. Traditional Catholic teaching concurs with this understanding.

What about Hell Fire?

This brings us to the second question: How did Jesus intend us to understand the image of hell fire?

Again, the answers Bible interpreters give to this question tend to fall into one of three categories: Jesus intended the image of fire to be taken—

- literally,
- symbolically,
- dramatically.

Literal interpreters hold that Jesus intended the word *fire* to refer to real, physical fire.

Contextual interpreters hold that Jesus never intended the word to be taken literally.

Some contextualists hold that Jesus used the word *fire* in a metaphorical sense—that he meant it in the same way that we speak of "burning with shame."

Other contextualists hold that Jesus used the word in a dramatic sense. That is, he used it to dramatize the urgency with which we should avoid hell. We would avoid it as we would avoid eternal physical fire. We should avoid eternal separation from God with every fiber of our being.

Regardless of how we interpret hell, we should be clear on one thing. Human freedom involves the possibility of freely separating ourselves from God—and bringing upon ourselves whatever suffering this entails. Looked at from this viewpoint, God does not punish us so much as we punish ourselves. Two simple analogies will help to illustrate.

If we refuse to breathe air, the air doesn't punish us by suffocating us. We do that ourselves. Or if we beat our fist against a brick wall, the wall doesn't punish us by making our fist hurt. We do that ourselves. It is something like this with the punishment of hell. In a very real sense, God does not punish us. We do that ourselves.

This brings us to the traditional teaching of the Catholic Church concerning hell. In general, this teaching may be summed up in two concise statements:

- Hell exists and is eternal.
- Hell involves suffering, primarily the loss of God, who fulfills human existence.

Purgatory

Someone once asked Samuel Johnson, the great British writer, what he thought about the Catholic teaching on purgatory. He surprised them, saying that he thought it made good sense. His explanation was interesting.

Johnson said that it was obvious that most people who die aren't bad enough for hell; nor are they good enough for heaven. So it is reasonable to conclude that there must be a kind of middle state after death, in which some sort of purgation or purification takes place.

The traditional biblical text implying the existence of what we call *purgatory* is 2 Maccabees 12:42. There the biblical author speaks approvingly of praying that the sin of the dead soldiers "might be completely blotted out."

Jesus taught us to use our talents to advance God's Kingdom on earth by living lives of love and service. But most of us fall short of this ideal because of ego-centeredness. The purpose of purgatory is to purge away this ego-centeredness and complete the process of dying to ourselves in order to rise with Christ to eternal life.

This brings us to the traditional Catholic teaching concerning purgatory. In general, it may be summed up in two concise statements:

- Purgatory exists and is temporary.
- Purgatory involves the purging away of whatever keeps us from final union with God in heaven.

Detail from Michaelangelo's Last Judgment *in the Vatican's Cistine Chapel.*

Jesus Teaches About Heaven

Jesus spoke about heaven often. In doing so, he used a variety of images. Consider just a few: *vision* of God, *union* with God, and *life* eternal with God. Here is what Jesus has to say about these images.

- Vision: *"Happy are the pure in heart; they will see God!"* MATTHEW 5:8
- Union: *"Father! May they be in us, just as you are in me and I am in you."* JOHN 17:21
- Life: *"The Son of Man . . . came down from heaven . . . so that everyone who believes in him may not die but have eternal life."* JOHN 3:13, 16

Let's take a brief look at each of these images.

Heaven

A young couple was walking down an airport ramp to board a plane. In front of them a little girl bounced along excitedly. Everything about her radiated joy and happiness.

"Where are you going?" her mother asked. Without missing a bounce, the little girl sang out, "To Grandma's! To Grandma's! To Grandma's!"

The little girl didn't say "to Chicago" or "to Cleveland," but "to Grandma's."

The little girl's answer makes an important point. Joy and happiness do not consist so much in going to a "place" as in going to a "person."

The little girl's answer recalls Jesus' words to Mary Magdalene, after his resurrection:

"Go to my brothers and tell them that I am going to . . .
my Father and their Father,
my God and their God."
JOHN 20:17

Heaven Involves Vision

Concerning the image of heaven as the vision of God, Saint Paul wrote to the Christian community at Corinth:

What we see now
is like a dim image in a mirror;
then we shall see face-to-face.
1 CORINTHIANS 13:12

And Saint John says of this same image:

We know that when Christ appears,
we shall be like him,
because we shall see him as he really is.
1 JOHN 3:2

Theologians call the vision of God the "beatific vision." The word *beatific* comes from the Latin word *beatus,* meaning "happy." The heavenly vision of God results in happiness beyond words.

Heaven Involves Union

Concerning the image of heaven as union with God, Saint Paul wrote this beautiful passage to the Christian community at Colossae:

> *Your life is hidden with Christ in God.*
> *Your real life is Christ*
> *and when he appears,*
> *then you too will appear with him*
> *and share his glory!*
> COLOSSIANS 3:3–4

Our union with God is the culmination of the destiny for which God made us. Saint Augustine expressed this destiny in these memorable words:

> *Our hearts are made for you, O Lord,*
> *and they will not rest*
> *until they rest in you.*

Heaven Involves Life

This brings us to a third image that Jesus used to refer to heaven: life eternal with God. Jesus said:

> *"The Son of Man . . .*
> *came down from heaven . . .*
> *so that everyone who believes in him*
> *may have eternal life.*
>
> *"For God loved the world so much*
> *that he gave his only Son,*
> *so that everyone who believes in him*
> *may not die but have eternal life."*
> JOHN 3:13, 15–16

On another occasion Jesus told his disciples:

> *"I have come*
> *in order that you might have life—*
> *life in all its fullness."*
> JOHN 10:10

What is Jesus' point? We were not made for *this* life. We were made for a more *glorious* life: life eternal with God. In the words of an ancient Jewish author:

> *The day of death*
> *is when two worlds meet with a kiss:*
> *this world going out*
> *and a more glorious world coming in.*

And so heaven involves *vision* of God, *union* with God, and *life* eternal with God. Heaven involves the culmination of God's re-creation of the human race and the world. Heaven involves joy beyond anything the human mind could ever dream of. In the words of Saint Paul:

> *"What no one ever saw or heard,*
> *what no one ever thought could happen,*
> *is the very thing*
> *God prepared for those who love him."*
> 1 CORINTHIANS 2:9

This brings us to the traditional teaching of the Catholic Church concerning heaven. In general, it may be summed up in two concise statements:

- Heaven exists and involves vision, union, and life with an all-loving God forever.
- Heaven is the culmination of God's re-creation of ourselves and our world.

Recap

An *individual* judgment awaits each of us at the end of our life on earth. It will take place immediately after our death and will culminate in—

- heaven: union with God,
- hell: separation from God, or
- purgatory: preparation for union.

A *last* judgment also awaits each one of us. It will take place at the end of history when Jesus returns in glory, and it will mark the culmination of God's re-creation of ourselves and our world.

The Parable of the Twins

Once, twins were conceived. Weeks passed and they developed. As they grew, they sang for joy, "Isn't it great to be alive!"

Together the twins explored the womb. When they found their mother's life cord, they shouted for joy, "How great is our mother's love that she shares her very life with us."

As weeks passed, the twins began to change. "What does this mean?" said the one. "It means that our life in the womb is coming to an end," said the second. "But I don't want to leave the womb. I want to stay here forever," said the first.

"We have no choice," said the second. "Besides, maybe there is life after birth." "How can that be?" said the first. "We will shed our mother's cord, and how is life possible without it? Besides, there is evidence that there were others in the womb before us, and none of them has ever come back to tell us there is life after birth. No, this is the end."

And so the first twin fell into despair, saying, "If life in the womb ends in death, what's its purpose? It's meaningless! Maybe we don't even have a mother. Maybe we made her up." "But we must have a mother," said the second. "How else did we get here? How else do we stay alive?"

And so the last days in the womb were filled with deep questioning and fear.

Finally, the moment of birth arrived. When the twins opened their eyes, they cried for joy. For what they saw exceeded their wildest dreams.

> *"What no one ever saw or heard,*
> *what no one ever thought could happen,*
> *is the very thing*
> *God prepared for those who love him."*
> 1 CORINTHIANS 2:9

(inspired by an unknown author)

Understanding Afterlife

Review

The Return of Jesus

1. What did Jesus tell his followers just before he ascended to heaven?

2. What point does Jesus make in his Parable of the Ten Young Women?

Judgment

3. List and explain (a) the two kinds of judgment that Scripture refers to, and (b) when each will take place.

4. Where does Jesus allude to the *individual* judgment in his teaching, and what two conclusions may we draw concerning it?

5. Where does Jesus refer to the *last* judgment in his teaching, and what two conclusions may we draw concerning it?

Hell

6. In what parable does Jesus speak about hell, and how does he refer to hell in this parable?

7. List and explain three positions Bible interpreters take concerning Jesus' teaching on (a) hell and (b) hell fire.

8. In general, what two statements sum up Catholic teaching about hell?

Purgatory

9. In general, what two statements sum up Catholic teaching about purgatory?

Heaven

10. List and briefly explain three images that Jesus used to describe heaven.

11. In general, what two statements sum up Catholic teaching about heaven?

Exercises

1. In one of his writings, novelist Somerset Maugham tells the story of a merchant in ancient Baghdad who sent his servant to the marketplace to buy supplies. Minutes later the servant returned, trembling from head to foot. "Master! Master!" he shouted. "As I walked through the crowded marketplace, someone jostled me. When I looked to see who it was, I saw it was Death. He peered at me threateningly. Lend me your swiftest horse that I may flee to far-off Samarra. He will never think of looking for me there." The merchant obliged and the servant sped off. Meanwhile the merchant went to the marketplace to buy the rest of the supplies. Lo and behold, who should he see but Death. The merchant said to Death, "Why did you give my servant such a threatening look this morning?" "That wasn't a threatening look," said Death. "It was a look of surprise. I was amazed to see your servant in Baghdad, for I had an appointment with him tonight in far-off Samarra."

What point does Maugham's story make? Suppose you knew that you had only twenty-four hours before dying. What would you do in those twenty-four hours? Write out a brief message that you would like to have read at your funeral Mass.

2. More than any scientist on earth, Wernher von Braun deserves credit for putting astronauts on the moon. *Time* magazine called him the "twentieth-century Columbus." Before he died, von Braun made a statement that surprised a lot of people. Writing in *This Week* magazine, he said:

> *Many people seem to think that science has somehow made "religious ideas" untimely or old-fashioned. But I think science has a real surprise for the skeptics. Science, for instance, tells us that nothing in nature, not even the tiniest particle, can disappear without a trace. Nature does not know extinction. All it knows is transformation. Now, if God applied this fundamental principle to the most minute and insignificant parts of his universe, doesn't it make sense to assume that he applies it also to the human soul? I think it does. And everything science has taught me, and continues to teach me, strengthens my belief in the continuity of our spiritual existence after death.*

Explain von Braun's point in your own words. What convinces you most that there is life after death?

3. While operating on a woman, Dr. Wilder Penfield, a Montreal neurosurgeon, made an amazing discovery. When he accidentally touched the temporal cortex of her brain with a weak electric current, the woman, who was under local anesthesia and was able to talk, reported reliving the experience of bearing her baby. Later another patient in a similar situation reported reliving a childhood experience. What amazed Penfield even more was that the patients felt again the emotion that the situation originally produced and were aware of the "same interpretations, true or false," that they gave the experience in the first place. *Time* magazine said, "Penfield's findings have led some scientists to believe that the brain has indelibly recorded every sensation it has ever received."

Explain how Dr. Penfield's discoveries lend support to the Catholic teaching concerning an *individual* judgment after death. Why is it especially significant that the patients were aware of the "interpretations, true or false," that they gave their experience at the time it occurred?

4. In one of his novels, Charles Dickens describes a boy and a girl who grew up together. They loved each other and promised to marry someday. Years passed, however, and they went their separate ways. The boy fell in with an evil crowd; the girl stayed innocent. One day they accidentally met again, and the memories of their love flooded back. With all his heart the young man wished he could purge away his sinful state, because he knew that he could never ask her to marry him now. At that moment he would have gladly endured *any pain* to be purged of his sins and made worthy, again, of her love.

Explain how the last line sheds light on the purpose of purgatory.

5. A queen had no heirs to succeed her after her death. So she issued a decree saying that she was searching for someone who would become her adopted child and rule after her. Those interested in applying needed two qualifications: a deep love of God, and a deep love of people. A poor peasant teenager felt moved to apply. The teenager worked long and hard to buy the proper clothes for an interview with the queen. Finally, the young person set out. After weeks of difficult travel, the teenager neared the palace. Just outside the large gate leading into the palace grounds was a beggar. Moved with pity, the teenager exchanged clothes with the beggar. Upon arrival inside the palace, the ill-dressed teenager was escorted into the throne room to be interviewed. Looking up at the queen, the young person stood stunned. On the throne sat the beggar, wearing the clothes the teenager had just given her. The queen smiled and said, "Welcome, my child."

What point does the story make? What Gospel passage concerning the last judgment does this story remind you of? Explain. Describe in writing a time when, like the teenager in the story, you made a big sacrifice to help someone. What keeps you from being more generous than you are, especially toward people in need?

Personal Reflection

When just a young man, Benjamin Franklin composed this inscription for his gravestone:

> *The body*
> *of B. Franklin, Printer,*
> *Like the Cover of an old Book*
> *Its Contents worn out*
> *and Stript of the Letter and Gilding,*
> *Lies here,*
> *Food for Worms.*
>
> *But the Work shall not be wholly lost:*
> *For it will, as he believed,*
> *appear once more,*
> *In a new & more perfect Edition*
> *Corrected and amended*
> *by the Author.*

What is Franklin referring to? Compose an inscription of your own that expresses your feelings about death and afterlife.

Bible Reading

Pick a passage. After reading it prayerfully, write out a brief prayer to God that reflects your personal feelings or thoughts about it.

1. Future judgment   2 Corinthians 5:1–10
2. Future glory   Romans 8:18–30
3. Future coming   Acts 1:1–11
4. Future destiny   1 John 2:26–3:3
5. Future home   Revelation 21:1–7

Part Two
Catholic Worship

10 Personal Prayer

Thomas Merton grew up with no religion. His parents died before he was sixteen. A few years later he became a communist. And at twenty-five he became a Catholic. Merton describes his faith journey in his autobiography, *The Seven Storey Mountain.* A milestone in that journey occurred in his late teens.

One night he was suddenly overwhelmed by the amount of evil present in his young life. He writes:

> *I was filled with horror at what I saw. . . .*
> *And now I think for the first time*
> *in my whole life I really began to pray—*
> *praying not with my lips*
> *and with my intellect and my imagination,*
> *but praying out of the very roots*

of my life and of my being. . . .
There were
a lot of tears connected with this,
and they did me good. . . .

I remember the morning
that followed this experience. . . .
I went to the Dominicans' Church . . .
knelt down and said slowly,
with all the belief I had in me,
the Our Father.

Merton's prayer experience was the first big step in his faith journey.

The powerful impact that praying had on Thomas Merton, and on people like him, makes us ask ourselves: What is prayer? Why does it have such a powerful impact?

Prayer

A boy was watching a sadhu (an Indian mystic) praying at the river's edge. When the sadhu finished, the boy said, "Teach me to pray!" The sadhu looked directly into the boy's eyes for a full minute. Then he took the boy's head, plunged it under water, and held it there. When the boy finally broke loose and got his breath back, he sputtered, "What did you do that for?" The sadhu said:

> *I just gave you your first lesson in prayer.*
> *When you want to pray*
> *as badly as you wanted to breathe*
> *when you were under water,*
> *only then will I be able to teach you.*

The sadhu's point is an important one. Praying is more a thing of the *heart* than of the *head.* The first condition for learning to pray is the desire to pray.

Praying is a lot like dieting. We can know all about dieting, but if we don't want to diet, our knowledge won't do us any good. It is the same with praying.

Why Pray?

If we stopped four people walking out of a church or a synagogue and asked them why they prayed, they would probably give us four different reasons. For example, they might say that praying gives them—

- peace that the world can't give,
- wisdom that education can't give,
- strength that friends can't give, and
- help that only God can give.

These are excellent reasons, but they cannot be the *primary* reason for praying. Why? Because they deal with the *usefulness* of praying. It's not that praying has no *useful* dimension. It certainly does! It's simply that usefulness can never be the *primary* reason for praying. Why? There are two reasons.

The first reason may be illustrated by an example. A friendship can serve many useful purposes. But if *usefulness* is the primary purpose for the friendship, there is no true friendship. We do not "use" a friend. The same is true of God. We do not "use" God.

The second reason that prayer cannot be evaluated in terms of usefulness is this: The day may come when the "usefulness" of praying seems to break down. For example, the day may come when prayer no longer brings us peace. Or the day may come when God no longer seems to answer our prayers. Should this happen, praying will seem useless, and we will be tempted to give it up.

What, then, should be the primary reason for praying?

Prayer Expresses Love

The primary reason for praying is this: Praying is an expression of love. It is an expression of love to God, who created us, redeemed us, and graces us continually.

Does this mean that we should not pray to God for such things as guidance or help? Of course not! Jesus himself taught us to pray for such things (Luke 11:9). It simply means that *usefulness* can never be the primary motive for praying. The primary motive must always be *love.*

Scripturally, prayer (as an expression of love) assumes four different forms, sometimes called the four purposes of prayer:

- adoration,
- contrition,
- thanksgiving, and
- supplication (petition).

The focus of *adoration* is the mystery of God's glory. The Apostle Thomas falls on his knees before the glorified Jesus and prays, "My Lord and my God!" (John 20:28).

The focus of *contrition* is the mystery of God's mercy. A tax collector stands at a distance and prays, "God, have pity on me, a sinner!" (Luke 18:13).

The focus of *thanksgiving* is the mystery of God's goodness. Jesus raised his eyes to heaven and thanked his Father before feeding the hungry crowd (Luke 9:16).

Finally, the focus of *supplication* is the mystery of God's loving concern for us. Jesus told his disciples, "Ask, and you will receive" (Luke 11:9).

Prayer Settings

Henry David Thoreau was a nineteenth-century naturalist. He lived a part of his life in a tiny hut on Walden pond outside of Concord, Massachusetts. Describing the simple furnishings of the hut that he built on the shores of this wilderness pond, Thoreau wrote in his book *Walden:*

> *I had three chairs . . .*
> *one for solitude,*
> *two for friendship,*
> *and three for society.*

Thoreau's description points to an important psychological fact about human nature. It has three dimensions, or sides:

- personal   (solitude),
- interpersonal   (friendship),
- social   (society).

In other words, there are times when we need to be alone. There are times when we need the support of family and close friends. And there are times when we need the support of the total community.

What is true of our *psychological* makeup is true also of our *spiritual* makeup. Sometimes we need to pray *alone,* sometimes we need to pray with *family and friends,* and sometimes we need to pray with the *community.*

The Gospel portrays Jesus praying in all three of these settings:

- in private   (Mark 1:35),
- with friends   (Luke 9:28),
- with the community (Luke 4:16).

Praying *daily* to God *in private* is as important as eating and sleeping. We need spiritual food as much as we need physical food. Furthermore, unless we learn to relate to God in private, we will find it next to impossible to relate to God in community. Praying in private is the key that unlocks the door to praying in community, especially the community gathered together in Sunday worship.

Prayer Steps

When a girl and a boy want to get to know each other better, they agree on places and times to meet. They don't leave these things to chance. Getting to know each other is too important for that.

It is the same with God and us. The *first* step in getting to know God better through praying is to find a good *place* for prayer.

Some people can pray in any place: on a beach, on a jogging trail, on a bus. But if we want to pray without interruption, we usually need privacy.

Jesus sought privacy to pray. The Gospel says that he "went up a hill to pray" (Luke 6:12). It also says that he "went out of town to a lonely place, where he prayed" (Mark 1:35).

The important thing about a *place* is that it helps us pray. The best way to find the *right* place is to experiment, to see what works best for us.

The *second* step in getting to know God better is to schedule into our day a *time* to meet God in prayer.

Some people pray best in the morning; other people pray best at night. Jesus seems to have prayed well at both times. Thus the Gospel says, "Very early the next morning . . . Jesus prayed" (Mark 1:35). And it says that Jesus "spent the whole night . . . praying" (Luke 6:12). Once again, the way to discover the *right* time for us is to experiment.

The *final* step in getting to know God better is to find a *posture* that is conducive to praying.

Some people pray best lying down. Other people pray best walking. Jesus seems to have used different postures at different times. For example, the Gospel says that Jesus "knelt down and prayed" (Luke 22:41). It also says that he "threw himself face downward on the ground and prayed" (Matthew 26:39).

And so the procedure for getting to know God better through prayer involves three steps: selecting a *place,* a *time,* and a *posture* that are conducive to praying.

Prayer Styles

A Chicago high school student wrote the following as part of a homework assignment. It is a simple but beautiful illustration of the three forms, or styles, that praying ordinarily takes.

One day after playing in the park,
I went to a nearby fountain for some water.
The cool water tasted good,
and I felt refreshment enter my tired body.

Then, I lay down
and began to think.
"We need water to drink.
But where does water come from?"

"Clouds!" I thought.
"But where do clouds come from?"
"Vaporized moisture."
This went on until I was left
with just one answer: God!

Then I talked to God for a little bit
in my own words.

For the next couple of minutes,
I just lay on the grass,
looking up at the sky,
resting in God's presence.
(slightly adapted)

This student's beautiful experience illustrates the three styles that praying ordinarily takes:

- meditation,
- conversation,
- contemplation.

Meditation Engages the Mind

A good name for *meditation* is *mind* praying. This style of prayer consists in taking an idea and probing it prayerfully with the mind. In other words, we do what the student did:

> *Then, I lay down*
> *and began to think.*
> *"We need water to drink.*
> *But where does water come from?"*
> *"Clouds!" I thought.*
> *"But where do clouds come from?"*
> *"Vaporized moisture."*
> *This went on until I was left*
> *with just one answer: God!*

Conversation Touches the Heart

A good name for *conversation* is *heart* praying. This style of prayer consists in talking to God from the heart. That is, we do what the student did:

> *Then I talked to God for a little bit*
> *in my own words.*

Contemplation Moves the Soul

A good name for *contemplation* is *soul* praying. This style of prayer consists in simply resting in God's presence. We do what the student did:

> *For the next couple of minutes,*
> *I just lay on the grass,*
> *looking up at the sky,*
> *resting in God's presence.*

Resting quietly in the divine presence helps us become aware of the activity of the Holy Spirit in the depths of our being. It helps us listen with the "ears" of our soul to the "voice" of the Spirit dwelling within us.

In brief, then, prayer normally takes three forms, or styles:

- meditation   (mind praying),
- conversation   (heart praying),
- contemplation (soul praying).

Often these three styles are so closely interwoven in one and the same prayer that it is hard to say where one starts and the other stops.

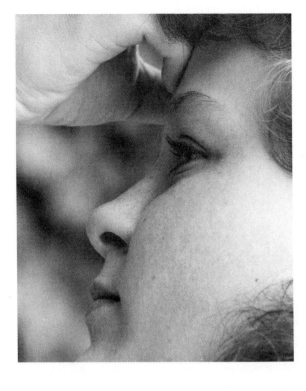

who dwells within us (1 Corinthians 6:19), and start praying.

Many people use *models* when they pray. A model is simply a guide to help us pray. It is a track to run on to keep us from going in circles. Two models that some people find helpful are—

- the daily-life model and
- the Scripture model.

Daily-Life Model

The *daily-life* model is both simple and practical. It makes an ideal night prayer. Before we begin to pray, we take our prayer posture and relax our body. Then we monitor our breathing until a mood of quiet sets in. When we feel at peace and in touch with our innermost self, we turn to God and begin our praying.

The daily-life model involves using the *high point* or the *low point* of our day as the subject of our prayer. The prayer procedure uses all three styles of prayer: meditation, conversation, and contemplation.

We Meditate

First, we replay our day rapidly and identify one of its high points—something good that we did or something good that happened to us. After we have identified a high point, we reflect on it prayerfully.

For example, let's say our high point was keeping our cool in a very tense situation. After identifying the high point, we reflect on it. For example, we consider what might have happened had we not kept our cool. Or we consider why we were able to keep our cool. Or we consider the benefits that resulted because we kept our cool.

Prayer Process

Praying is a lot like jogging. When we take jogging seriously, we don't step out-of-doors and immediately start jogging. First we go through a preparation process: stretching and loosening our muscles. If we start jogging right away, we risk straining or pulling a muscle.

When we take prayer seriously, we do something similar. We don't begin praying immediately. We go through a *pre-prayer* process. The purpose of this process is to ready ourselves for prayer. It consists of two parts.

The first part involves relaxing the three tension areas of the body: the forehead, the jaw, and the chest. We start with the forehead and relax any tightness there. Next, we move down to the jaw and relax any tightness there. Then, we move down to the shoulders and chest and relax any tightness there.

The second part involves setting up a pattern of rhythmic breathing and monitoring it until a mood of quiet sets in. When we are quiet and in touch with our inner self, we turn to the Spirit,

Journeying with Jesus

An ancient painting portrays Jesus being taken down from the cross. A moving detail of the painting shows one of the disciples holding the crown of thorns that has just been removed from Jesus' head. The disciple is pressing a finger against one of the thorns to get an idea of the pain Jesus felt when the crown was on his head.

Catholics have always been devoted to Jesus in his Passion (suffering and death). One form their devotion takes is a prayer model called the "Way of the Cross." It involves journeying in spirit with Jesus to Calvary and contains fourteen stations, or "stopping points." The procedure for praying each station is as follows:

- meditation: *think* about the station;
- conversation: *speak* to Jesus about it;
- contemplation: *listen* for Jesus' reply.

Here is a brief guide for meditating on each station. (A fifteenth station—the Resurrection—is used by some Catholics and is included here.)

1. *Jesus is condemned to death.*
We see Jesus unjustly accused and convicted. We hear the mob shouting, "Crucify him!"

2. *Jesus carries his cross.*
We see Jesus shoulder his cross. We recall that he said that if you want to come with him, you must pick up your cross and follow him (Matthew 16:24).

3. *Jesus falls the first time.*
We see Jesus fall and struggle to his feet. As we watch, we ask ourselves, "When we fall, do we get up and resolve to follow Jesus again—even more closely?"

4. *Jesus meets his mother.*
We see Jesus' eyes meet his mother's eyes. We wonder what each is thinking.

5. *Jesus is helped by Simon.*
We see Simon help Jesus. We recall that Jesus said, "Whenever you did this for one of the least important of these . . . you did it for me!" (Matthew 25:40).

6. *Jesus' face is wiped by Veronica.*
We see a woman do a courageous thing. We wonder where she got the courage to do it.

7. *Jesus falls a second time.*
We see Jesus fall again. We think of these words: "The hardest thing we can do is to fall down, get up again, and praise God."

8. *Jesus comforts the women.*
We see Jesus comfort others. We wonder what gives him the power to comfort others, even when he needs comfort more than they do.

9. *Jesus falls a third time.*
We see Jesus fall once more. We think of these words: "Our greatest glory is not in never falling but in getting up each time we fall."

10. *Jesus is stripped of his clothes.*
We see Jesus standing alone. We think of his words: "I was . . . naked and you clothed me" (Matthew 25:35-36).

11. *Jesus is nailed to the cross.*
We listen to the sound of the hammer. We wonder why Jesus suffered so much—for us.

12. *Jesus dies.*
We look at Jesus framed against the sky. We recall his words: "The greatest love a person can have for his friends is to give his life for them" (John 15:13).

13. *Jesus is taken down from the cross.*
We hold Jesus in our arms. We recall that there are times when God asks nothing of us except silence and trust.

14. *Jesus is laid in the tomb.*
We help place Jesus in the tomb. These words come to mind: "Tears may flow in the night, but joy comes in the morning" (Psalm 30:5).

15. *Jesus rises from the dead.*
Sing with all of creation: "Bloom in every meadow, / leaves on every bough, / Speak His sorrow ended, / hail His triumph now" (Fortunatus).

We Converse

After reflecting on our high point, we express our feelings to God about it. For example, we say to God something like this:

> *Lord, you know what a short fuse I have.*
> *Sometimes, the slightest thing sets me off.*
> *But today you helped me remain cool*
> *in a tough situation.*
> *Thank you, Lord!*
> *I couldn't have done it without your help.*

We Contemplate

After we have expressed our feelings to God, we simply rest quietly in the divine presence for a while. We listen in the depths of our consciousness for whatever the Spirit may wish to say to us in reply.

The Spirit will not speak to us in a "voice" that we can hear with our ears. The Holy Spirit will speak to us in a much more subtle way: a movement of our heart, an idea, an inspiration.

We Can Repeat the Process

After praying over the high point of the day, some people repeat the process and pray over the low point also. They ponder some wrongful thing they did or some unfortunate thing that happened to them. They follow the same prayer procedure as they did for the high point: meditation, conversation, and contemplation.

Scripture Model

A second prayer model that people use is the *Scripture* model. It is a way to pray the Scriptures and extract from God's word its deeper meaning. The Scripture model makes a good morning prayer. It works better when we are fresh.

The procedure is simple. We open the Bible to the passage that we have picked for prayer. Next, we prepare ourselves for prayer, using the *pre-prayer* process: relaxing our body and monitoring our breathing until a mood of quiet sets in. Then we read the Scripture passage prayerfully. For example:

> *While Jesus*
> *was having a meal in Matthew's house,*
> *many tax collectors and other outcasts*
> *came and joined Jesus and his disciples*
> *at the table.*
>
> *Some Pharisees saw this*
> *and asked his disciples,*
> *"Why does your teacher eat with such people?"*
> *Jesus heard them and answered,*
> *"People who are well do not need a doctor,*
> *but only those who are sick."*
> MATTHEW 9:10–12

We Meditate

After we have read the passage, we begin our meditation. This involves reflecting on two questions: (1) What might the Holy Spirit be trying to say to us through God's word? and (2) How ought we to respond to what the Spirit seems to be saying to us?

For example, the point of this episode is stated clearly by Jesus: "People who are well do not need a doctor, but only those who are sick." This explains why Jesus welcomes the tax collectors and the outcasts: they need a doctor.

An application of this point to our lives might be this: We should approach Jesus just as the Pharisees and outcasts did—knowing that he welcomes us with open arms. It is for people like us that Jesus came into the world.

We Converse

After deciding how the point applies to our lives, we speak to the Spirit. For example, we say:

> *Spirit of God, help me see myself as I really am.*
> *Help me see that parts of me*
> *are spiritually sick and need healing.*
>
> *Give me the courage to approach you for healing*
> *in the sacrament of Reconciliation,*
> *a sacrament that I've been avoiding.*
>
> *Help me realize that in this sacrament*
> *I encounter your spiritual healing,*
> *just as truly*
> *as did the tax collectors and the outcasts.*

We Contemplate

After speaking to the Spirit, we become quiet and simply rest in the Spirit's presence. We listen for whatever the Spirit may wish to say to us in the depths of our consciousness.

Here we should keep in mind that the Spirit does not always respond to us immediately. Sometimes the Holy Spirit responds later, outside the time of prayer, in the turmoil of our day.

Recap

The first condition for learning to pray is the *desire* to pray. Prayer is, above all, an *expression of love to God,* who is love.

Prayer takes place in one of three *settings:* alone, with family and friends, with the larger community. Prayer usually works better if preceded by a *pre-prayer* process of getting in touch with ourselves before seeking to get in touch with God.

Prayer normally follows three forms, or *styles:* meditation, conversation, contemplation. Prayer often flows better if we follow a prayer *model:* a guide to help us pray.

Mini-Gospel

A priest spent twelve years in China in prisons and doing hard labor in factories. He was also obliged to attend lectures on communism. Instead of listening to the lectures, he would pray the *rosary* on his fingers.

Traditionally, the rosary has been a popular prayer model for Catholics. The best way to describe the rosary is to think of it as a kind of mini-Gospel. It is made up of fifteen *mysteries* (events from Jesus' life). These fifteen mysteries are broken down into three sets: five *joyful* (infancy and childhood), five *sorrowful* (suffering and death), and five *glorious* (risen life).

Joyful mysteries (infancy and childhood)

1.	Annunciation	Mary learns she will be a mother.
2.	Visitation	Mary visits Elizabeth.
3.	Nativity	Jesus is born.
4.	Presentation	Jesus is presented in the Temple.
5.	Finding	Jesus is found in the Temple.

Sorrowful mysteries (suffering and death)

1.	Agony	Jesus prays in Gethsemane.
2.	Scourging	Jesus is beaten by the soldiers.
3.	Crowning	Jesus is crowned with thorns.
4.	Way of Cross	Jesus carries his cross.
5.	Crucifixion	Jesus dies on the cross.

Glorious mysteries (risen life)

1.	Resurrection	Jesus rises.
2.	Ascension	Jesus returns to the Father.
3.	Pentecost	Jesus sends the Spirit.
4.	Assumption	Jesus takes his mother to heaven.
5.	Crowning	Jesus honors his mother in heaven.

Many Catholics try to pray one set of five mysteries a day. The procedure is simple. After making the Sign of the Cross, we pray the Apostles' Creed while holding the crucifix. Next, we pray an Our Father on the first bead and a Hail Mary on each of the next three beads. After the final Hail Mary, we pray the Glory to the Father.

We are now ready to pray the mysteries. Each is prayed the same way. Meditate on the mystery while reciting one Our Father (large bead) and ten Hail Marys (smaller beads). Reciting these prayers acts as a mantra ("background music") and a "timing device" for our meditation.

After we have completed one set of five mysteries, we may conclude by speaking briefly to God (conversation) and resting quietly in God's presence for a minute, listening to whatever God may wish to say to us (contemplation).

Understanding Personal Prayer

Review

Prayer

1. What is the first condition for learning to pray?

2. List and explain two reasons why the useful benefits we get from prayer cannot be the primary reason for praying.

3. What is the primary reason for praying?

Prayer Settings

4. List the three dimensions of human nature and explain how they relate to the three settings in which Jesus prayed.

Prayer Steps

5. List the three preliminary steps we must take to get to know God better through prayer. Illustrate by examples from the Gospel to show how Jesus took these same three preliminary steps.

Prayer Styles

6. List and explain the three forms, or styles, that prayer ordinarily takes.

Prayer Process

7. What is the purpose of the *pre-prayer* process? Briefly describe its two parts.

8. What is a prayer *model?*

Daily-Life Model

9. Explain and illustrate the three steps of the daily-life model.

Scripture Model

10. Explain and illustrate the three steps of the Scripture model.

Journeying with Jesus

11. What is the "Way of the Cross," and how is it prayed?

Mini-Gospel

12. Explain the following: (a) why the rosary is called a mini-Gospel, (b) the twofold purpose of the recitation of the Our Father and the Hail Marys, and (c) the names of the rosary's three sets of mysteries and the period of Jesus' life each focuses on.

Exercises

1. A lay minister headed for Room 201. A nurse told her a patient was there from her hometown. When she got to the room, however, the expected patient was not there. The lay minister apologized to the occupant, saying she probably got her numbers mixed up. But the patient said, "Please stay! It's no mistake that you came here today. I've been praying for the courage to talk with someone like you, but I couldn't bring myself to do it."

On a scale of one (little) to ten (lots), how much confidence do you have that God answers prayers? How do you explain the fact that some prayers do not seem to be answered? Recall a time when you prayed for something and your prayer was answered.

2. Explain the point that each of the following statements makes.

   a. A young lady married a terrific guy. A friend said to her, "Kim, you're so lucky to get a guy like Jay!" Kim replied, "I've been praying for a guy like Jay all my life."

   b. "God hears our heart, not our voice." (Saint Cyprian)

   c. "Prayer is like turning on an electric switch. It does not create the current; it simply provides a channel through which the electric current may flow." (Max Handel)

3. Charlie Rumbaugh grew up in reform schools, jails, and hospital wards. At the age of seventeen, he escaped from a manic depressive ward, found a gun, and held up a jewelry store. A scuffle followed and the jeweler was killed. A Texas judge sentenced Charlie to death.

During his stay on death row, guards treated Charlie badly on several occasions. Shortly before being executed, Charlie asked a friend to pray that he'd be able to forgive the guards before he died. Moments before he received the lethal injection, Charlie said to all involved, "You may not forgive me my transgressions, but I forgive your transgressions against me." Then he said to the warden, "I'm ready."

How did Charlie's final moments resemble Jesus' final moments on the cross? Describe a time when you found it hard to forgive someone.

4. A cartoon showed a tiny insect peering up at a giant insect. After staring at the giant for a while, the tiny insect said, "What kind of a bug are you?" "I'm a praying mantis," came the reply. "That's absurd!" said the tiny insect. "Insects don't pray!" With that, the giant insect grabbed the tiny insect around the throat and began to squeeze. The little bug's eyes began to bulge. Then rolling its eyeballs heavenward, the tiny insect screamed, "Lord, help me!"

Explain the cartoon's point. Answer the following questions on an unsigned slip of paper:

- How frequently do you pray (for example, daily, weekly, rarely)?
- If you pray daily, when and where do you usually pray?
- If you don't pray daily, what are some reasons for not doing so?
- Does your family ever pray at mealtime?

Have several people collect the slips of paper and read them aloud as a secretary records the answers on the chalkboard. Discuss the results.

5. One winter night a high school student and her friend were driving down an icy road. They noticed something on the side of the road. It turned out to be an old man who had fallen on the ice. They put the man in the car. While her friend ran to a nearby house to call the paramedics, the other student asked the man, "Do you believe in God?" The injured man nodded. With that, the student prayed the Our Father a sentence at a time, pausing to let the old man repeat the words after her. Later, the student said, "That Our Father was the most meaningful prayer of my life."

Why did the Our Father have such an impact on the student? Describe a time when you and a friend helped someone as the two friends did. Recall one of the most meaningful prayers you ever prayed.

6. Byron Dell grew up on a farm in Nebraska. When he was eight years old, he had a pony named Frisky, which sometimes lived up to its name. One morning when Byron was herding the cows, Frisky became frightened and bolted off at breakneck speed. Byron held on for dear life and remained unhurt. That night Byron's father accompanied him upstairs to bed and asked his son to kneel with him to thank God that he was not hurt. That incident took place over fifty years ago, and Byron has never forgotten it. It inspired him to make prayer a regular part of his daily life.

Describe a happening from your childhood that still continues to have an impact on you. Did any of your parents ever pray with you? Explain.

Personal Reflection

Prayer often occurs after we experience a "natural high." Here are seven "natural highs" that one girl said "raise my mind and heart to God and move me to want to give thanks."

- having your last class canceled on a spring day
- listening to your headphones as you jog along on a sunny fall afternoon
- watching your baby brother do something for the first time after you've taught him
- seeing a falling star on a clear night
- enjoying a hot shower after a strenuous workout on a winter day
- sledding down a hill while big snowflakes are falling
- watching your dog jump around because it's glad to see you

List seven "natural highs" that "raise your mind and heart to God and move you to want to give thanks."

Bible Reading

Pick a passage. After reading it prayerfully, write out a brief prayer to God that reflects your personal feelings or thoughts about it.

1.	Pray with humility	Luke 18:9–14
2.	Pray with generosity	2 Chronicles 1:7–12
3.	Pray with simplicity	Matthew 6:5–13
4.	Pray with vigor	Luke 11:5–13
5.	Pray with perseverance	Luke 18:1–8

11 Baptism and Confirmation

Robert was one of Esther Thompson's favorite young people. After Esther's husband died, Robert did all her odd jobs, like shoveling snow and mowing her lawn. A real friendship developed between them.

Thus, Esther faced an embarrassing dilemma when Robert invited her to attend his Confirmation. All of her life Esther had a mistrust of the Catholic faith, especially its "magic" rituals.

After anguishing over the invitation, she finally pushed aside her distrust and attended. Esther was totally unprepared for what happened. She wrote later:

> *The Confirmation service*
> *dissolved my years of ignorant distrust. . . .*
> *The Catholic faith was beautiful.*
> *Three years have passed and*
> *I'm a Catholic now.*
> *I thank God every day that Robert invited me*
> *to attend the sacrament of Confirmation.*

Suppose an unchurched friend asked you, "What is the sacrament of Confirmation, and why do Catholics receive it?" How would you answer your friend's question?

Jesus' New Presence

Before Jesus ascended and returned to his Father, he revealed something amazing to his disciples. He revealed that although he would no longer be present on earth in a flesh-and-blood way, he would be present in another way. He said:

> *"When I go,*
> *you will not be left all alone;*

> *I will come back to you. . . .*
> *When that day comes, you will know*
> *that I am in my Father*
> *and that you are in me,*
> *just as I am in you."*
> JOHN 14:18, 20

These words of Jesus revealed that he would be present on earth in a new way. The exact nature of this new presence remained a mystery until Pentecost.

Jesus Is Present in His Church

On Pentecost the Holy Spirit came upon Jesus' followers and empowered them to live as Jesus' "mystical body," the Church. At that moment, they began to realize that the risen Jesus is present on earth in and through his followers.

Recall how Saint Paul experienced this new presence. One day, while persecuting the Church, a light flashed around him.

> *He fell to the ground*
> *and heard a voice saying to him,*
> *"Saul, Saul! Why do you persecute me?"*
> *"Who are you, Lord?" he asked.*
> *"I am Jesus, whom you persecute,"*
> *the voice said.*
> ACTS 9:4–5

This experience led Paul to an incredible realization: Jesus and his Church form *one body* (Ephesians 1:23). To persecute the Church was to persecute Jesus.

And so on Pentecost the Spirit introduced Jesus' disciples into an incredible mystery: Jesus is present on earth in a new way: through his "mystical body," the Church.

Jesus Acts through His Church

On Pentecost something else happened. The disciples began to realize that Jesus not only is present in his Church but also acts through it. The Church is his new body: his new arms, his new legs, his new mouth. It became the new way that Jesus will reach out to people until the end of history.

Now Jesus' disciples understood what he meant when he said to them earlier, "Whoever listens to you listens to me" (Luke 10:16). Jesus meant that the day would come when he would teach through them, forgive through them, and heal through them. Thus when people watched amazed one day as Peter healed a cripple, Peter said:

> *"Why are you surprised at this,*
> *and why do you stare at us?*
> *Do you think that it was by means*
> *of our own power or godliness*
> *that we made this man walk?"*
> ACTS 3:12

Peter then goes on to explain to the people that it was not him, but Jesus acting through him, that enabled the cripple to walk.

And so Jesus not only is *present* in his Church, but also *acts* through it. Church members are joined to Jesus by the Holy Spirit and made to share in Jesus' continuing mission in and to the world. Referring to the mysterious unity of the Church and Christ, Saint Augustine said, "When the Church baptizes, it is Christ himself who baptizes."

The Sacraments

In the years after Pentecost, Jesus' followers gradually came to realize that certain Church actions were extra special. For example, they realized that when they baptized new members, or when they celebrated the Eucharist together, Jesus acted through them in an extra special way. So they gave these actions a special name; they called them *sacraments.*

One of the first uses of this word occurs in the ancient writings of a Christian named Tertullian. He compared baptism to the *sacramentum* by which Roman recruits were initiated into the Roman army. In a similar way, Christians were initiated into the Body of Christ through the *sacramentum* of Baptism.

The word caught on. Unfortunately, some Christians began to apply it to lesser Church actions as well. At one point someone listed thirty actions of the Church that people referred to as sacraments.

Eventually, the Church reserved the word *sacrament* for those seven special moments when the risen Jesus acts through the community of his followers in a special way. These seven sacraments may be grouped as follows:

- Sacraments of initiation: Baptism, Confirmation, Eucharist
- Sacraments of healing: Reconciliation, Anointing of the Sick
- Sacraments of commitment: Marriage, Holy Orders

This brings us to the heart of what is meant by the word *sacrament.*

Jesus no longer reaches out and encounters people through his own *physical* actions, because he is no longer present in our midst through his *historical* body. But Jesus is present through his *mystical* body. And it is through the *sacramental* actions of this body that he continues to encounter people.

And so a sacrament may be described as *a tangible encounter with the risen Jesus.* By *tangible* we mean in a way that involves our senses. And by *encounter* we mean a meeting in which Jesus communicates with us personally—just as he did with people in Gospel times.

Rite of Christian Initiation of Adults

Imagine you have been transported back into time to the year A.D. 300. Suddenly you find yourself in a large house in Rome. It is Holy Saturday night. About a hundred Christians are present.

As you listen to what is going on, you discover that several people are to be initiated into the Christian community that night. These catechumens, as they are called, are gathered around a garden pool in a courtyard adjacent to a big room. They have been preparing for a long time for this memorable moment. A presbyter (priest) and two deacons are preparing them for the initiation rite. A bishop presides over the gathering.

The first sacrament of the initiation rite is Baptism. Each candidate renounces Satan and evil. Next, a deacon accompanies each catechumen down the pool steps into the water to be baptized.

When all catechumens have been baptized, they are led into a large room where the community is gathered for the second sacrament of the initiation rite: Confirmation. This sacrament begins with the bishop calling each of the newly baptized forward by name. Next, he lays hands on them, praying that they may be worthy to receive the Holy Spirit. He then anoints them with oil, embraces them, and admits them to the Christian community.

The third sacrament of the initiation rite is the Eucharist. It begins with singing and a procession of people carrying loaves of bread and cups of wine. The bread and wine are placed on a table in the center of the room. The bishop prays over them, just as Jesus did at the Last Supper. Finally, the presbyter and the deacons distribute the loaves and the wine (which have become the Body and Blood of Christ) to the whole community, including the new members.

This imaginary scene illustrates how the early Church celebrated the sacraments of Christian initiation. It celebrated them in a *single celebration* composed of three sacraments.

As the Church grew, the bishops could no longer preside over every ceremony in every parish at the Easter Vigil. Since they wanted to stay personally involved in the initiation of each Christian, the bishops reserved to themselves the celebration of Confirmation. The Confirmation rite became detached from Baptism and was celebrated when the bishops were available.

Another change took place as the Church grew. Many of those to be initiated into the community were the infants of members. This led to the practice of introducing infants to the first stage of the initiation ceremony, but postponing the latter two stages until the infants had reached the age of reason and could participate more personally in the rite.

This situation prevailed until modern times, when the Church restored the Rite of the Initiation of Christian Adults to its original integrity. Now adults are normally initiated into the community at a single ceremony at the Easter Vigil.

Sacrament of Baptism

Years ago, anthropologist Thor Heyerdahl suggested that ancient South Americans could have migrated to Polynesia on rafts. All they had to do was to let the current of the water carry them. To prove his point, he built a tiny raft and floated it from South America to Polynesia.

A surprising part of this story is that Thor once had a deathly fear of water. How could someone who once feared water cross four thousand miles of ocean on a tiny raft?

Something happened to Thor to remove his fear. One day while on military maneuvers, his canoe capsized near a waterfall. His body plunged down into the watery depths of the river. As the waters closed over him, he began to pray. A burst of energy surged through him, and he struggled to the surface. Then he battled the waters as they swept him toward the waterfall. Minutes later, he reached shore.

That experience transformed Thor. Somewhere in the watery depths of the river, the old, fearful Thor *died* and a new, courageous Thor was *born*. The waters of that river were for Thor an agent of *death* and an agent of *new life*.

Thor's death-life experience introduces us to a prominent biblical theme:

> *Water is an agent of death*
> *and an agent of birth.*

The Book of Genesis portrays a great flood destroying all human life except for Noah's family. Thus the flood *waters* act as an agent of *death* (to an old world of sin) and as an agent of *birth* (to a new world of grace).

In a similar way, the Book of Exodus portrays the Israelites escaping from Egypt through the waters of the Red Sea. Thus the sea *waters* act as an agent of *death* (to their old life of slavery) and as an agent of *birth* (to their new life of freedom).

The Christian Scriptures continue this theme. For example, John's baptisms at the Jordan portray the river *waters* as being an agent of *death* (to an old life of sin) and an agent of *birth* (to a new life of repentance).

And so Scripture often uses water in a symbolic way: as an agent of *death* to an *old life* and as an agent of *birth* to a *new life*.

Meaning of Baptism

Jesus told the Jewish leader Nicodemus that unless a person be baptized ("born of water and the Spirit"), that person cannot enter the Kingdom of God. Jesus added, "A person is born physically of human parents, but he is born spiritually of the Spirit" (John 3:6).

And at the end of his life, just before ascending to his Father, Jesus instructed his disciples:

> *"Go, then, to all peoples everywhere*
> *and make them my disciples:*
> *baptize them in the name of the Father,*
> *the Son, and the Holy Spirit."*
> MATTHEW 28:19

These two instructions form the basis for our understanding of Baptism. The *liturgy* ("sacred ritual") of Baptism involves two central actions:

- immersing a person in water (or pouring water over the person) while
- pronouncing the words, "I baptize you in the name of the Father, and of the Son, and of the Holy Spirit."

Baptism Is a Death-Birth Agent

Water is used in Baptism much as it is used in Scripture: as a *death-birth* agent. It is used to symbolize a passage from death to life.

Recall that the first sin doomed the human race to spiritual death. Referring to this tragic fact, Saint Paul writes:

> *Sin came into the world . . .*
> *sin brought death with it.*
> *As a result,*
> *death has spread to the whole human race*
> *because everyone has sinned.*
> ROMANS 5:12

This first sin doomed the human race. Our only hope was that God had promised to have mercy on us and save us. And that is just what God did.

God sent God's only Son into the world to save us. The Son of God, Jesus, became human, died for our sins, and rose to new life. Referring to the saving act of Jesus' death and resurrection, Saint Paul writes:

> *As the one sin*
> *condemned all mankind,*
> *in the same way*
> *the one righteous act*
> *sets all mankind free and gives them life.*
> ROMANS 5:18

Baptism Extends Jesus' Saving Act

Through the sacrament of Baptism, the risen Jesus unites us to himself and shares with us the new life he won by his death and resurrection.

And this is where the use of water comes in. Water symbolizes our passage from spiritual death to spiritual rebirth in Christ. It symbolizes our

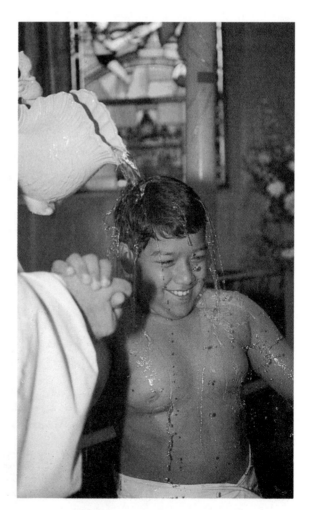

spiritual dying and rising with Christ. Saint Paul writes:

> *By our baptism . . .*
> *we were buried with him and shared his death,*
> *in order that,*
> *just as Christ was raised from death*
> *by the glorious power of the Father,*
> *so also we might live a new life.*
>
> *For since we have become one with him*
> *in dying as he did,*
> *in the same way we shall be one with him*
> *by being raised to life as he was.*
>
> ROMANS 6:4–5

Paul's words explain why early Christians began baptizing new members by immersing them in a large pool of running water—a practice the Church approves and recommends today. This way of baptizing new members better symbolizes their participation in Jesus' death and resurrection. An ancient Christian writing describes the symbolism this way:

> *You were led down*
> *to the font of holy baptism*
> *just as Christ was taken down from the cross*
> *and placed in the tomb. . . .*
> *You were plunged in the water. . . .*
> *It was night for you and you could not see.*
> *But when you rose again,*
> *it was like coming into broad daylight.*
> *In the same instant*
> *you died and were born again;*
> *the saving water was both*
> *a tomb [agent of death] and*
> *a womb [agent of life].*
>
> JERUSALEM CATECHESIS

And so Baptism may be described as *a tangible encounter with the risen Jesus in which he unites us to himself, makes us participants in his death and resurrection to new life, pardons our sins, and makes us adopted children of God.*

Signs Say It Better

Athletes share "high fives" to celebrate a great play. Families eat cake to celebrate a birthday. People shake hands to celebrate an agreement.

This raises a question. Why do we do these things? Why don't we simply use words? It's much easier to say "Nice play!" than to give someone a "high five." The answer is that on certain occasions signs are better expressions of what we feel than words are. They engage our hearts and our emotions better than words do.

Jesus was human. He knew the importance of signs. He knew that in certain situations, signs are more expressive than words. And so Jesus used signs to express certain spiritual realities. For example, he anointed people's eyes to say that he was healing their blindness (John 9:6). Jesus also taught his followers to use signs (Mark 6:13).

And so Jesus' disciples, following Jesus' example and his instruction, used certain signs to convey certain special spiritual realities. We call these special signs *sacraments,* because they do more than *signify* a spiritual reality. They *make it present.* For example, they make present in a tangible way the "life-giving power" of God (Baptism), the "forgiving power" of God (Reconciliation), and the "healing power" of God (Anointing of the Sick).

Some people ask, "Did Jesus institute all the sacraments?" The answer is yes, but not in the way that some people think. For example, Jesus did not pause after anointing a sick person and say, "What I just did was to institute the sacrament of the Anointing of the Sick." Nor did Jesus pause after the Last Supper and say, "What I just did was to institute the sacrament of the Eucharist." Rather, Jesus instituted all the sacraments in the sense that their existence and power ultimately come from him.

Someone compared Jesus' institution of the sacaments to God's creation of the universe. We don't know the details of how each creature came into being. But we do know that, ultimately, each owes its existence to God. In a similar way, we don't know the details of how each sacrament came into being. But we know that, ultimately, each owes its existence and power to Jesus.

Sacrament of Confirmation

"One Tooth" was an old man in New Guinea. He got his name from the fact that he had only one tooth in his upper jaw. One Tooth had just become a Christian and spent a part of each day reading the Gospel to outpatients in the waiting room of the local mission hospital.

One day, One Tooth had trouble reading. So he went to the hospital doctor. The doctor checked his eyes and gave him the tragic news: he was going blind. The next day, One Tooth did not show up at the hospital. Nor did he show up the day after that.

Later, the doctor learned that One Tooth had gone to a deserted part of the island. So the doctor went to see him. One Tooth explained what he was doing, saying:

> *"Ever since you told me I was going blind,*
> *I've been reading and memorizing*
> *the most important parts of the Gospel.*
> *I've memorized Jesus' birth,*
> *his important miracles and parables,*
> *and his death and resurrection.*
> *I've been repeating them over and over*
> *to make sure I have them right.*
> *Soon I'll be back at the hospital again,*
> *doctor, telling the outpatients about Jesus."*

That story makes a fitting introduction to the sacrament of Confirmation. It illustrates the fact that Confirmation continues our initiation into the Church community as the Holy Spirit empowers us—

- to witness to Jesus, and
- to continue his work.

Before seeing how Confirmation celebrates this mystery, let us explore its biblical background.

The Holy Spirit Is Promised

Before returning to his Father, Jesus told his disciples to go back to Jerusalem, saying:

> *"Wait for the gift I told you about,*
> *the gift my Father promised. . . .*
> *In a few days*
> *you will be baptized with the Holy Spirit. . . .*
> *When the Holy Spirit comes upon you,*
> *you will be filled with power,*
> *and you will be witnesses for me . . .*
> *to the ends of the earth."*
> ACTS 1:4–5, 8

The Holy Spirit Comes

On the day of the Jewish feast of Pentecost, the Apostles with Mary the mother of Jesus and some disciples were gathered in prayer in a house in Jerusalem.

> *Suddenly there was a noise from the sky*
> *which sounded like a strong wind blowing,*
> *and it filled the whole house. . . .*
> *They were all filled with the Holy Spirit*
> *and began to talk in other languages,*
> *as the Spirit enabled them to speak.*
> ACTS 2:2, 4

The Holy Spirit Is Communicated

The Apostles, in turn, imparted the Holy Spirit to the newly baptized.

> *The apostles in Jerusalem heard*
> *that the people of Samaria*
> *had received the word of God,*
> *so they sent Peter and John to them.*
> *When they arrived,*
> *they prayed for the believers*
> *that they might receive the Holy Spirit. . . .*
> *Then Peter and John*
> *placed their hands on them,*
> *and they received the Holy Spirit.*
> ACTS 8:14–15, 17

It is against this biblical background that we must view Confirmation. It is the sacrament by which we receive the fullness of the Holy Spirit that the disciples received on Pentecost.

Laying On of Hands

The laying on of hands on a person's head has its origin in Old Testament times. For example, when God picked Joshua to succeed Moses, he told Moses:

> *"Take Joshua son of Nun . . .*
> *and place your hands on his head. . . .*
> *Give him some of your own authority,*
> *so that the whole community of Israel*
> *will obey him. . . ."*
>
> *Moses did as the LORD had commanded him. . . .*
> *Moses put his hands on Joshua's head*
> *and proclaimed him as his successor.*
> NUMBERS 27:18, 20, 22–23

And so the rite of placing of hands on a person's head symbolized the calling and the empowering of that person to perform a special service.

Anointing with Oil

Anointing a person with oil has its origin in the Bible also. For example, God told Moses:

> *"This is what you are to do*
> *to Aaron and his sons*
> *to dedicate them as priests. . . .*
> *Dress Aaron in the priestly garments. . . .*
> *Then take the anointing oil . . .*
> *and anoint him."*
> EXODUS 29:1, 5, 7

Meaning of Confirmation

The newly baptized continue their Christian initiation by receiving the sacrament of Confirmation. The liturgy ("sacred ritual") of Confirmation involves three central actions:

- laying on of hands,
- anointing the baptized person's forehead,
- saying, "Be sealed with the Gift of the Holy Spirit."

Similarly, God instructed Samuel to anoint David as king of Israel, saying:

"Get some olive oil and go to Bethlehem,
to a man named Jesse,
because I have chosen one of his sons
to be king."

Jesse sent for David. . . .
The Lord said to Samuel,
"This is the one—anoint him!"
Samuel took the olive oil and anointed David.
1 SAMUEL 16:1, 12–13

Finally, the Bible speaks of prophets being "anointed." God says to Elijah:

"Anoint Elisha . . .
to succeed you as prophet."
1 KINGS 19:16

And so the rite of anointing the forehead with oil was highly symbolic. It signified the calling and empowering a prophet, priest, or king for special service to the community.

Sharing food with poor.

Sealing with the Spirit

Ancient kings tattooed the hand of their soldiers with a sign, or "seal." Referring to this practice, an ancient writing addresses new Christians as follows:

The soldier chosen for service . . .
receives on his hand
the seal showing what king he will serve.
So with you.
You were chosen for the king of heaven,
and will henceforth bear his seal.

And another ancient writing addresses new Christians in these words:

Come near
and receive the sacramental seal
so that you may be recognized by the Master.

These examples help us understand the words "Be sealed with the Gift of the Holy Spirit." They signify—

- that the same Holy Spirit whom Jesus communicated to his disciples on Pentecost is now communicated to us, and
- that the Holy Spirit's presence in us is the special sign, or "seal," that we belong to Jesus and have been called and empowered to witness to him and to continue his work.

And so the sacrament of Confirmation may be described as *a tangible encounter with the risen Jesus in which we are sealed with the fullness of the Gift of the Holy Spirit and are called and empowered to witness to Jesus and to continue his work.*

Recap

On Pentecost the Holy Spirit came upon the disciples and formed them into *one body,* with Jesus as *head* of the body (Colossians 1:18). From that moment on, the risen Jesus not only became present in the Church but also began *to act through it.* Seven actions of Jesus are special and are called *sacraments.* Two of these sacraments are Baptism and Confirmation.

Baptism may be described as a tangible encounter with the risen Jesus in which he unites us to himself, makes us participants in his death and resurrection to new life, pardons our sins, and makes us adopted children of God.

Confirmation may be described as a tangible encounter with the risen Jesus in which we are sealed with the fullness of the Gift of the Holy Spirit and are called and empowered to witness to Jesus and to continue his work.

Finally, we use the word *mystery* to refer to the saving event of Jesus' death and resurrection. Early Christians called this mysterious event the "paschal mystery." The word *paschal* derives from the Jewish Passover Festival. During this festival a "Passover lamb" is sacrificed to commemorate Israel's *passover* from slavery to freedom as God's Chosen People. Saint Paul relates the Passover Festival to Jesus' death and resurrection, saying:

> *Our Passover Festival is ready,*
> *now that Christ,*
> *our Passover lamb,*
> *has been sacrificed.*
> 1 CORINTHIANS 5:7

In other words, by Jesus' death and resurrection we Christians "pass over" from slavery to sin to freedom as God's adopted children. This is the paschal mystery that we celebrate (proclaim and make present) in the sacraments—especially during the Rite of Christian Initiation of Adults at the Easter Vigil.

> *Thus, by baptism, [Christians] are plunged*
> *into the paschal mystery of Christ:*
> *they die with Him,*
> *are buried with Him, and rise with Him . . . ;*
> *they receive the spirit of adoption as [children]*
> *"by virtue of which we cry: Abba, Father." . . .*
> *In like manner,*
> *as often as they eat the supper of the Lord*
> *they proclaim the death of the Lord . . .*
> *[and] celebrate the paschal mystery . . .*
> *in which "the victory and triumph*
> *of [the Lord's] death are again made present."*
> CONSTITUTION ON THE SACRED LITURGY, 6

The paschal mystery is beautifully summed up in these words of the eucharistic acclamation:

> *Christ has died,*
> *Christ has risen,*
> *Christ will come again.*

The Paschal Mystery

The word *mystery* is used in different ways. For example, we use it as Saint Paul does in referring to Christ's union with the Church (Ephesians 5:32, NAB). This mysterious union exceeds anything we can imagine.

> *The church is Christ's body,*
> *the completion of him*
> *who himself completes all things everywhere.*
> EPHESIANS 1:23

We also use the word *mystery* as Saint Paul does in referring to God's plan.

> *This plan, which God will complete*
> *when the time is right,*
> *is to bring all creation together,*
> *everything in heaven and on earth,*
> *with Christ as head.*
> EPHESIANS 1:10

Understanding Baptism and Confirmation

Review

Jesus' New Presence

1. What did Jesus promise his disciples shortly before returning to his Father, and when did he fulfill this promise?

2. How is Jesus present and active in a new way starting with Pentecost?

3. Explain how Paul experienced that the risen Jesus and his followers form one body.

The Sacraments

4. Explain where the word *sacrament* comes from and why the early Christians first began to use it.

5. Define the word *sacrament* as we now use it of the "seven sacraments."

6. Explain the parallel between the way people encountered the historical Jesus in Gospel times and the way we encounter the risen Jesus today.

7. List the three groups into which the sacraments are divided and the sacraments that belong to each group.

Sacrament of Baptism

8. Explain the symbolic way in which water is often used in the Hebrew Scriptures, and use Israel's crossing of the Red Sea to illustrate your answer.

Meaning of Baptism

9. What two instructions of Jesus form the basis of our understanding of the liturgy of Baptism? What are the two central actions of the liturgy of Baptism?

10. Explain how Baptism relates to Jesus' salvation (saving) of the human race.

11. Explain how baptizing in a large pool of water enabled early Christians to better symbolize that Baptism is a sharing or participation in Jesus' death and resurrection.

12. Describe the sacrament of Baptism.

Sacrament of Confirmation

13. What two actions does the sacrament of Confirmation call and empower us to do?

14. How is the sacrament of Confirmation related to Pentecost?

Meaning of Confirmation

15. List and briefly explain the biblical or ancient background of the three central actions of the liturgy of Confirmation.

16. Describe the sacrament of Confirmation.

Rite of Christian Initiation of Adults

17. Explain how the Rite of Christian Initiation of Adults became fragmented.

Signs Say It Better

18. In what sense did Jesus institute the sacraments? In what sense do sacramental signs do more than merely *signify* the presence of a spiritual reality?

The Paschal Mystery

19. Explain what is meant by the "paschal mystery."

Exercises

1. October 23, 1945, was the day Jackie Robinson became baseball's first black athlete. Jackie's entry into baseball was not easy. Racial slurs and insults were a common occurrence. One day in Boston's Fenway Park, the situation got especially bad. At one point the all-star shortstop, Pee Wee Reese, called time, walked over to second base, put his arm around Jackie, and just stood there looking at the fans.

List some other kinds of prejudice, besides racial. On a scale of one (low) to ten (high), how strong is prejudice in your school? How do you account for the amount of prejudice that is there? Describe a time when, like Pee Wee Reese, you took a stand against some prejudice (racial or otherwise).

2. Upon entering a church, Catholics take holy water and bless themselves. This practice began as a symbolic renewal of our baptismal commitment. Some churches, following an ancient tradition, locate the baptismal font near the entrance of the church. When this is not done, a small holy water font is put in its place to remind us that it was by the water of Baptism that we first entered, or became members of, the Church. When a high school girl learned the meaning of taking holy water and blessing herself, she said, "That makes this practice so much more meaningful. But I'll bet most Catholics don't know the meaning of it."

To test the girl's thesis, ask three Catholics if they know the meaning of taking holy water and blessing themselves upon entering a church. Why is there so much ignorance concerning practices like taking holy water upon entering a church? List two other Catholic customs and the purpose behind each one.

This combination baptismal–holy water font portrays John baptizing Jesus.

3. Fifty-two Americans were held hostage by Iran for 444 days in 1980–81. On Christmas, three American ministers were permitted to enter Iran, hold services, and give the hostages messages from loved ones. One message to hostage Barry Rosen was especially moving. The minister began by saying to Barry, "I saw your wife, Barbara, and your son, Alexander, in New York. Alexander is a lovely boy; he told me to give you this." Then he kissed Barry on the cheek. Barry had all he could do to fight back the tears.

Why do you think kissing the boy's father was more effective than saying, "Your son sends his love"? How was the real kiss (relayed through the minister) somewhat like a *sacrament?* Why do we often become less affectionate (outwardly) as we grow older, and is this good or bad?

4. Consider two stories. The first concerns seventy-nine-year-old Clara Hale. In the twenty years after her own family had grown up, she served as foster mother to over five hundred babies born of drug-addicted mothers. These babies enter life with a drug dependency themselves. "When a baby is crying for a drug," she says, "all you can do is hold it close and say to it, 'I love you, and God loves you, and your mama loves you. Your mama just needs a little time.' " The second story concerns an elderly woman in a Georgia nursing home. Even though writing is a task for her, she corresponds with fourteen prison inmates. "All of them need a grandmother," she says.

How do these two stories illustrate the purpose of the sacrament of Confirmation? Give an example of some adult you know who performs a similar service for others.

Personal Reflection

The following prayer is a reflection on the sacraments. It was composed by a well-known twentieth-century theologian.

> *Lord, your salvation*
> *is bound up with a visible Church. . . .*
> *Your grace comes to us in ways*
> *that we can see, hear, and feel. . . .*
> *It warms my heart*
> *to know that I can be sure*
> *of your powerful life-giving presence*
> *in the water of Baptism,*
> *in the word of Reconciliation,*
> *and in the bread of the Eucharist.*
> Karl Rahner (slightly adapted)

Compose a similar prayer to Jesus about the sacraments in general or one sacrament in particular. For example, you might speak to Jesus about the sacrament of Reconciliation or the sacrament of the Eucharist. What are your feelings about the sacrament? Why don't you receive it as often as you could? How might you make it more meaningful in your life?

Bible Reading

Pick a passage. After reading it prayerfully, write out a brief prayer to God that reflects your personal feelings or thoughts about it.

1. Baptism   Acts 8:26–40
2. Confirmation   Acts 8:14–17
3. New Christian life   Ephesians 2:1–17
4. One Spirit, many gifts   1 Corinthians 12:1–11
5. One body, many gifts   1 Corinthians 12:27–31

12 Eucharist

Gift table.

Mary Reilly's father was leaving for work. As usual, he was about a half-hour early. Mary said, "Dad, why don't you relax at home for an extra half-hour rather than go to work so early?" Her dad said, "I don't go right to work, Mary. I usually try to catch the eight o'clock Mass at Holy Trinity."

Mary was surprised. She said later, "I was really impressed. I sometimes complained to Dad because he insisted we take part in Sunday Mass together as a family. But he never once said to me, 'Hey, Mary, I go every day; the least you can do is to join us on Sunday.' "

How do your parents feel about the frequency of your participation in Mass?

Eucharistic Worship

The Eucharist is the coming together of God's people, who have been initiated into Christ's Body by Baptism and Confirmation. The celebration of the Eucharist completes our initiation by uniting us more fully to Christ and to one another.

To understand the Eucharist (Mass), we need to go back to Gospel times. In those days, Jews worshiped publicly in two different places: the synagogue and the Temple. A synagogue was located in every town. But there was only one Temple, in Jerusalem.

Both the synagogue and the Temple had their own special worship service. The synagogue was mainly a place of prayer and *instruction*. People gathered there to listen to God's word. The Temple was mainly a place of prayer and *sacrifice*. People gathered there to make offerings to God. Jesus worshiped in both the synagogue and the Temple (Luke 2:46, 4:16).

The Mass (Eucharist) reflects the synagogue service and the Temple service. The synagogue service is reflected in the first major part of the Mass, called the *Liturgy of the Word*. The Temple service is reflected in the second major part of the Mass, called the *Liturgy of the Eucharist*.

We begin with the Liturgy of the Word. It may be viewed as being made up of three rites:

- ■ Gathering Rite,
- ■ Penitential Rite, and
- ■ Reading Rite.

Liturgy of the Word

The Mass is the center of Catholic life. It expresses, celebrates, and strengthens our union with Christ and one another. It is the focal point of everything we believe, everything we do, and everything we hope for.

In response to the Lord's invitation at the Last Supper, "Do this in memory of me," we gather every Lord's Day—

- to *recall* and be *nourished* by the Lord's Word and the Lord's Supper, and
- to *proclaim* to the world the "good news" that "Christ has died, Christ is risen, Christ will come again."

Gathering Rite

The Mass begins with the Gathering Rite. Everyone stands and sings as the celebrant and the other ministers enter the assembly in procession. The focal point of the *procession* is the book of God's word, from which we will read during the Liturgy of the Word. It is held high for all to see.

Ancient Jews kept the sacred scroll of God's word near the throne. Jewish generals carried it into battle. Modern Jews carry it in procession around the synagogue before reading from it. It is in the spirit of this ancient tradition that the book of God's word is held high and reverenced in the procession.

After the procession reaches the sanctuary, the book is reverently placed on the lectern.

The celebrant then kisses the altar, a symbol of Jesus Christ, and goes to the presider's chair. There he greets the "gathering" and leads them in the Penitential Rite.

Penitential Rite

The Penitential Rite carries out Jesus' command in the Sermon on the Mount. Jesus said that if we gather to worship and have not forgiven a brother or a sister, we should forgive that person first. Only then should we begin our worship (Matthew 5:23–24).

The purpose of the Penitential Rite is to exchange forgiveness with one another and to ask God's forgiveness for our sins.

Next, the celebrant leads us in a hymn of *thanks* and *adoration* (praise). Called the *Gloria,* this ancient hymn begins:

> *Glory to God in the highest,*
> *and peace to his people on earth.*
>
> *Lord God, heavenly King,*
> *almighty God and Father,*
> *   we worship you, we give you thanks,*
> *   we praise you for your glory.*

The celebrant ends with a prayer of *supplication:* asking God's help in some area of our lives. For example, the celebrant prays:

> *Almighty God, ever-loving Father,*
> *your care extends beyond the boundaries*
> *   of race and nation*
> *to the hearts of all who live.*
>
> *May the walls,*
> *   which prejudice raises between us,*
> *crumble beneath the shadow*
> *   of your outstretched arm.*
>
> *We ask this through Christ our Lord.*
> TWENTIETH SUNDAY OF THE YEAR

We respond, "Amen," which is a Hebrew word meaning "So be it." Our "Amen" prepares us for the final and most important rite of the Liturgy of the Word.

Reading Rite

A beautiful description of the Reading Rite is this passage from the Gospel according to Luke:

> *Jesus stood up [in the synagogue]*
> *to read the Scriptures*
> *and was handed the book of the prophet Isaiah.*
> *He unrolled the scroll*
> *and found the place where it is written,*
>
> *"The Spirit of the Lord is upon me,*
> *because he has chosen me*
> *to bring good news to the poor.*
> *He has sent me to proclaim*
> *liberty to the captives and*
> *recovery of sight to the blind,*
> *to set free the oppressed*
> *and announce that the time has come*
> *when the Lord will save his people."*
>
> *Jesus rolled up the scroll,*
> *gave it back to the attendant,*
> *and sat down.*
> *All the people in the synagogue*
> *had their eyes fixed on him,*
> *as he said to them,*
> *"This passage of scripture*
> *has come true today,*
> *as you heard it being read."*
>
> *They were all well impressed with him*
> *and marveled at the eloquent words*
> *that he spoke.*
> LUKE 4:16–22

This passage capsulizes what happens during the Liturgy of the Word.

- We listen to God's word.
- A priest or deacon opens up the meaning of God's word.
- We apply God's word to our lives.

The *first reading* is usually from the Hebrew Scriptures. We listen to the same words that touched Jesus' heart when he heard them read in Nazareth.

The first reading is followed by the singing of a *responsorial* psalm. We give it the name *responsorial* because we usually punctuate it with responses, like "Your word, O Lord, is a lamp for my feet." This psalm acts as a prayerful reflection on the first reading.

The *second reading* is taken from the Christian Scriptures, usually one of Paul's letters. These letters deal with early Christian problems, which were surprisingly like our own.

The *third reading* is the high point of the Liturgy of the Word. It is always taken from one of the four Gospels. We show the importance of this reading in the following twofold way:

- by introducing it with a *chant,* and
- by *standing* and *signing* ourselves before it is proclaimed to us.

Signing dates back to the early Christians. It consists of tracing a small cross on the forehead, the lips, and the heart. While signing themselves, some Catholics pray silently in words like these:

> *May God's word be in my mind,*
> *on my lips, and in my heart*
> *that I may worthily proclaim it*
> *by word and example.*

The Gospel proclamation puts us in touch with Jesus. It puts us in touch with what we believe as Christians.

The reading from the Gospel is followed by the *homily:* explaining and applying God's word to our lives.

A homily is difficult to preach for two reasons. The first is that most congregations are composed of people with vastly different needs, ages, and backgrounds. This makes it hard to appeal equally to everyone in the congregation. The second reason is that not all homilists are gifted speakers.

And so the delivery of the homily is not always as inspiring as we might like it to be. But we look beyond the homilist's delivery and remember what Jesus said to his disciples: "Whoever listens to you listens to me" (Luke 10:16). Thus, if we listen to the homily with an open mind and an open heart, we will be inspired. Jesus does speak to us through it in some special way.

The Liturgy of the Word ends with the *Creed* and the *General Intercessions.*

The *Creed* is a profession of faith in God's word, which we have just heard, and what we believe as Catholics. Think of the Creed this way: If someone asked us to summarize the Catholic faith in sixty seconds, could we do it? The answer is yes. That's what the Creed is: a concise statement of Catholic belief.

The *General Intercessions* are an expression of the Church's needs and the needs of the world. For example, we pray—

- that the victims of child abuse may be healed of their rage and learn to forgive those who abused them. We pray to the Lord.
- that the victims of prejudice may not forfeit their dignity and integrity by sinful, retaliatory actions. We pray to the Lord.

The celebrant concludes the General Intercessions by praying in words like these:

God our Father,
your Son, Jesus, taught us
not to curse the darkness of our world,
but to light candles to illuminate it.
Help us carry out this teaching.
We make our prayer through Christ our Lord.

We believe in one God,
the Father, the Almighty,
maker of heaven and earth,
of all that is seen and unseen.

We believe in one Lord, Jesus Christ,
the only Son of God,
eternally begotten of the Father,
God from God, Light from Light,
true God from true God,
begotten, not made, one in Being with the Father.
Through him all things were made.
For us men and for our salvation
*   he came down from heaven:*
by the power of the Holy Spirit
*   he was born of the Virgin Mary, and became man.*

For our sake he was crucified under Pontius Pilate;
*   he suffered, died, and was buried.*
On the third day he rose again
*   in fulfillment of the Scriptures;*
he ascended into heaven
*   and is seated at the right hand of the Father.*
He will come again in glory to judge the living and the dead,
*   and his kingdom will have no end.*

We believe in the Holy Spirit, the Lord, the giver of life,
who proceeds from the Father and the Son.
With the Father and the Son he is worshiped and glorified.
He has spoken through the Prophets.
We believe in one holy catholic and apostolic Church.
We acknowledge one baptism for the forgiveness of sins.
We look for the resurrection of the dead,
*   and the life of the world to come. Amen.*

Listening to God's Word

The Broadway play *The Royal Hunt of the Sun* deals with Spain's conquest of ancient Peru. In one scene a Spaniard gives an Indian leader a Bible, saying that it is God's word. Filled with curiosity, the leader raises the Bible to his ear and listens. Hearing nothing, the leader slams the Bible to the ground.

That scene raises an important question: How do we listen to God's word in the Bible?

First, we listen with our *body*. This means that we listen with reverence and attention. This kind of listening requires special effort. An early Christian preacher used to tell the congregation: "You receive the *Body of the Lord* with special care and reverence, lest even a tiny crumb fall to the floor. You should receive the *Word of the Lord* the same way."

Second, we listen with our *mind*. This means that we listen with our imagination. It means that we try to make the passage come alive in our imagination. It means that we try to visualize the scene and feel the excitement Jesus' disciples did as they watched it unfold.

Third, we listen with our *heart*. This means that we "take to heart" God's word. An example will help to illustrate.

A few years ago a chaplain formed a prayer group with some inmates at the maximum-security prison at Riker's Island, New York. They would read a parable like the Good Samaritan. Then they would reflect on the passage in silence. Finally, they would share their thoughts on it.

One night it was cold and there was little heat in the room. One of the inmates was not warmly dressed and was shivering, while another had come prepared and was wrapped in two blankets. Suddenly, in the midst of their reflection, the well-prepared inmate walked over and put one of his blankets around the inmate who was cold. The inmate who gave away his blanket had "taken to heart" the parable they were reflecting on.

Finally, we listen with our *soul*. This means that we listen with faith. It means that we believe that God's word has the power to transform us. All we can do is to open ourselves to the word. Beyond that, we can do nothing. God's word has the power to penetrate to our soul and transform us. Again, a story will illustrate.

A young camper was canoeing with a friend in the Canadian wilderness. They were tired and needed rest. When they spotted a trapper's cabin on the river bank, they beached their canoe and went into the cabin. It was empty, except for a cot. On the cot lay an open Bible and a note, which said: "Your cabin saved my life. I had taken seriously ill and needed shelter. Your cabin provided it. I cannot repay you with money, only with God's blessing. Read the Bible passage beneath this note." The campers lifted the note and read:

> *"Then the King will say to the people*
> *on his right,*
> *'Come, you that are blessed by my Father!*
> *Come and possess the kingdom*
> *which has been prepared for you*
> *ever since the creation of the world.*
> *I was hungry and you fed me . . .*
> *I was a stranger*
> *and you received me in your homes . . .*
> *I was sick and you took care of me. . . .'*
> *Whenever you did this*
> *for one of the least important of these . . .*
> *you did it for me!"*
> MATTHEW 25:34-36, 40

The campers said later that they had heard that passage many times, but it never touched them so deeply as it did at that moment.

And so the final way to listen to God's word is with our soul—with faith—knowing that it has the power to touch us. This means that we may hear it read many times before it touches us. But if we persevere in listening, the day will come when it will touch us.

Van Gogh's Good Samaritan.

De Juanes's Last Supper.

Liturgy of the Eucharist

Charles Butler went to visit his son, who was working in the Amazon Basin in Brazil. When Charles arrived in Brazil, he took a small plane to a tiny town in the Basin. There he and the pilot went to a local cafe for a meal.

An old-timer in the cafe began talking to the pilot. They soon discovered that they were both from the same province in Brazil. Next they discovered that they were from the same town.

When Charles and the pilot finished their meal, the old-timer said to the pilot jokingly, "You know, if we keep talking, we might discover that we're from the same family."

That story makes a good introduction to the Liturgy of the Eucharist. During the Eucharist we Christians discover, in a special way, that we are a family. We celebrate and strengthen our unity as brothers and sisters: members of the one Body of Christ. Saint Paul says of the Eucharistic Meal:

> *Because there is the one loaf of bread,*
> *all of us, though many, are one body,*
> *for we all share the same loaf.*
> 1 CORINTHIANS 10:17

To understand and appreciate the great mystery of the Liturgy of the Eucharist, we need to go back to the Last Supper, the final Passover meal that Jesus ate with his disciples. Describing what happened at that meal, Saint Luke writes:

> *Jesus took his place at the table*
> *with the apostles. . . .*
> *Then he took a piece of bread,*
> *gave thanks to God, broke it,*
> *and gave it to them, saying,*
> *"This is my body,*
> *which is given for you.*
> *Do this in memory of me."*
> *In the same way,*
> *he gave them the cup after the supper,*
> *saying, "This cup is God's new covenant*
> *sealed with my blood,*
> *which is poured out for you."*
> LUKE 22:14, 19–20

Luke's description of the Last Supper gives us an insight into what the Eucharist is. It is a holy meal that recalls the Last Supper, celebrates and deepens our unity with Christ, and anticipates the eternal banquet of God's Kingdom in heaven.

Luke's narrative shows that the Last Supper had three dimensions. It was—

- a memorial meal,
- a sacrificial meal, and
- a covenant meal.

These same three dimensions are found in the Eucharist.

Jewish Passover meal.

Memorial Meal

When Jews ate the Passover meal, as Jesus and the Apostles did at the Last Supper, they did more than recall the event that freed their ancestors from slavery. *By faith they brought that event into the present.* They relived it and participated in it, just as if they had been present at the original event. In this way they shared in its original blessing.

It was this special kind of "remembering" that Jesus had in mind when he told his Apostles, "Do this in memory of me."

When we celebrate the Eucharist in memory of Jesus, we bring the "paschal mystery" (Jesus' passion, death, and resurrection) into the present in a sacramental way. Jesus becomes really present, and we relive and participate with him in this great mystery.

Sacrificial Meal

The word *sacrifice* is not well understood today. To get an idea of its meaning, consider a story that Mother Teresa told when she received the Nobel Peace Prize in Oslo, Norway. She said:

> *The other day I received $15 from a man*
> *who has been on his back for twenty years.*
> *The only part of his body that he can move*
> *is his right hand.*
> *And the only companion that he enjoys*
> *is smoking. And he said to me:*
> *"I do not smoke for one week,*
> *and I send you this money."*

> *It must have been a terrible sacrifice*
> *for him. . . .*
> *And with that money I bought bread*
> *and gave it to those who are hungry. . . .*
> *He was giving and the poor were receiving.*

Keeping this story in mind, recall Jesus' words over the bread at the Last Supper: "This is my body, which is *given for you.*" Recall also Jesus' words over the cup: "This cup is God's new covenant sealed with my blood, which is *poured out for you.*"

Both of these expressions speak of *sacrifice.* They speak of "giving up" something for another. The whole context of the Last Supper was sacrifice. It was directly linked to Jesus' death on the cross, which took place the following day. When we celebrate the Eucharist, Jesus is really present with us. With him we relive and participate in his sacrifice. Paul makes this clear when he says:

> *The cup we use in the Lord's Supper . . .*
> *when we drink from it,*
> *we are sharing in the blood of Christ.*
> *And the bread we break:*
> *when we eat it,*
> *we are sharing in the body of Christ.*
> 1 CORINTHIANS 10:16

The holy sacrifice of the Mass, the Eucharistic Meal, is the very same one that Jesus began at the Last Supper. In some mysterious way, we bring it into the present. And we participate in it with Jesus just as truly as if we had been there ourselves.

Covenant Meal

Like the word *sacrifice,* the word *covenant* is not well understood today. When Jesus said, "This cup is God's new *covenant* sealed with my blood," he did so in the rich Judaic tradition of the covenant, which both symbolized and expressed Israel's unique relationship with God.

Jesus was aware of the new covenant that God had promised through the prophet Jeremiah:

> *"I will make a new covenant*
> *with the people of Israel*
> *and with the people of Judah. . . .*
> *I will be their God,*
> *and they will be my people. . . .*
> *I will forgive their sins*
> *and I will no longer remember their wrongs."*
> JEREMIAH 31:31–34

It is this new covenant that Jesus inaugurated at the Last Supper. It is this new covenant that we celebrate in each Eucharist.

When Jesus said "sealed with my blood," his words recalled God's first covenant with the Israelites at Mount Sinai. It was sealed with the blood of animals. The Book of Exodus says:

> *Moses took the book of the covenant . . .*
> *and read it aloud to the people. . . .*
> *Then Moses took the blood in the bowls*
> *and threw it on the people. He said,*
> *"This is the blood that seals the covenant*
> *which the LORD made with you."*
> EXODUS 24:7–8

The new covenant that Jesus inaugurated at the Last Supper was "sealed" not with the blood of animals, but with the blood of Jesus himself.

And so we may describe the Eucharist as *a holy meal that recalls the Last Supper, celebrates and deepens our unity with Christ, and anticipates the eternal banquet of God's Kingdom in heaven.*

We now turn to the Liturgy of the Eucharist as it is celebrated in each Mass.

We Do What Jesus Did

At the Last Supper, Jesus "took a piece of bread, gave thanks to God, broke it, and gave it to [his Apostles], saying, 'This is my body. . . .' In the same way, he gave them the cup after the supper" (Luke 22:19–20). This is exactly what we do during the Liturgy of the Eucharist.

The priest, acting as the representative of the community, *takes* the bread and wine and prepares them. We call this the Preparation Rite.

Next, the priest *blesses* the bread and wine. We call this the Eucharistic Prayer Rite.

Finally, the priest *gives* the bread and wine (now the Body and Blood of Christ) to the community. We call this the Communion Rite.

What Jesus did at the Last Supper corresponds this way to the three main parts of the Liturgy of the Eucharist:

Eucharistic Liturgy	*Last Supper*
Preparation Rite	Jesus took
Eucharistic Prayer Rite	Jesus blessed
Communion Rite	Jesus broke/gave

Preparation Rite

The Liturgy of the Eucharist begins the way the Liturgy of the Word begins: with a procession. Representatives of the community carry bread and wine to the altar. These are given to the celebrant, who prepares them for the Eucharistic Meal. He takes the bread in his hands and prays:

Blessed are you, Lord, God of all creation.
Through your goodness
  we have this bread to offer,
which earth has given
  and human hands have made.
It will become for us the bread of life.

In a similar way, the celebrant prepares the cup of wine. Then he invites us to pray that our gifts of bread and wine (symbols of ourselves and our lives) may be acceptable to God. We pray:

May the Lord
  accept the sacrifice at your hands
for the praise and glory of his name,
for our good,
  and the good of all his Church.

The celebrant then leads the assembly in the Prayer over the Gifts, praying in words like these:

Lord our God,
may the bread and wine
you give us for our nourishment on earth
become the sacrament of our eternal life.

We ask this through Christ our Lord.
FIFTH SUNDAY OF THE YEAR

This brings us to the heart of the Liturgy of the Eucharist.

Eucharistic Prayer Rite

The Eucharistic Prayer Rite begins with the celebrant inviting us to lift up our hearts and to give thanks to God.

The high point of the prayer occurs when the celebrant takes the bread in his hands and says:

Before [Jesus] was given up to death,
a death he freely accepted,
he took bread and gave you thanks.
He broke the bread,
gave it to his disciples, and said:

"Take this, all of you, and eat it:
this is my body
  which will be given up for you."

Then the celebrant takes the cup of wine in his hands and says:

When supper was ended, he took the cup.
Again he gave you thanks and praise,
gave the cup to his disciples, and said:

"Take this, all of you, and drink from it:
this is the cup of my blood,
the blood of the new and everlasting covenant.
It will be shed for you and for all men
so that sins may be forgiven.
Do this in memory of me."

In this prayer, the entire congregation joins Jesus in acknowledging the works of the Father and in offering sacrifice.

The celebrant continues the Eucharistic Prayer by recalling Jesus' death and resurrection. Then he concludes by holding up the Body and Blood of Jesus, saying:

Through him, with him, in him,
in the unity of the Holy Spirit,
all glory and honor is yours,
almighty Father, for ever and ever.

The community then responds with a resounding "Amen."

Communion Rite

Holy Communion follows. The priest introduces it by inviting the community to join in praying the Lord's Prayer. This prayer is an especially appropriate way to prepare the congregation for Holy Communion, for the words "give us this day our daily *bread*" recall these unforgettable words of Jesus:

> *"I am the living bread*
> *that came down from heaven.*
> *If anyone eats this bread,*
> *he will live forever.*
> *The bread that I will give him is my flesh,*
> *which I give*
> *so that the world may live. . . .*
> *Whoever eats my flesh and drinks my blood*
> *has eternal life,*
> *and I will raise him to life on the last day."*
> JOHN 6:51, 54

What happens when we eat the consecrated bread and drink the consecrated wine is the direct opposite of what happens when we eat and drink at ordinary meals. At ordinary meals, what we eat becomes a part of us. In Holy Communion, we become a part of what we eat, the Body of Christ.

The celebrant brings the Communion Rite to a close, praying in words like these:

> *Lord,*
> *you have nourished us with bread from heaven.*
> *Fill us with your Spirit,*
> *and make us one in peace and love.*
>
> *We ask this through Christ our Lord.*
> SECOND SUNDAY OF THE YEAR

Dismissal

The Mass concludes with the dismissal of the congregation. The priest or deacon exhorts us to live what we have celebrated, saying to all, "Go in peace to love and serve the Lord." Concerning this solemn moment, Ernest Southcott says:

> *The holiest moment of the church service*
> *is the moment when God's people—*
> *strengthened by preaching and sacrament—*
> *go out of the church door into the world*
> *to be Church.*

The celebrant and the ministers leave the assembly in procession, to the accompaniment of singing.

Recap

The Mass (Eucharist) is made up of two major parts: the *Liturgy of the Word* and the *Liturgy of the Eucharist.*

The Liturgy of the Word may be viewed as being made up of three parts: Gathering Rite, Penitential Rite, Reading Rite. The highpoint of the liturgy is the reading of the *Gospel.*

The Liturgy of the Eucharist may also be viewed as being made up of three parts: Preparation Rite, Eucharistic Prayer Rite, Communion Rite. The highpoint occurs when the priest prays in Jesus' name the words Jesus spoke at the Last Supper:

> *Take this, all of you, and eat it:*
> *this is my body. . . .*
> *Take this, all of you, and drink from it:*
> *this is the cup of my blood.*

Liturgy and Liturgical Year

The *liturgy* is Jesus acting in modern times through his mystical body, as he acted in Gospel times through his flesh-and-blood body. The liturgy is celebrating Mass. It is celebrating Baptism. It is celebrating Reconciliation. In the words of the Second Vatican Council, the liturgy is Jesus continuing his "work of redemption" on earth. A scene from John Steinbeck's *The Winter of Our Discontent* illustrates the important point that the Council makes. Steinbeck writes:

> *Aunt Deborah read the Scripture to me*
> *like a daily newspaper and I suppose*
> *that's the way she thought of it,*
> *as something going on, happening eternally*
> *but always exciting and new.*
> *Every Easter,*
> *Jesus really rose from the dead,*
> *an explosion, expected but nonetheless new:*
> *it wasn't two thousand years ago to her;*
> *it was now.*

That is what the liturgy is. It is not something that happened two thousand years ago. It is something "expected but nonetheless new." It happens now.

This brings us to the *liturgical year*. Jesus' "work of redemption" is so vast that our finite minds cannot grasp it all at once. We must break it down. This is what the liturgical year does. It breaks down the events of Jesus' life into bite-size units so that we can

relive them and be nourished by them. It does infinitely more. It really makes them present so that we can participate in them. Thus Pope Pius XII writes in *Mediator Dei:*

> *The liturgical year . . .*
> *is not a cold and lifeless representation*
> *of the events of the past. . . .*
> *It is rather Christ himself*
> *who is ever living in his Church.*
> *Here he continues the journey . . .*
> *which he lovingly began in his mortal life.*

The liturgical year revolves around two main feasts: Christmas and Easter. Each feast gives rise to its own season: the Christmas season and the Easter season. We may think of these seasons as being made up of three parts:

- the main feast,
- the period of preparation, and
- the period of prolongation.

The feast of Christmas celebrates God's entry into human history in the person of Jesus. It is God living among us, as one of us.

The period of preparation is called *Advent* ("coming"). The coming of Jesus that we prepare for is not just the liturgical celebration of Jesus' first coming, but also the anticipation of Jesus' Second Coming at the end of time.

The period of prolongation is called *Ordinary Time*. Ordinary Time takes two forms: the time that prolongs Christmas and the time that prolongs Easter.

The Ordinary Time that prolongs Christmas leads to the second and the *most important* season of the liturgical year: Easter.

The feast of Easter celebrates the "paschal mystery," Jesus' death and resurrection. It is the event that reversed the course of history.

The period of preparation for Easter is called Lent. It begins with Ash Wednesday and lasts forty days. Catholics mark their foreheads with ashes on this day for two reasons. First, the ashes remind us that, like Jesus, who died on Good Friday, we too shall die. Second, they remind us that if we are to rise to new life, as Jesus did on Easter, we must repent our sins and undergo a conversion of heart.

The Ordinary Time that prolongs Easter recalls the life and ministry of Jesus and inspires us to model our own lives after his.

The liturgical year ends with the celebration of the feast of Christ the King. This feast acts as a crowning reminder of our mission as Catholics. It is to complete the work of the Kingdom of God (the *re-creation* of all things), which Jesus began.

Understanding Eucharist

Review

Eucharistic Worship

1. List the following: (a) the two worship places in Israel in Jesus' time, (b) the kind of service held in each place, (c) how these services are reflected in the Mass.

Liturgy of the Word

2. List and briefly explain the three rites of the Liturgy of the Word.

3. List and explain (a) the normal sources for each of the three Sunday readings, (b) the purpose of the *responsorial* psalm, (c) three things we do to highlight the reading of the Gospel.

4. Explain the following: (a) two reasons why homilies are hard to preach, (b) in whose name the homilist speaks, (c) why we should listen to the homilist with openness, (d) the Creed, (e) the General Intercessions.

Liturgy of the Eucharist

5. Explain how the Eucharist is (a) a memorial meal, (b) a sacrificial meal, (c) a covenant meal.

6. List and briefly explain the three rites of the Liturgy of the Eucharist.

7. With what similar activity do the Liturgy of the Word and the Liturgy of the Eucharist begin, and what is the focal point of each activity?

8. List and explain (a) the three main parts of the Liturgy of the Eucharist, (b) the highpoint of the Eucharistic Prayer, (c) why the Lord's Prayer is a fitting introduction to the Communion Rite, (d) how eating the consecrated bread and drinking the consecrated wine differ from eating and drinking ordinary meals.

Listening to God's Word

9. List and briefly explain the four ways we should listen to God's word.

Liturgy and Liturgical Year

10. How does *Mediator Dei* describe the liturgical year?

11. List and briefly describe the two main feasts around which the liturgical year revolves.

Astronaut Neil Armstrong.

Exercises

1. Neil Armstrong and Ed Aldrin landed on the moon July 20, 1969. While Armstrong prepared for his moon walk, Aldrin unpacked bread and wine and put them on the abort guidance system computer. Then he poured wine into a small chalice, noting that "in the one-sixth gravity of the moon the wine curled slowly and gracefully up the side of the cup." To prepare for Communion, Aldrin read John 15:5: "I am the vine, and you are the branches. . . . You can do nothing without me." After his Communion, Aldrin paused in silent prayer. Commenting on this experience, Aldrin said, "I sensed especially strong my unity with our church back home, and the Church everywhere."

Do you think it was appropriate for Aldrin to perform such a personal religious act on the moon? Explain.

2. Regina Riley prayed for years that her two sons would return to the practice of their faith. One Sunday she looked up and saw them across the aisle. After Mass, she asked them what brought them back. They said that while vacationing in Colorado, they had picked up an old man one Sunday morning. It was pouring rain, and he was getting soaked as he trudged along. He told them that he was on his way to Mass three miles up the mountain road. When they got to church, they decided to take part in Mass with the man and take him home afterward. "You know," the younger brother told his mother, "it felt so right—like returning home after a long trip."

What are some reasons why young people stop practicing their faith for a while? What are some of the reasons why they begin again?

3. A pastor began his homily by holding up a huge triangle. "My homily this morning," he said, "is like this triangle. It has three points. The first point is that we don't love others as Jesus commanded us. As a result, millions of people are starving and homeless. The second point is that most people don't give a damn about this. The third point is that some of you are more disturbed that I just said *damn* than you are about the millions who are starving and homeless." Then the pastor sat down to let the people think about what he had just said.

How would you evaluate the pastor's homily, and why? Describe the most creative homily you ever heard. If you could preach one homily over national television, what topic would you choose, and why?

4. A national survey shows that Catholics give far less to the Church than do Protestants. Moreover, the Catholics surveyed earned more than the Protestants surveyed. One disturbing statistic was that young Catholics give less than half of what young Protestants give.

How would you account for this difference in generosity in supporting Christ's work? On an unsigned slip of paper, list what you usually give. Collect the slips and tally the results on the chalkboard.

Personal Reflection

The Sunday after his child was born, Steve Garwood brought the Body of Christ home to his wife. She was still recuperating. When he opened the door, he saw that some friends had dropped in to see the baby. So he placed the pyx (container housing Christ's Body) on a shelf in the living room. Visitors streamed in all day. By the time the last one left, he had not had time to be alone with his wife, who had just fallen asleep. As he passed through the darkened living room on his way to bed, he knelt before the Body of Christ on the shelf. As he did, he was overwhelmed by a sense of Christ's presence. He wrote later: "Blood pounded in my ears and all the hairs of my body stood on end. 'Lord Jesus Christ,' I said, 'have mercy on me, an ungrateful sinner. You are here before me, in my house, and you have blessed me so much.' "

Compose a prayer that you could put in your wallet and pray in preparation for Communion. Compose a second prayer that you could pray after Communion.

Bible Reading

Pick a passage. After reading it prayerfully, write out a brief prayer to God that reflects your personal feelings and thoughts about it.

1. Synagogue worship — Acts 10:34–43
2. Temple worship — Leviticus 16:1–28
3. Liturgy of the Word — Luke 4:14–21
4. Liturgy of the Eucharist — Luke 22:14–20
5. Eucharist and Paul — 1 Corinthians 11:17–29

13 Reconciliation

milie Griffin was a New York advertising executive when she decided to become a Catholic. One thing that bothered her, however, was the sacrament of Reconciliation. She writes in her book *Turning:*

The notion of confessing my sins
was hateful to me.
It was not a question of unwillingness
to confess my sins
before another human being;
it was in fact
an unwillingness to confess my sins at all.
I could not admit myself to be a sinner.

But the more Emilie thought about it, the more she began to admit to herself that she needed forgiveness and healing. And with that admission came a change of attitude toward the sacrament of Reconciliation.

When it finally came time for Emilie to celebrate the sacrament, it was not the ordeal she had expected. It was just the opposite. It was an experience of peace and joy.

What kind of feelings do you have toward the sacrament of Reconciliation? What is the reason for those feelings?

Sin

ome years ago the Detroit Zoo was forced to beef up its security force. The reason was not to protect people from animals. Rather, it was to protect animals from people.

Over a period of time a growing number of animals had been brutalized by zoo spectators. Consider just two examples. An Australian wallaby was stoned to death by rock-throwing youths. A pregnant reindeer had a miscarriage when rowdies "bombed" her with firecrackers, sending the frantic animal into convulsions.

When we finish reading reports like this, we feel like the person who said, "If I were God, my heart would break at all the cruelty and sin in the world."

But there is something even worse than all the cruelty and sin in the world. It is the denial of sin or cruelty. For example, some people deny that they are brutalizing animals; they are just "having fun." Others deny that they are taking human life; they are just "terminating a pregnancy." Others deny that they are being unfaithful to a spouse; they are just "fooling around."

Commenting on the refusal of people to admit that they sin, Louis Evely writes:

The worst evil lies not in committing evil
but in committing evil
while pretending it is good. . . .
It is better to sin with sincerity
than to lie to one's self
in order to stay virtuous.
IN HIS PRESENCE

Scripture is even more outspoken when it comes to people who deny they sin, saying:

If we say that we have no sin,
we deceive ourselves, and . . .
make a liar out of God.
1 JOHN 1:8, 10

We all have need of forgiveness and healing.

Need for Forgiveness

Each of us has been incorporated into Christ's Body, the Church, by the sacraments of initiation. Our incorporation into Christ transformed us into new beings. "When anyone is joined to Christ," says Saint Paul, "[that person] is a new being; the old is gone, the new has come" (2 Corinthians 5:17).

But even after our incorporation into Christ, we remain fragile human beings. As a result, we sometimes turn aside from our early love and even break off our relationship with God (Revelation 2:4). When this happens, we have need of forgiveness and healing.

This is why Jesus instituted the sacrament of Reconciliation: to extend forgiveness and healing to us for sins committed after Baptism. Novelist Somerset Maugham speaks for many when he writes:

> *I have committed follies.*
> *I have a sensitive conscience*
> *and I have done certain things in my life*
> *that I am unable to entirely forget:*
> *if I had been fortunate enough to be a Catholic,*
> *I could have delivered myself of them*
> *at confession*
> *and after performing the penance imposed,*
> *received absolution*
> *and put them out of my mind forever.*

And so we turn to Scripture to look at two important dimensions of Jesus' life and ministry:

- how he exercised a ministry of reconciliation, and
- how he entrusted this ministry to his Church.

Jesus' Ministry of Reconciliation

One day some religious leaders were listening to Jesus teach. Suddenly, some people came carrying a man who was paralyzed. When Jesus saw the man, he was moved with pity and said to him, "Your sins are forgiven" (Luke 5:20).

When the religious leaders heard this, they grew angry, thinking to themselves, "God is the only one who can forgive sins!" (Luke 5:21).

Jesus knew their thoughts
and said to them,
"Why do you think such things?
Is it easier to say,
'Your sins are forgiven you,'
or to say, 'Get up and walk'?
I will prove to you, then,
that the Son of Man has authority on earth
to forgive sins."
So he said to the paralyzed man,
"I tell you, get up,
pick up your bed, and go home!"

At once the man got up in front of them all,
took the bed he had been lying on,
and went home, praising God.
They were all completely amazed!
LUKE 5:22–26

That passage needs no explanation. It reveals Jesus exercising a ministry of reconciliation. It reveals Jesus reaching out to people and inviting them to open their minds and hearts to the forgiveness and healing that he came to bring.

Jesus reaches out and invites us to open ourselves to forgiveness and healing.

Jesus Shared His Ministry

But Jesus did more than forgive sins. He shared his ministry to forgive and reconcile with his Church.

One day Jesus asked his disciples, "Who do you say I am?" Simon Peter answered, "You are the Messiah, the Son of the living God" (Matthew 16:15–16). Jesus answered:

"And so I tell you, Peter:
you are a rock,
and on this rock foundation
I will build my church. . . .
I will give you the keys
of the Kingdom of heaven;
what you prohibit on earth
will be prohibited in heaven,
and what you permit on earth
will be permitted in heaven."
MATTHEW 16:18–19

Again, the point is clear. Jesus not only forgave sins but also shared this ministry with his Apostles. He gave Peter the "keys of the Kingdom of heaven."

Then came the moment when Jesus sent the Holy Spirit upon his Apostles to empower them to go forth into the world and to continue his ministry of reconciliation. He did this on Easter Sunday evening. The Apostles were gathered together. Then Jesus appeared to them and said:

"Peace be with you.
As the Father sent me, so I send you."
Then he breathed on them and said,
"Receive the Holy Spirit.
If you forgive people's sins,
they are forgiven;
if you do not forgive them,
they are not forgiven."
JOHN 20:21–22

And so Jesus' Easter gift to his Apostles is the power to continue his ministry of reconciliation.

At first, this sounds like a strange Easter gift. But a little thought shows that it is not. Rather it is the *perfect* Easter gift. This is why Jesus came into the world: to free people from the tyranny of sin and to reconcile everyone to God and one another. Jesus' Easter gift empowers his Apostles to communicate his saving power to all peoples of all times.

We Continue Jesus' Ministry

The Apostles carried out their ministry of reconciliation in the same way that Jesus did: by inviting people to open their hearts to repentance and faith. Thus we find Peter exhorting the crowd that had gathered on Pentecost:

> *"Each one of you*
> *must turn away from [your] sins*
> *and be baptized in the name of Jesus Christ,*
> *so that your sins will be forgiven;*
> *and you will receive God's gift,*
> *the Holy Spirit."*
> ACTS 2:38

And so the first way the Church continues Jesus' ministry of reconciliation is through the sacrament of Baptism.

A second way the Church continues its ministry of reconciliation is through the sacrament of Reconciliation. It is the *chief* way by which sins committed after Baptism are forgiven.

Perhaps the best way to understand the sacrament of Reconciliation is to view it against the background of the Parable of the Prodigal Son. Recall the parable.

A man had two sons. One day the younger son decided to leave home. So he demanded his inheritance. This was a cruel demand. In effect, it took away part of the security that his parents would need in old age. But the father gave it to his son anyway, and the boy left home.

In no time the boy spent all his money. Coming to his senses, he said to himself:

> *"All my father's hired workers*
> *have more than they can eat,*
> *and here I am about to starve!*
> *I will get up and go to my father and say,*
> *'Father,*
> *I have sinned against God*
> *and against you.*
> *I am no longer fit to be called your son;*
> *treat me as one of your hired workers.' "*
> *So he got up and started back to his father.*
>
> *He was still a long way from home*
> *when his father saw him;*
> *his heart was filled with pity,*
> *and he ran, threw his arms around his son,*
> *and kissed him.*
> *"Father," the son said,*
> *"I have sinned against God*
> *and against you.*
> *I am no longer fit to be called your son."*
>
> *But the father called to his servants.*
> *"Hurry!" he said.*
> *"Bring the best robe and put it on him.*
> *Put a ring on his finger*
> *and shoes on his feet.*
> *Then go and get the prize calf and kill it,*
> *and let us celebrate with a feast!*
> *For this son of mine was dead,*
> *but now he is alive; he was lost,*
> *but now he has been found."*
> *And so the feasting began.*
> LUKE 15:17–24

The Son Does Four Things

A closer look at the parable shows that when the son came to his senses, he did four things. He—

- *examined* his sinfulness ("I am about to starve!"),
- *repented* his sinfulness ("I will get up and go to my father"),
- *confessed* his sinfulness ("Father, I have sinned"),
- *made satisfaction* for his sinfulness ("Treat me as one of your hired workers").

The Father Does Four Things

The father's response to the boy is especially beautiful. "His heart was filled with pity, and he ran, threw his arms around his son, and kissed him." In other words, the father *welcomed* his son with all the warmth at his command.

Next, the father did something highly symbolic. He had shoes put on his son's feet. This symbolized that he was *forgiving* his son totally. In ancient times, slaves went barefoot; sons wore shoes. The shoes took away the sign that said the boy was somebody's slave and gave to him the sign that said he was somebody's son.

Then the father did something equally symbolic. He had a ring put on his son's finger. This symbolized that he was *restoring* the son to the *full* status he had before he left home. Undoubtedly, the ring was a signet ring, containing the family seal. To possess it was to possess the power to act in the family's name.

Finally, the father ordered a feast in his son's honor. This *celebration* recalls Jesus' words: "There will be more joy in heaven over one sinner who repents than over ninety-nine respectable people who do not need to repent" (Luke 15:7).

And so the parable shows the father doing four beautiful things for his son. He—

- *welcomed* him home (kissed him),
- *forgave* him (put shoes on his feet),
- *restored* him to full family status (put a ring on his finger),
- *celebrated* with him (shared a feast).

Forgiveness

An old ballad concerns Judas, the Apostle who betrayed Jesus. After Judas commits suicide, his soul searches for a place to put his body. But he is unsuccessful. Hell refuses his body, the sun won't shine on it, and the soil rejects it. So the soul keeps searching.

One night in the polar regions of the north, the soul happens upon a lighted hall. It lays the body down in the snow. Then, with weary feet, it runs up and down, moaning like a wolf, trying to see inside the hall. Finally, it finds a slit in the curtain and looks. It can't believe what it sees.

'Twas the Bridegroom sat at the table-head,
And the lights burned bright and clear—
"Oh, who is that?" the Bridegroom said,
"Whose weary feet I hear?"

'Twas one looked from the lighted hall,
And answered soft and slow,
"It is a wolf runs up and down
With black track in the snow."

The Bridegroom in his robe of white
Sat at the table-head—
"Oh, who is that who moans without?"
The blessed Bridegroom said.

'Twas one looked from the lighted hall,
And answered fierce and low,
" 'Tis the soul of Judas Iscariot
Gliding to and fro."

'Twas the soul of Judas Iscariot
Did hush itself and stand,
And saw the Bridegroom at the door
With light in his hand. . . .

'Twas the Bridegroom stood at the open door,
And beckoned, smiling sweet;
'Twas the soul of Judas Iscariot
Stole in, and fell at his feet.

"The Holy Supper is spread within,
And the many candles shine,
And I have waited long for thee
Before I poured the wine!"

Robert Buchanan (1841-1901)

We Confess Our Sins

Almost all people find the third step to be the hardest step of all.

Interestingly, Alcoholics Anonymous has a similar step in the AA program. Known as "Step Five," it reads: "We admitted to God, to ourselves, and to another human being the exact nature of our wrongs." The AA manual then says:

> *Scarcely any step is more necessary.*
> *So intense though*
> *is our fear and reluctance to do this*
> *that many AAs at first*
> *try to by-step Step Five. . . .*
>
> *Somehow, being alone with God*
> *doesn't seem as embarrassing*
> *as facing another person. . . .*
> *When we are honest*
> *with another person,*
> *it confirms that we have been honest*
> *with ourselves and with God.*

What Must We Confess?

When it comes to the sacrament of Reconciliation, we are obliged to confess all *mortal* sins. A mortal sin is one that breaks off our relationship with God and God's family—as the prodigal son broke off his relationship with his father and his family.

Moreover, all mortal sins must be confessed according to *kind* (what we did) and *number* (how often we did it). For example, we confess that we stole expensive items from a small retailer on two different occasions to support a drug habit.

Lesser *(venial)* sins need not be confessed. But it is highly advisable to so, at least in a general way. For example, we confess that we have a *regular* tendency to be impatient with others.

Our celebration of the sacrament of Reconciliation truly restores our friendship with God and with our brothers and sisters (whom we often harm by sins). And so we look to the future with new joy and hope as we—

- take to heart the priest's counsel,
- perform the penance assigned,
- make a reasonable effort to repair any damage caused by our sins, and
- make a reasonable effort to avoid situations that tempt us to sin.

Liturgy of Reconciliation

The Parable of the Prodigal Son is a perfect picture of what happens in the sacrament of Reconciliation. We do what the son did, and the priest does what the father did.

First, consider what the son did after "coming to his senses." He reviewed his sins, repented his sins, confessed them, and made satisfaction for them. That is exactly what we do in the sacrament. We—

- review our sins: *examination,*
- repent our sins: *contrition,*
- confess our sins: *confession,*
- make up for our sins: *satisfaction.*

Second, consider what the father of the prodigal son did: he welcomed his son home, forgave him, restored him to full family status, and celebrated with him. That is exactly what the priest does in the sacrament. He *absolves* us; that is, he—

- *welcomes* us home,
- *forgives* us,
- *restores* us,
- *celebrates* with us.

Let us now take a closer look at, perhaps, the most difficult thing that we do in the liturgy of the sacrament.

Two Kinds of Sin

No matter how hard we try, we often fail to live and love as Jesus did. We call this moral failure *sin*. Catholic tradition distinguishes two kinds of sin: *mortal* and *venial*.

Mortal sin involves a total rejection of Jesus and our commitment to live and love as he did. This means that not only do we choose to perform a certain act, but in the process we also choose to *become* the kind of person that the act makes us to be. Thus the act involves our *total being in a total way*.

Catholic tradition holds that for sin to be *mortal*, three conditions must be present:

- grave matter,
- sufficient reflection,
- full consent of the will.

By grave matter, we mean that what we do is *objectively grave*. For example, we kill someone or we commit adultery.

By sufficient reflection, we mean that we are fully aware of the grave evil we are about to do. In spite of this, we choose to go ahead and do it anyway.

By full consent of the will, we mean that we *freely* decide to act. We are not under any compulsion or pressure that destroys our free will.

Having listed these three conditions, however, we must add that they are only a guide. Like all guides, they need to be understood properly, or they could be misleading.

For example, under ordinary circumstances, stealing a loaf of bread and a jug of water would *not* be considered grave matter. If, however, we stole these items from someone who needed them to survive until a rescue party came, they would *become* grave matter. In other words, the *circumstances* surrounding an action can change its moral gravity.

Consider another example. Under ordinary circumstances, it would be a grave matter to take another's life. If, however, we took another's life in *justifiable self-defense,* it would not be gravely wrong. In fact, it would not be morally wrong at all. In other words, the *reasons* for performing an act can also affect its moral gravity.

This brings us to the second type of sin. Besides *mortal* sin, which is *total* rejection of God, there is what is called *venial* sin, which is *partial* rejection of God. It is an action that falls short of being a mortal sin.

For example, a person does something that does not involve grave matter (such as stealing a small article); or a person does something that involves grave matter, but does it without sufficient reflection or full consent (for example, commits adultery while deprived of full reason by alcohol).

Venial sin, itself, admits of varying degrees of seriousness. For example, telling a lie to embarrass someone does not involve grave matter, but it is still more reprehensible than simply speaking harshly to someone in a moment of frustration.

"I make all things new!" REVELATION 21:5

How Often Should We Celebrate?

People often ask, "How often should we celebrate the sacrament of Reconciliation?" There are two ways of answering this question.

First, we should celebrate it as often as the Spirit touches our heart to do so.

Second, we should celebrate it when "coming to our senses" after a serious break with God and God's family (mortal sin). In such a case, the celebration will climax a process of sorrow and repentance, as it did with the prodigal son.

Apart from these two special situations, the frequency in celebrating the sacrament will vary. During certain periods of our life we will experience the need or desire to seek reconciliation more often than in others. Again, we should strive to be sensitive to the movement of the Spirit in this regard.

In his encyclical on the Mystical Body, Pope Pius XII lists the benefits of celebrating the sacrament regularly (say every two months)—even when we have no mortal sins to confess. This practice—

■ sharpens spiritual sensitivity,
■ combats spiritual laziness,
■ heals spiritual weaknesses, and
■ deepens spiritual unity with God and with the Christian family.

Recap

Jesus forgave sin. He *shared* this power and ministry with his Church. The Church exercises this power and ministry, in a *special* way, in the sacrament of Reconciliation.

The best way to understand the sacrament of Reconciliation is to view it against the backdrop of the Parable of the Prodigal Son. What the *son* and the *father* did in the parable, the *sinner* and the *priest* do in the sacrament of Reconciliation.

Understanding Reconciliation

Review

Sin

1. What is even worse than all the sin and cruelty in the world?

2. What does Scripture say about people who deny that they sin?

Need for Forgiveness

3. Describe when, where, and how Jesus (a) claimed and proved that he had the power to forgive sin, (b) shared this power with his Apostles.

4. Why was the power to forgive sins a perfect Easter gift? How does the Church exercise its power to forgive sins?

5. List and explain (a) the four things the son did in the Parable of the Prodigal Son and (b) the four things the father did in the same parable.

Liturgy of Reconciliation

6. List and explain (a) the four things the sinner does in the sacrament of Reconciliation and (b) the four things the priest does in the same sacrament.

7. For most people, which of the four things they do in the sacrament of Reconciliation is the most difficult and why?

8. What sins are we obliged to confess, and what are we obliged to confess about them?

9. Explain the difference between a *mortal* sin and a *venial* sin.

10. After we have confessed our sins, what four things remain to be done?

11. What are two ways to answer the following question: How often should we celebrate the sacrament of Reconciliation?

12. List four spiritual benefits of celebrating the sacrament of Reconciliation regularly, say every two months.

Two Kinds of Sin

13. Explain the difference between a mortal sin and a venial sin.

14. List the three conditions that must be present for a mortal sin.

15. Explain how the circumstances surrounding an action and the reasons for performing an action can affect its moral gravity.

Exercises

1. Lee Iacocca has been called an "American legend." He won fame by rescuing the Chrysler Corporation from bankruptcy. In his autobiography, he says of the sacrament of Reconciliation:

> *In my teens I began to appreciate the importance of the most misunderstood rite in the Catholic Church. I not only had to think out my transgressions against my friends; I had to speak them aloud.... The necessity of weighing right from wrong on a regular basis turned out to be the best therapy I ever had.*
> IACOCCA: AN AUTOBIOGRAPHY

Why do you think Iacocca began to "appreciate the importance" of the sacrament in his teens? Why is it the "most misunderstood rite in the Catholic Church"? Explain Iacocca's final sentence.

2. On November 2, 1984, in Raleigh, North Carolina, Velma Barfield became the first woman in twenty-two years to be executed in the United States. She had been convicted of killing four people. But the Velma Barfield who was executed was totally different from the person who entered prison in 1978. During her six years of imprisonment, she had undergone a remarkable conversion. A high point in it came when she wrote on the flyleaf of her Bible:

> *Sin is being called all kinds of fancy names nowadays but it's time we came to grips with ourselves and call sin what it really is—SIN. It's the ancient enemy of the soul. It has never changed. Tonight I'm making a new commitment to my Lord. I'm going to start ... naming my sins before the Lord and trust him for deliverance.*
> WOMAN ON DEATH ROW

Why are people today reluctant to "call sin what it really is—SIN"? On an unsigned sheet of paper, answer these three questions: (a) When was the last time you named your sins "before the Lord" in the sacrament of Reconciliation? (b) What led you to do it then? (c) What keeps you from celebrating this sacrament more frequently?

3. Greek Orthodox Catholics celebrate the sacrament of Reconciliation standing and facing an icon (picture) of the Risen Christ.

Why do you think they stand, rather than kneel or sit? Why do you think they face an icon, rather than face each other?

4. Babe Ruth is one of the most famous names in sports. At one point in his life Ruth drifted from practicing his Catholic faith. But he did not abandon it completely. He wrote in *Guideposts* magazine:

I did have my own altar, a big window in my New York apartment overlooking the city lights. Often I would kneel before that window and say my prayers. I would feel quite humble then. I'd ask God to help me.

Then, one December night, near the end of his career, Ruth took seriously ill. With him at the hospital was Paul Carey, one of his closest friends. After a while, Carey said, "Babe, they're going to operate in the morning. Don't you think you should see a priest?" Ruth said, "Yes, Paul! I'd like to see a priest." That night Ruth celebrated the sacrament of Reconciliation. It was a moving experience. He wrote later: "As I lay in bed that evening, I thought to myself what a comfortable feeling to be free from fear and worries. I could simply turn them over to God."

Recall a moving celebration of Reconciliation that you experienced. What made it special? Did you ever help someone spiritually, as Paul Carey helped Babe Ruth? Explain.

Personal Reflection

Psychologists talk about the *persona.* It is that part of ourselves that we like. It is that part that we show to others. The underside of the persona is the *shadow.* It is that part of ourselves that we hide from others. It is a weakness of character that we try to sweep under the rug and forget about.

But the shadow never forgets about us. It goes right on living in our subconscious. Occasionally, it pops out without warning. For example, we might have a jealous side that we try to keep hidden. Then one day it pops out to embarrass us.

The first step in controlling our shadow is to admit it. An example of someone who did this is Charles Colson, a White House aide who went to prison in the Watergate scandal. His persona was his ability to get things done. His shadow was his pride of achievement. The thing that helped him face up to his shadow was this passage from C. S. Lewis's book *Mere Christianity:*

Pride leads to every other vice: it is the complete anti-God state of mind. . . . As long as you are proud you cannot know God. A proud man is

always looking down on things. . . . As long as you are looking down, you cannot see something that is above you.

After a short period of reflection, briefly describe two things on a sheet of paper: (1) your persona and (2) your shadow.

Bible Reading

Pick a passage. After reading it prayerfully, write out a brief prayer to God that reflects your personal thoughts or feelings about it.

1. Jesus came for sinners   Luke 5:27–32
2. Jesus visits sinner's home   Luke 19:1–10
3. Jesus defends sinful woman   Luke 7:36–50
4. Jesus forgives paralyzed man   Luke 5:17–26
5. Jesus teaches us to forgive   Matthew 18:21–35

14 Anointing of the Sick

Rain streaked down the window of Jane Lindstrom's hospital room. It deepened the feeling of isolation and depression that came over her after her surgery. Then a nurse came in with a letter and gave it to her. Jane opened it and read:

> Dear Jane,
>
> My class is about to begin,
> but I must write these few words
> before my students arrive.
> I missed your smile and your wave this morning,
> just as I have every morning
> since you've been ill.
> I pray you'll be well soon. . . .
> The world is a less happy place without you.

That brief note was better than any medicine for Jane. It melted her loneliness and depression and gave her a spiritual shot in the arm.

Jane's story dramatizes something we tend to forget. Prolonged serious sickness can weaken not only the body but also the spirit. It can create in us a feeling of isolation and deep loneliness. It can plunge us into a state of mental depression that can weaken our faith and affect our attitude toward God and others.

Why does sickness sometimes make us feel isolated and lonely?

Why does mental depression sometimes weaken our faith and affect our attitude toward God and others?

The Sick

Eighty-eight-year-old John lives alone. On Sunday mornings his rocking chair moves a little faster as he anticipates seeing a special person. That person is Marie, a college student, who is a eucharistic minister in her parish. A dimension of her ministry is to bring Communion to the sick.

When Marie arrives at John's apartment around eleven o'clock, she begins by reading the Sunday Gospel to John. Then she summarizes the homily that she has just listened to at the ten o'clock Mass. Finally, she and John join hands and pray together the Lord's Prayer in preparation for John's Communion.

After John receives Communion, Marie reads slowly from a prayer book. John especially likes this prayer:

> *Lord, Holy Father . . .*
> *free your servant from sickness,*
> *restore him to health,*
> *raise him up by your right hand,*
> *strengthen him by your power,*
> *protect him by your might,*
> *and give him all that is needed*
> *for his welfare,*
> *through Christ, our Lord.*

Following the prayers, John and Marie share with each other what they did during the week.

As Marie hugs John good-bye, she realizes something beautiful. She realizes that she has not only brought him Communion but has also given him the loving assurance that people care about him.

> *In receiving*
> *the body and blood of Christ,*
> *the sick are united sacramentally*
> *to the Lord and are reunited*
> *with the eucharistic community*
> *from which illness has separated them.*
> INTRODUCTION TO PASTORAL CARE OF THE SICK, 51

The true story of John and Marie dramatizes that the Church, following Jesus' example, has a special love for the elderly and the sick.

Jesus Ministered with the Sick

The Gospel is filled with stories of Jesus' ministry with the sick. Consider the following:

> *Simon's mother-in-law*
> *was sick in bed with a fever,*
> *and as soon as Jesus arrived,*
> *he was told about her.*
> *He went to her, took her by the hand,*
> *and helped her up.*
> *The fever left her. . . .*
>
> *After the sun had set and evening had come,*
> *people brought to Jesus all the sick*
> *and those who had demons.*
> *All the people of the town*
> *gathered in front of the house.*
> *Jesus healed many who were sick . . .*
> *and drove out many demons.*
> MARK 1:30–34

Also, consider this moving example of Jesus' special compassion for certain sick people who were often shunned and treated as outcasts by the rest of society.

> *A man suffering from a dreaded skin disease*
> *came to Jesus, knelt down,*
> *and begged him for help.*
> *"If you want to," he said,*
> *"you can make me clean."*
> *Jesus was filled with pity,*
> *and reached out and touched him.*
> *"I do want to," he answered. "Be clean!"*
> MARK 1:40–41

Jesus Shared His Healing Ministry

Jesus did more than heal the sick himself. He also shared this healing ministry with his disciples.

> *Jesus called the twelve disciples together*
> *and gave them power and authority*
> *to drive out all demons and to cure diseases.*
> *Then he sent them out*
> *to preach the Kingdom of God*
> *and to heal the sick. . . .*
> *The disciples left*
> *and traveled through all the villages,*
> *preaching the Good News*
> *and healing people everywhere.*
> LUKE 9:1–2, 6

From that moment on, ministry with the sick became an important dimension of the Church's life. A letter to early Church members instructs them as follows:

> *Is there anyone who is sick?*
> *He should send for the church elders,*
> *who will pray for him and rub olive oil on him*
> *in the name of the Lord.*
> *This prayer made in faith*
> *will heal the sick person;*
> *the Lord will restore him to health,*
> *and the sins he has committed will be forgiven.*
> JAMES 5:14–15

This passage introduces us to the sacrament of the Anointing of the Sick. Through this sacrament the Church continues Jesus' healing ministry in a special way.

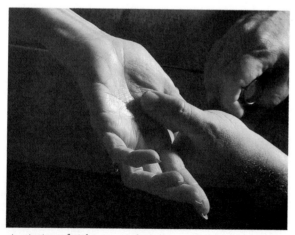

Anointing of sick person's hands.

Sacrament of Anointing

A Vietnam veteran was recuperating in Walter Reed Hospital in Washington, D.C. In a letter to a friend, he described a remarkable experience that took place shortly after he had been hit by mortar fire on the battlefield. He writes:

> *From the split second I was hit,*
> *I was completely alone.*
> *I've heard it said, but never realized it—*
> *when you're dying there's no one but you.*
> *You're all alone.*
>
> *I was hurt bad, real bad;*
> *a 4.2 mortar shell*
> *landed about six feet behind me*
> *and took off my left leg,*
> *badly ripped up my left arm,*
> *hit me in the back,*
> *head, hip, and right heel and ankle.*
> *Shock was instantaneous, but I fought it—*
> *knowing that if I went out*
> *I'd never wake up again.*
>
> *There were three or four medics*
> *hovering over me,*
> *all shook up, trying to help me. . . .*
> *I tried to pray but couldn't.*
> *I asked the guys to talk to me*
> *to keep me conscious, and most of all,*
> *if anyone could help me pray.*
> *I felt like there was no one but me;*
> *those around me*
> *I could only hear talking over me.*
>
> *Well, with a hell of a lot of stubbornness*
> *and luck (providence),*
> *I lived to make it to the chopper*
> *two hours after being hit.*
>
> *After they carried me*
> *into the first-aid station,*
> *I felt four or five people*
> *scrubbing my body in different places.*
> *This brought me to open my eyes,*
> *and I could see about a foot in front of me—*
> *and not too well at that.*
>
> *Anyway, someone bent over me*
> *and began to pray.*
> *I wasn't sure who it was,*
> *but I thought*
> *it looked like our battalion chaplain;*

his nose was practically on mine.
After I saw him place his hands on my head,
I started to go out—
I figured for the last time.
When I talked I could only whisper,
and this took all I had.

As I was going out,
my eyes closed and I heard Father say,
"Are you sorry for your sins?"
With my last breath and all I had,
I whispered, "Hell, yes!"

Then a split second before I went out,
I felt oil on my forehead.
And something happened
which I'll never forget—
something which I never experienced before
in my life!
All of a sudden, I stopped gasping
for every inch of life;
I just burst with joy. . . .
I felt like I had just got
a million cc's of morphine.
I was on Cloud Nine.
I felt free of body and mind.

After this,
I was conscious about three or four times
during the next ten-day period;
I never worried about dying.
In fact, I was waiting for it.

That soldier's letter is a beautiful description of his experience of celebrating the sacrament of the Anointing of the Sick. By this sacrament the same compassionate Jesus who healed people in Gospel times continues to heal people today. The only difference is the way he does this.

In Gospel times Jesus healed people through the *physical* actions of his *historical* body. He touched them and prayed over them, using his own flesh-and-blood body. Today, Jesus heals people through the *sacramental,* or *liturgical,* actions of his *mystical* body, the Church.

A closer look at the Vietnam soldier's description of his experience of the sacrament of the Anointing of the Sick reveals three points. He describes the chaplain as—

■ praying over him,
■ laying hands on him, and
■ anointing his forehead with oil.

These three actions introduce us to the liturgy of the sacrament of the Anointing of the Sick.

Liturgy of Anointing

The sacrament of the Anointing of the Sick may be celebrated anywhere: at home, in a hospital, on a battlefield. An ideal time and place is during the celebration of the Mass for the Anointing of the Sick.

The reason this is the ideal time and place is that the celebration of this sacrament is not a *private* action involving only the priest and the sick person. It is a *communal* action involving the whole Body of Christ. As Saint Paul says:

> *There is no division in the body. . . .*
> *If one part of the body suffers,*
> *all the other parts suffer with it.*
> 1 CORINTHIANS 12:25–26

In other words, the body of the Church is like a human body. If one member is sick, the entire body is affected in a spiritual way. And so it is fitting that others (especially family and friends of the sick person) are present during the celebration of the sacrament.

In most cases, however, the condition of the sick person is such that he or she is unable to be anointed during Mass. When this is the case, the sacrament, normally, is celebrated in the following manner.

First, the priest greets all, sprinkles them with holy water, speaks briefly about the mystery of the sacrament, and invites all to join in a short penitential rite.

Next, a passage from Scripture is read and the priest applies it to the lives of those present.

The actual Liturgy of Anointing begins with a series of prayers. After the prayers are completed, the priest lays his hands on the head of the sick person in silence. (He may invite those present to lay hands on the sick person as well.) This beautiful gesture is one that Jesus used in healing the sick (Mark 6:5).

Finally, the priest takes oil, gives thanks, blesses the oil, and anoints the person's forehead, praying:

> *Through this holy anointing*
> *may the Lord in his love and mercy help you*
> *with the grace of the Holy Spirit.*

The priest then anoints the hands of the sick person, praying:

> *May the Lord who frees you from sin*
> *save you and raise you up.*
> INTRODUCTION TO PASTORAL CARE OF THE SICK, 124

At the end of each prayer, the sick person responds, "Amen."

If the sick person is not to receive Holy Communion, the rite ends with all present praying the Our Father and the celebrant offering a final prayer.

If the sick person is to receive Holy Communion, this takes place immediately after praying the Lord's Prayer.

If the sick person wishes to celebrate the sacrament of Reconciliation, this takes place before celebrating the sacrament of the Anointing of the Sick.

Sacrament Recipients

Father Joe was called to a Los Angeles hospital to anoint an elderly woman, named Gladys. She was in a coma and was not expected to live. When Father Joe arrived, Gladys's family, the resident doctor, and the nurse who had so devotedly cared for her were in the room. Father Joe asked them to gather around the bed and after reading from the Scriptures, he invited them to place their hands on Gladys before he annointed her. Gladys went on to recover.

This true story of Gladys raises a question about the sacrament of Anointing: Who may receive the sacrament?

It surprises some Catholics that the sacrament of the Anointing of the Sick was celebrated with Gladys while she was in a coma. They are not aware that the Church celebrates this sacrament with us whether we are fully awake and conscious, in a coma, in a confused state, or under sedation. The assumption is that we would want to receive this sacrament now, if we were able to make the choice.

It also surprises some Catholics that Anointing may even be celebrated with a baptized person who is not a Catholic, if that Christian asks for it and believes that Christ acts through it.

In general, the sacrament of the Anointing of the Sick may and should be celebrated with people who—

- are seriously ill,
- are seriously weakened by advanced age,
- are scheduled for serious or life-threatening surgery,
- "take a turn for the worse" or develop a new sickness (for example, pneumonia), even though they have received the sacrament a few days before.

Serious illness does not mean terminal illness. Nor does it mean an illness that puts a person in immediate danger of death. Serious illness means any illness that seriously impairs the health of a person.

People suffering from serious illness often suffer from anxiety. They may even be tempted to lose their trust in God. To such people as this, especially, the sacrament of the Anointing of the Sick is the occasion of special grace from the Holy Spirit.

*By this grace
the whole person is helped and saved,
sustained by trust in God,
and strengthened against . . . temptations . . .
and against anxiety. . . .
Thus the sick person is able
not only to bear suffering bravely,
but also to fight against it.
A return to physical health
may follow the reception of this sacrament. . . .
If necessary,
the sacrament also provides the sick person
with the forgiveness of sins. . . .*
INTRODUCTION TO PASTORAL CARE OF THE SICK, 6

A fitting conclusion to our discussion of the sacrament of Anointing of the Sick is this Opening Prayer from the Mass for the Anointing of the Sick:

*Father
you raised your Son's cross
as the sign of victory and life.*

*May all who share in his suffering
find in these sacraments
a source of fresh courage and healing.*

*We ask this through our Lord Jesus Christ,
your Son,
who lives and reigns with you
and the Holy Spirit,
one God, for ever and ever.*
(paragraph 136)

Recap

The Church has a special ministry with the sick and the elderly. By healing the sick and the elderly, Jesus gave us an example of the kind of love and attention with which we are to care for them. The Church continues Jesus' healing ministry with the sick, especially through the sacrament of the Anointing of the Sick.

The mystery of the sacrament of Anointing is best celebrated at Mass with family, friends, and other community members present. But it may be celebrated at any time and in any place, depending on the needs of the sick person.

Understanding Anointing of the Sick

Review

The Sick

1. Explain why the very sick and the very aged often need the special love and concern of the Church community.

2. Briefly describe one Gospel episode where Jesus (a) displayed special concern for the sick, (b) shared his healing power with his disciples.

3. Give an example from Scripture that witnesses to the fact that the early Church continued the healing ministry of Jesus.

Sacrament of Anointing

4. Explain the precise difference between how Jesus healed people in Gospel times and how he continues to heal them today.

5. List the three things the chaplain did in the course of celebrating the sacrament of the Anointing of the Sick with the young Vietnam soldier after he was wounded.

Liturgy of Anointing

6. Explain (a) why an ideal setting for celebrating the sacrament of Anointing is within Mass, and (b) how Saint Paul explains that this is the preferred setting.

7. Explain the rites that the celebration of the sacrament of Anointing outside Mass normally follows.

8. When the sick person wants to celebrate the sacrament of Reconciliation and receive Holy Communion along with the sacrament of Anointing, in what order should these three sacraments be celebrated?

Sacrament Recipients

9. In general, what four groups of people may and should request the sacrament of Anointing?

10. Under what conditions may the following receive the sacrament of Anointing: (a) non-Catholics, (b) adults in a coma or in a confused or sedated state?

Exercises

1. Old age can make people feel useless and even a burden to others. This is tragic, because the elderly can give to others (especially the young) something no one else can give them in quite the same way. To illustrate, consider this excerpt from an essay by a third-grader:

> *Grandmothers don't have to be smart, only answer questions like, "Why isn't God married?" and "How come dogs chase cats?" A grandmother is a lady with no children of her own. . . . She likes other people's little girls and boys. Everyone should have a grandmother, especially if they don't have TV.*
> (quoted by Dr. James Dobson)

Describe an experience you had with a grandparent (or other older person) that gave you an appreciation of the important role older people can play in the lives of younger people. Explain how younger people can also play an important role in the lives of older people.

2. Brother Michael Newman has nursed the sick not only bodily but also spiritually. One day he prayed over a patient named Alice, who was in a coma. Three days later, she came out of the coma, saying that she recalled Brother Mike's prayer and how much it meant to her. On another occasion, Brother Mike was praying over a woman close to death. He told her that she was at heaven's door and should knock. She made a knocking motion and died.

Brother Mike gives these guidelines for dealing with people near death, even when they appear completely unconscious:

- Talk to the people, since there is a good chance they can still hear you.
- Address them by name and in an adult way.
- Pray over them out loud and slowly, using familiar prayers like the Lord's Prayer.
- Suggest that they pray with you in their minds.

Did you ever see a person die? What are some of the feelings you experienced on this occasion? Describe a time when you prayed for (or with) a sick person. What impact did the prayer have on you?

3. *The American Journal of Nursing* describes a fascinating experiment that was done at New York University. It dealt with nurses "laying hands on patients with the intention of healing them." The patients involved in the experiment improved dramatically over a similar group not treated in this way.

Commenting on the experiment, Francis MacNutt says in his book *Power to Heal:*

> *These studies provide evidence to show that, simply in the* natural *order, the patients' power to recover improves when the nurses lay on hands. . . . The way they understand it is that there is a* natural *power of life in loving people which is communicated in a special way through the power of touch.*

In other words, loving people radiate healing, just as the sun radiates warmth.

If God can use "loving hands" to heal people, why do we need the sacrament of the Anointing of the Sick? Can you think of an everyday example in which placing loving hands on someone can help the person immensely? Describe a time when someone's love and concern produced an emotional or spiritual healing in you.

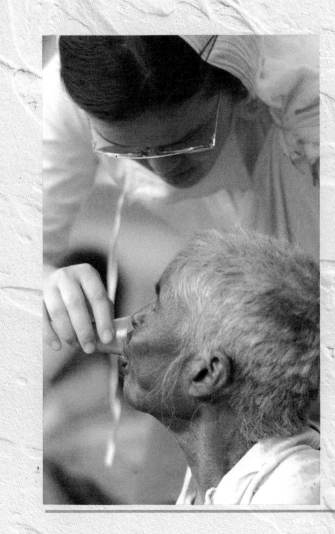

4. In the movie *Little Big Man,* the Indian Old Lodgeskin made a final prayer to God before dying, saying:

> *I thank you for making me a human being.*
> *I thank you for my defeats.*
> *I thank you for my sight.*
> *And I thank you for my blindness*
> *which has helped me see even further.*

Explain the meaning of Old Lodgeskin's final sentence. Give an example (preferably from your own life) to illustrate it. Imagine you are alone and have only a few minutes to live. Compose a prayer you would like to make to God at that time.

Personal Reflection

To prepare yourself for this personal reflection, do the following:

Relax completely. Set up a pattern of slow, rhythmic breathing. As you inhale, imagine God's powerful love flowing into your body through the pores of your skin. As this love flows into your body, imagine that it remains trapped inside you.

Now imagine your body becoming a great lamp, radiating love to the world about you. Rest there quietly, allowing God's love to build up inside you and radiate from you to all the world. Recall Jesus' words: "I love you just as the Father loves me. . . . Love one another, just as I love you" (John 15:9, 12). Let this teaching of Jesus penetrate you.

When you feel ready, mentally visit any person you know who has special need of God's love. Place both hands on that person's head. As you exhale, imagine God's love flowing out from your body, through your hands, into the other person. Stay with the person as long as you feel you are needed.

Whom did you pray for? Why this person? Did you have the feeling that your prayer was really helping the person? Explain.

Bible Reading

Pick a passage. After reading it prayerfully, write out a brief prayer to God that reflects your personal thoughts or feelings about it.

1. Jesus heals the sick	Luke 7:1–10
2. Jesus shares his healing power	Luke 10:1–9
3. Jesus' disciples heal the sick	Luke 10:17–24
4. The early Church heals the sick	Acts 5:12–16
5. Ask for the Church's healing	James 5:13–20

15 Marriage

Psychologist Eugene Kennedy recommends this "test of friendship." He says that if we don't really enjoy being with someone unless we are doing something—like bowling or going to a movie—then that person may not be as good a friend as we think.

The true test of a friendship, says Kennedy, is that we can do nothing together and still be happy. In other words, we enjoy each other so much that we don't need the glue of activity to hold us together.

On a scale of one (not at all) to ten (totally), how much do you agree with Kennedy's friendship test? Explain. To what extent might the test have special relevance for two people thinking of marriage?

Love

In the movie *Shadow of the Hawk,* a young couple and a native American guide are making their way up a mountainside. At one point the young woman slumps to the ground and says, "I can't take another step."

The young man lifts her to her feet and says, "But, darling, we must go on. We have no choice." She shakes her head and says, "I can't do it." Then the guide says to the young man, "Hold her close to your heart. Let the strength and love from your body flow into her body."

The young man does this, and in a few minutes the woman smiles and says, "Now I'm ready. I can go on."

We can all relate to that episode. There are times when we, too, don't think we have the strength to go on. Then someone holds us close and lets their love and strength flow into our body. And that gives us the strength to go on.

Love Is the Human Vocation

The number-one power in the world is love. Theologian Teilhard de Chardin was moved by this conviction when he wrote:

> *Someday, after mastering the winds,*
> *the waves, the tides, and gravity,*
> *we shall harness for God the energies of love,*
> *and then, for the second time*
> *in the history of the world,*
> *we will have discovered fire.*

The discovery of fire eighty thousand years ago saved the human race from extinction. This discovery inspired Jean-Jacques Arnaud to produce a movie called *Quest for Fire.* It dramatized how the discovery and harnessing of fire saved humankind from destruction.

Teilhard de Chardin was concerned, as many others are today, that the human race is again in danger of extinction. This time it is not from an absence of fire. Rather, it is from the absence of something much more basic: love. Nuclear capability and human inability—or unwillingness—to love one another are threatening survival on our planet.

Unless we rediscover love and harness its energies, we may not make it through another century. Concerned people wonder:

> *Eighty thousand years from now*
> *will someone produce another movie*
> *called* Quest for Love
> *to celebrate the discovery of love—*
> *just in time to save the human race?*

Jesus Put Love First

If we had to pick one word to summarize Jesus' teaching, it would be *love.* "Love one another," said Jesus, "just as I love you" (John 15:12).

Love is the only human power capable of saving and transforming the world. It is the only power capable of reversing "the tidal wave of evil" that the first sin unleashed. Consider an example to illustrate love's power over evil.

A woman was about to board a crowded bus. Suddenly a man charged in ahead of her, almost knocking her down. The woman said with *mock* sincerity, "Forgive me for blocking your way!" The man was taken aback by her response and said with *true* sincerity, "I'm sorry! That was rude of me! I don't know what I was thinking about. I'm ashamed of myself."

Now the woman was taken aback. The man had responded to her counterfeit love as if it were real. And it had deeply moved him.

Later, the woman thought about what had happened. Then it hit her. Love is the world's greatest power. It can even conquer sin. It can arrest the tide of evil in the world and change it into a tidal wave of good (Romans 12:21).

Love is the vocation of every human being. Our life on earth will not be judged by the fame we achieved or the fortune we acquired. Rather, it will be judged by the love we showed. Mother Teresa put it this way:

> *At the hour of death*
> *when we come face to face with God,*
> *we are going to be judged on love;*
> *not how much we have done,*
> *but how much love we have put into the doing.*

Jesus Blessed Married Love

There are many kinds of love. For example, there is the love of a parent for a child, a child for a parent, a spouse for a spouse, a brother for a sister, a sister for a brother, a friend for a friend of the same sex, a friend for a friend of the opposite sex. You can go on and on.

One love, however, stands out above all others. It is the love that Jesus blessed and raised to the level of a sacrament. It is the love between a woman and a man in marriage.

Sacrament of Marriage

There is an ancient story about a young man who knocked at the door of a house. A voice from within said, "Who is it?" The young man said, "It is I. I've come to ask permission to marry your daughter." The voice from within said, "You're not ready; come back in a year."

A year later the young man returned and knocked again. The voice from within said, "Who is it?" The young man said, "It is your daughter and I. We've come to ask your permission to marry." The voice from within said, "You are now ready. Please come in."

Marriage is an "event of grace" in which God joins a man and a woman so intimately that "the two will become one" (Mark 10:8). It is an "event of grace" in which God merges the lives of two people so intimately that they become a symbol of God's love for the human race.

Marriage Symbolizes God's Love

Saint John described God as love, saying, "God is love, and whoever lives in love lives in union with God and God lives in union with him" (1 John 4:16). A poet went a step further and described God as "love generating life."

The poet's point is a good one. It is the nature of love to generate life. Thus, theologians speak of God's love "generating" *creation* in its myriad forms of life. In other words, *created* life, especially *human* life, is a "sacrament" of God's love. It is a "sacrament" in the sense that it is a "mysterious, tangible manifestation" of God's love.

But God may be described as "love generating life" in yet another sense: a "redemptive" sense. By this we mean that God's love is *faithful* and *forgiving.* When the human race separated itself from God by sin, God's love was revealed as "redemptive" as well as "creative." God entered into a covenant with Israel that blossomed into the coming of Jesus. "God loved the world

*L*ove is patient and kind;
it is not jealous
or conceited or proud;
love is not ill-mannered
or selfish or irritable;
love does not keep a record
of wrongs;
love is not happy with evil,
but is happy with the truth.
Love never gives up;
and its faith, hope, and patience
never fail.
Love is eternal.

1 CORINTHIANS 13:4-8

so much" that God sent Jesus into the world "to be its savior" (John 3:16–17).

In Jesus Christ, the love of God became Incarnate (took flesh and lived among us). This "redemptive," covenant love of God continues among us in the Church, Christ's Body.

It is against this background that the Church understands the mystery of Christian marriage. Thus, the Church prays in the liturgy:

> *Father . . .*
> *through Jesus Christ our Lord . . .*
> *you entered into a new covenant*
> *   with your people.*
> *You restored [us] to grace*
> *   in the saving mystery of redemption.*
> *You gave [us] a share in the divine life*
> *through [our] union with Christ. . . .*
>
> *This outpouring of love*
> *   in the new covenant of grace*
> *is symbolized in the marriage covenant*
> *that seals the love of husband and wife*
> *and reflects your divine plan of love.*
> PREFACE OF THE MASS: MARRIAGE II

It was this mystery of Christian marriage that led Saint Paul to compare marital love to the love of Christ for his Church (Ephesians 5:25).

And so Christian marriage is a symbol of God's "creative" love in that it is life-giving, and it is a symbol of God's "redemptive" love in that it is forgiving and faithful.

And so Christian marriage involves the lofty *vocation* of showing forth to the world God's covenant love for the human race.

Think of it this way. As the Holy Spirit united Jesus' followers into one body in Christ, so the Holy Spirit unites husband and wife into "one flesh" in Christ (Matthew 19:5). And as the Holy Spirit united Jesus' followers into the "universal Church," the sacrament of God's covenant love in the world, so the Holy Spirit unites husband and wife into the "domestic Church," the sacrament of God's covenant love in the home.

Consider what this means in everyday married life.

Marriage Is a Covenant

Today much is said about "marriage contracts." But is that what marriage is really about—each partner protecting her or his material possessions, time, career, and so on?

Marriage is not so much a contract as it is a *covenant.* A contract protects the parties in advance. It spells out what is expected of each party. A *covenant* does not. A covenant is built on a commitment to love and serve the other. A covenant is a mutual pledge to be faithful to one another forever: in good times and in bad times, in sickness and in health, for better or for worse.

Purpose of Marriage

The purpose of Christian marriage is twofold: to grow in love for one another and God, and to join God in creating new life. Or to put it another way, the purpose is both—

- unitive: love-giving and forgiving, and
- procreative: life-giving and life-nourishing.

First, consider *unitive.* By unitive we mean that Christian marriage is *love-giving.* That is, the love of husband and wife never stops but continues to grow each day. In other words, their love imitates God's unending love for us. By unitive we also mean that Christian marriage is *forgiving.* That is, husband and wife forgive the hurts they inflict upon one another, either intentionally or unintentionally. In other words, their forgiveness of one another imitates God's forgiveness of us.

Second, consider *procreative.* By procreative we mean that Christian marriage is *life-giving.* That is, the love of husband and wife ushers forth into new life. In other words, their love imitates God, whom the poet described as "love generating life." By procreative we also mean that Christian marriage is *life-nourishing.* That is, it creates the climate of unconditional family love in which new life can grow and mature into Christian adulthood.

This brings us to a question of which we are all painfully aware in our world.

Marriage is life-giving and love-giving.

What about Divorce?

The Catholic Church has taught for centuries that the marriage bond cannot be dissolved or broken. It bases its teaching on Jesus' words: We "must not separate, then, what God has joined together" (Mark 10:9).

The Church tolerates a married couple to separate or to divorce *without remarriage,* but only for very serious reasons. It permits remarriage only when the death of one of the spouses occurs, or when an annulment is applied for and granted.

Divorced Catholics whose first marriage has never been annulled may not remarry while the spouse of their first marriage is living. In the eyes of the Church, they remain married to the first spouse. Nonetheless, they are invited to continue to attend Mass and to remain active in the parish, but they are not free to receive Communion.

A divorced Catholic is advised to consult a priest to see if grounds exist for an annulment of his or her first marriage.

Interfaith Marriage

All religions recognize that a marriage between persons of different faiths is a serious step. An interfaith marriage should be entered into only after profound reflection, frank communication, and mutual prayer for guidance. There are many issues that need to be honestly faced in advance. Consider just one example.

The Catholic partner in an interfaith marriage must affirm his or her commitment to the Catholic faith and to sharing that faith with his or her children. The other partner must respect these commitments, but need not sign anything to that effect.

If each partner has a strong faith commitment to his or her own tradition and desires to rear the children in that tradition, can such a conflict be resolved? If not, the couple might be counseled to reconsider whether they should marry.

An interfaith marriage may take place in either a Catholic church or the place of worship of the other partner. Since marriage partners confer the sacrament on one another (their mutual consent is the basis of the sacrament), a priest or a deacon—or a rabbi or a minister (with the Church's approval)—may perform the ceremony.

One final point is in order here. A Catholic who married outside of the Church and wants to be reunited with the Church should consult a priest about the possibility of validating his or her marriage in a private ceremony.

Preparing for Marriage

Once a couple decide upon marriage, they should contact the parish priest as soon as possible. Under normal conditions, most dioceses require up to six months' preparation. This includes:

- interviews with a priest or deacon,
- presentation of recent certificates of Baptism, First Communion, and Confirmation,
- personal and liturgical preparation.

The Church loves us and wants to help us in any way possible. This is what the interviews are about.

A baptismal certificate establishes one's Catholic identity. It may be obtained by calling or writing the parish where the baptism took place.

Marriage is one of the most important steps we will ever take. Therefore, we should prepare for it spiritually and psychologically. Most dioceses provide a variety of preparation options: Pre-Cana conferences, Engagement Encounters, and the like.

Dynamic of Marriage

Most marriages go through a four-phase cycle. An understanding of this cycle can spell the difference between a happy marriage or a painful one.

First, there is the *attraction* phase: that exhilarating experience of being drawn to one another in a way that makes life pulsate with new excitement. This attraction takes place at four human levels: the physical, the emotional, the intellectual, and the spiritual.

The challenge of this phase is to keep the four levels of attraction in harmony and balance. The danger is to let one level roam out of control and overwhelm the others. If a couple meet the challenge and survive the danger, their attraction will flower into a commitment to marry.

The *integration* phase comes next. Once a couple marry, they begin the necessary process of integrating the excitement of love with the ordinariness of life.

The challenge of this phase is to retain love as the couple's top priority. It is to keep love from becoming routine. The danger is to begin to take love for granted and subordinate it to other things.

Third, there is the *conflict* phase. It begins when marriage partners fail the challenge or fall into the danger of the second phase. When this happens—and it does *to some degree* in most marriages—the relationship enters a sensitive stage. Faults and foibles that were once overlooked now ignite conflict. The "adoring spouse" becomes a "nagging adversary."

The challenge of this phase is to steer conflict into constructive directions. The danger is to avoid or suppress conflict rather than deal with it. If it is suppressed, communication breaks down and resentment builds.

The fourth phase is the *maturation* phase. It begins when the partners resolve to deal constructively with conflict and rediscover love. It can be the most beautiful period in a marriage. To understand how this phase works, think of human intimacy as having a "rubber band dimension." Andrew Greeley explains it this way:

> *The two lovers drift apart,*
> *indeed are often driven apart by one another;*
> *but the residual power*
> *of their affection (pair bonding)*
> *is often, indeed usually, sufficiently strong*
> *to impel them back to one another.*
>
> *Awkwardly, clumsily, blunderingly,*
> *they stumble into one another's arms,*
> *forgive each other, and begin again*
> *in a new burst of romantic love.*
> THE BOTTOM LINE CATHECHISM

The challenge of this phase is to forgive the other's faults and to rediscover his or her goodness. The danger is to give up and let love die, rather than to let it be reborn.

If marriage partners meet the challenge and avoid the danger, the residual power of their affection will launch them into a dimension of married love that will be more beautiful and more romantic than the love they first shared.

Recap

Jesus' teaching may be summed up in one word: *love.* Of all the loves a person can enjoy, only one was raised by Jesus to the level of a sacrament: married love.

The purpose of marriage is twofold: *unitive* (to grow in love of one another and God) and *procreative* (to join God in creating new life). Because marriage is such an important step in life, it should be preceded by extended courtship, serious reflection, honest discussion, and mutual prayer.

Most marriages follow a four-phase dynamic: attraction, integration, conflict, and maturation.

Marriage Annulment

Living the sacrament of Marriage involves "good times and bad," "sickness and health," "better and worse." Sometimes during a marriage the "worse" overpowers one or both spouses. They begin to admit things they denied before they married. Sometimes their worst fears come true. Things they hope marriage would solve or remedy continue—even grow worse.

When harsh realities like this set in, the couple can best express genuine love and concern for one another by consulting a professionally trained counselor or a priest. Either or both of these people can greatly assist them in prayerfully exploring their problems.

More often than not, spouses discover that problems that once seemed insurmountable can be turned into opportunities to grow. They discover that with professional help these problems can lead to a deeper and more mature love for one another.

In some cases, a prayerful exploration of marital problems may bring to light that a true sacramental marriage does not exist between them. In fact, it never existed from the beginning. In such cases an annulment may be requested from the Church. An annulment is not the dissolution (breaking up) of an existing marriage. It is a judgment by the Church that what seemed to be a marriage was never a marriage to begin with.

An annulment is granted when it can be shown that some essential defect made a particular marriage invalid from the start, despite outward appearances and the good faith of the partners. Some grounds for annulment are—

- lacking maturity to marry,
- lacking the requisite freedom to marry,
- feigning consent in a ceremony,
- hiding a serious defect in oneself to gain a partner's consent.

Understanding Marriage

Review

Love

1. List four kinds of love people can enjoy. Which is the only love that Jesus raised to the level of a sacrament?

Sacrament of Marriage

2. What is meant by the statement that marriage is not so much a contract as it is a covenant?

3. To what love does Paul compare the love of two married people?

4. List and briefly explain the twofold purpose of marriage.

5. Upon what words of Jesus does the Church base its teaching that there can be no remarriage after a divorce while both parties are alive?

6. What is the Church's teaching concerning "separation" or "divorce without remarriage"?

7. In the eyes of the Church, what is the status of a divorced Catholic who enters into a second marriage, and what is the attitude of the Catholic community toward such a Catholic?

Interfaith Marriage

8. What is the attitude of all religions toward interfaith marriages, and what do they recommend for those considering such a marriage?

9. What obligation does a Catholic partner have concerning the children of an interfaith marriage? If the other partner wishes to bring up the children in his or her own faith, what might a couple considering an interfaith marriage be counseled to do?

10. Where may an interfaith marriage take place, and who may perform it?

Preparing for Marriage

11. How far in advance should a couple begin wedding preparations? Explain the three elements of this preparation.

Dynamic of Marriage

12. Describe the four phases through which most marriages pass, and indicate the challenge and the danger that each phase presents.

Marriage Annulment

13. What is an annulment, and what are three examples of "grounds for an annulment"?

Exercises

1. There is a scene in the movie *My Fair Lady* in which Eliza Doolittle grows weary of Freddy's daily letters telling her how much he loves her. In a burst of frustration, she begins to sing the song "Show Me." In the song she says she is sick of words. She is sick of all this talk of stars "burning above." "If there's really any love burning in your heart, show me" (adapted).

Doesn't Eliza's point contradict the point that psychologist Eugene Kennedy makes in the opening statements of this chapter? Explain.

2. In an interview with President and Mrs. Reagan, Barbara Walters asked them this question: "How have you managed to keep your love alive across thirty-five years of married life?" When they didn't answer right away, Barbara tried to help them, saying, "Was it because both of you were so willing to give and take on a fifty-fifty basis?" The first lady broke into a gentle laugh and said, "Oh my! Married life never breaks that evenly. Sometimes it's more like ninety-ten. So one of us has had to give up so much more than the other." The president nodded. That was a high point of the interview, because it made such an important point: When it comes to love, we can't keep score. The day a husband and wife begin to keep score in a marriage is the day the marriage begins to die.

Explain the statement "When it comes to love, we can't keep score." To what extent does the statement apply to (a) the love of family members for one another, (b) the love of two friends for one another?

3. In his book *You Are the Light of the World*, John Catoir writes:

> *A study conducted over a seven-year period at the University of Virginia found that within one year of their divorce, 60 percent of the husbands and 73 percent of the wives felt that they might have made a mistake. Even those who thought their marriages were destructive relationships said that maybe they could have worked out their marital problems if they had tried harder.*

From your own family experience, make a list of four or five reasons why husbands and wives run into marriage problems. Show your list to a married friend or to one or both of your parents and ask them to critique the reasons. What reasons would they delete or modify? What reasons would they add?

4. People in India have two ways of getting a marriage partner. The first is called the *love* way. This means the two people seek each other out, date, and decide. The second way is called the *family* way. This means the two families decide.

A third way of getting married in modern times is the *computer* way. This means data on two possible partners is fed into a computer, and the computer decides. Here are six actual questions taken from a computer-dating application.

- How much formal education have you had?
- What music do you enjoy most?
- How religious are you?
- What is your favorite leisure-time activity?
- How touchy are you about neatness and grooming?
- What financial status are you accustomed to?

List three pros and three cons on each of these ways (love, family, computer) of getting a marriage partner. List three additional questions that you think should be on a computer-dating application, bringing the total to nine. Pick a person you have dated (or would like to date), ask that person the nine questions, record his or her answers, and share them with the class without revealing the name of the person you interviewed.

5. Explain the following and tell to what extent you agree with each statement.

a. "The most important thing a father can do for his children is to love their mother." (Theodore Hesburg)

b. "My mother was dead for five years before I knew that I had loved her very much." (Lillian Hellman)

6. In his book *Born Again,* Charles Colson, a top Nixon aide sentenced in the Watergate scandal, says of his wife, Patty: "In the ten years we've been married, I realized we'd never discussed . . . the living God, the faith deep down inside each one of us."

To what extent does your family discuss these kinds of things at home? Recall a good discussion you had in your home recently. What was it about? How did it start? What did you find especially good about it?

Personal Reflection

List five things you admire about any two members of your family. If you could make one suggestion to your father and/or your mother about how to improve the situation in your home, what would it be?

Bible Reading

Pick a passage. After reading it prayerfully, write out a brief prayer to God that reflects your personal thoughts or feelings about it.

1.	Love story	Ruth 1:1–4:22
2.	Love song	Song of Songs 1:1–8:14
3.	Loving wife	Proverbs 31:10–31
4.	Gift of love	John 2:1–12
5.	Perfect love	1 John 4:7–12

16 Holy Orders

Ordination ceremony.

Tom Dooley joined the navy as a doctor right after medical school. One day his ship spotted a thousand Vietnamese refugees adrift on a large fishing boat. Many were sick and diseased. Tom was the only doctor on board ship and had to direct the crew in treating them.

That night Tom was so tired he could hardly walk. But he was also so happy he could hardly talk. He had experienced, as never before, the power of medicine to help people.

Dooley's experience changed him forever. When he left the navy, he went back to Asia to minister to the needy—people like those on the fishing boat. In time, he was joined by hundreds of volunteers.

One of Dooley's favorite Bible passages was "Happy are those who mourn" (Matthew 5:4). Explaining why he liked this passage, he said:

To mourn
is to be more aware
of sorrow in the world
than of pleasure.
If you're extra sensitive to sorrow,
and do something,
no matter how small,
to make it lighter—
you can't help but be happy.
That's just the way it is.
THE GUIDEPOSTS TREASURY OF FAITH

Tom Dooley had discovered the deep satisfaction that comes from serving those in need. He had discovered the joy of ministry.

List some service organizations in your area that depend on volunteers to help them. List some reasons why you think more people do not volunteer their help.

Christian Ministry

The word *ministry* means "service." Christian ministry means to imitate Jesus, who said that he had come "to serve" (Mark 10:45). In other words, it means to walk in the footsteps of Jesus and do what he did.

Christian ministry is not an option. By Baptism and Confirmation we were all *called* to some form of ministry (Matthew 25:31–46, 28:16–20). Moreover, the Holy Spirit has *graced* each one of us with special gifts to minister with others.

> *The Spirit*
> *gives one person a message full of wisdom,*
> *while to another person the same Spirit*
> *gives a message full of knowledge.*
> *One and the same Spirit*
> *gives faith to one person,*
> *while to another person*
> *he gives the power to heal.*
> *The Spirit*
> *gives one person the power to work miracles;*
> *to another,*
> *the gift of speaking God's message. . . .*
> *But it is one and the same Spirit*
> *who does all this. . . .*
> *He gives a different gift to each person.*
>
> 1 CORINTHIANS 12:8–11

Every Catholic has been called and graced for Christian ministry. Every Catholic has the vocation to continue the work of Jesus in some concrete way.

Ordained Ministry

By Baptism every Catholic is called to serve others, or to minister with others. Besides this call, some Catholics are called to a *special* ministry. It is the *ordained* ministry: pastoral leadership in the Church. This special ministry is conferred by the sacrament of Holy Orders.

The specific word *order,* or *orders,* comes from Scripture, where we read, "You will be a priest forever, in the priestly order of Melchizedek" (Hebrews 5:6). Scripture uses three Greek words to refer to the three forms that ordained ministry can take:

- *episcopoi*   (Acts 20:28),
- *presbyteroi*   (Acts 14:23),
- *diakonoi*   (Acts 6:1–6).

From these words come the English words *episcopate* ("bishops"), *presbyterate* ("priests"), and *diaconate* ("deacons").

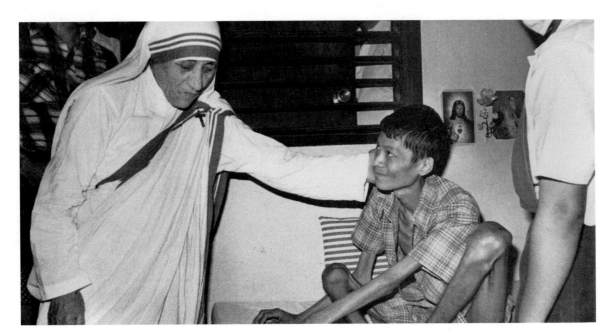

Ministry of Bishops

The sacrament of Holy Orders confers on bishops the responsibility to continue the work of the Apostles. As the successors of the Apostles, they exercise the same leadership that the Apostles did. They have the threefold responsibility to—

- shepherd the Church,
- lead it in worship and service, and
- teach it in the way of salvation.

The bishops' ministry to "teach" deserves our special attention. Before returning to the Father, Jesus said to his Apostles:

> *"I have been given all authority*
> *in heaven and on earth.*
> *Go, then, to all peoples everywhere and . . .*
> *teach them to obey everything*
> *I have commanded you."*
> MATTHEW 28:18–20

> *"What you prohibit on earth*
> *will be prohibited in heaven,*
> *and what you permit on earth*
> *will be permitted in heaven."*
> MATTHEW 18:18

> *"Whoever listens to you listens to me."*
> LUKE 10:16

But Jesus did more than authorize his Apostles to teach in his name. He also promised them the help of the Holy Spirit in doing this, saying:

> *"I will ask the Father,*
> *and he will give you another Helper,*
> *who will stay with you forever.*
> *He is the Spirit,*
> *who reveals the truth about God."*
> JOHN 14:16–17

> *"The Helper, the Holy Spirit,*
> *whom the Father will send in my name,*
> *will teach you everything*
> *and make you remember*
> *all that I have told you."*
> JOHN 14:26

> *"When . . . the Spirit comes,*
> *who reveals the truth about God,*
> *he will lead you into all the truth."*
> JOHN 16:13

And so Jesus not only commissioned and authorized his Apostles and their successors to teach in his name, but also assured them that the Holy Spirit would guide them in this difficult mission. In other words, in a world filled with confusion and contradictory voices, the Apostles and their successors enjoy a special *charism* (gift of the Holy Spirit) to help them carry out their teaching mission.

Among the Apostles, Peter exercised a special leadership role. For example, the Scriptures make it clear that Peter—

- held the keys of the Kingdom (Matthew 16:19),
- acted as spokesperson (Acts 2–5),
- taught other leaders (Galatians 1:18),
- headed all lists of Apostles (Luke 6:14, etc.).

Just as Peter exercised a special leadership role among the Apostles, so his successor, the bishop of Rome, exercises a special leadership role among the other bishops. This prompted eleventh-century Christians to give the bishop of Rome a special title: *pope,* which means "father of the fathers."

A dimension of the Church's *magisterium* ("teaching office") is what is called *infallibility.* This means that when the pope or the college of bishops teaches with the fullness of their authority in matters of faith or morals, the Holy Spirit protects them from error.

Ministry of Priests

As the early Church grew in numbers, the bishops could no longer serve all the people assigned to their care. Therefore, each bishop ordained assistants to help him. Called presbyters (priests), they were entrusted with smaller units (eventually called parishes) of the bishop's assigned territory.

Like their bishop, the priests remain celibate (unmarried). This practice dates back to early Christian times. It did not, however, become a *universal* practice in the Western Church until the twelfth century.

Celibacy served a number of purposes. Two purposes, especially, are noteworthy: a *spiritual* one and a *functional* one.

To appreciate the *spiritual* purpose, we need to keep in mind that celibacy, ultimately, models itself on Jesus, who lived a celibate life. Therefore, priestly celibacy serves as a sign of Jesus' continued presence in his Church.

Celibacy also has a *functional* purpose. By freeing the priest *from* the demands of family life, it makes him available *for* greater service to the community (1 Corinthians 7:32–35).

The priest's unique role in the Christian community and the world is beautifully summed up by the following statement:

> *To live in the midst of the world*
> *without wishing its pleasures.*
> *To be a member of each family,*
> *yet belonging to none.*
> *To share all sufferings,*
> *to penetrate all secrets,*
> *to heal all wounds. . . .*
> *To have a heart of fire for charity,*
> *and a heart of bronze for chastity.*
> *To teach, and to pardon, console,*
> *and bless always.*
> *My God! What a life!*
> *And it is yours,*
> *O Priest of Jesus Christ.*
> Lacordaire, "Thou Art a Priest Forever"

No priest ever measures up to this lofty ideal. But that's not what ideals are for.

> *Ideals are like stars;*
> *you will not succeed*
> *in touching them with your hands.*
> *But like seafaring men on the desert of waters,*
> *you choose them as your guides.*
> Carl Schurz

Church Organization

Vatican City is referred to by the news media as "the Vatican." It is a tiny independent state within the city of Rome. Politically, it has the status of any other nation on earth, enjoying a full diplomatic corps. Spiritually, it is the heart and soul of the world Catholic community. The pope and his staff reside in the Vatican.

Just as the president of the United States has a cabinet to help administer the office of president, so the pope has something similar to help him. Called the *Curia,* it helps coordinate and oversee the day-to-day operations of the worldwide Catholic community. The various departments of the Curia are normally headed by a bishop or cardinal.

Cardinal is an honorary title, usually given to a bishop who has distinguished himself in some way. A duty of the cardinals is to elect the pope. Another honorary title is that of *monsignor,* usually given to a priest who has distinguished himself in some way.

A somewhat simplified organizational chart of the Catholic Church might look something like this.

- *Parish:* the local Catholic community. Each parish is served by a pastor, usually with a pastoral team of ordained and lay associates.
- *Diocese:* a church territorial division, usually containing a number of parishes. Each diocese is served by a bishop and a team of ordained and lay associates, who coordinate Church activity at a diocesan level.
- *National Conference:* an organized structure of the bishops of a nation. Each national conference is served by committees of bishops, who coordinate Church activity at a national level.
- *Universal Church:* all Catholic communities of the world. It is served by the Holy Father and the Curia, who coordinate Church activity at an international level.

Bishops of the world gathered in Rome.

Two Kinds of Priests

Priests fall into two groupings: diocesan (secular) and religious. Diocesan priests work in a given diocese under the authority of the bishop of the diocese. Religious priests belong to a religious community and are under the authority of the religious superior.

Each religious community has its own particular spirit or spirituality. It is tailored to helping its members carry out the particular ministry to which the community is committed: education of the young, service to the poor, preaching the Gospel in mission countries.

Sisters serve as administrators in many parishes where no priest is in permanent residence.

Other Religious Communities

Besides religious communities of priests, there are also religious communities of women (sisters). They embrace a life-style and ministry in the Church similar to those of religious priests. There are also religious communities of brothers. Each of these communities has a particular spirituality that is tailored to the special ministry to which that community is committed.

Members of religious communities often take vows of poverty, chastity, and obedience. They vow poverty (forgoing personal ownership of goods) to try to better imitate Jesus, who sacrificed ownership of material things for the sake of God's Kingdom (Matthew 19:21). Similarly, they vow chastity to better imitate Jesus, who sacrificed the joys of marriage for the sake of God's Kingdom (Matthew 19:12). Finally, they vow obedience to try to better imitate Jesus, who sacrificed his own personal will for the sake of God's Kingdom (Luke 22:42, Philippians 2:8).

Taking vows of poverty, chastity, and obedience does not, of itself, make a person any holier than someone who does not take them. It is simply a different way of committing oneself to strive for the same perfection to which every Christian is called (Matthew 5:48).

Ministry of Deacons

Deacons complete the pastoral leadership team. They are single or married men who have felt God's call to ordained ministry.

Today, deacons serve the Catholic community in a variety of ways. They preach, baptize, marry, and conduct funerals. They cannot, however, be the celebrants of Confirmation, the Eucharist, Reconciliation, Anointing of the Sick, or Holy Orders.

More and more, deacons are assuming greater responsibility in the day-to-day life of the Church. The role of deacons is likely to continue to grow, rather than diminish, in the years to come.

Recap

The word *ministry* means "service." Christian ministry means to imitate Jesus, who came to serve and not to be served. By Baptism and Confirmation, all Catholics are called and graced for Christian ministry. Besides the *general* call to Christian ministry, there is a *special* call to *ordained* ministry: pastoral leadership in the Church. This ministry is conferred by the sacrament of Holy Orders.

The sacrament of Holy Orders commissions bishops, priests, and deacons to follow in the footsteps of the Apostles and to share in their same threefold leadership responsiblity to—

- shepherd the followers of Jesus,
- lead them in worship and service, and
- teach them in the way of salvation.

Understanding Holy Orders

Review

Christian Ministry

1. What is meant by Christian ministry?

2. What two sacraments call and grace every Catholic for Christian ministry?

Ordained Ministry

3. What is meant by *ordained* ministry? How is it conferred, and what three forms does it take?

Ministry of Bishops

4. List the threefold responsibility of bishops.

5. Cite biblical passages that show that Jesus (a) authorized the Apostles to teach in his name, and (b) assured the Apostles that the Holy Spirit would guide them in this task.

6. Cite three examples from Scripture that indicate that Peter exercised a special leadership among the Apostles.

7. The bishop of what city is the modern successor of Peter? How did he get the name *pope,* and what does the word mean?

8. Explain the following terms: (a) *magisterium,* (b) *infallibility.*

Ministry of Priests

9. Explain how priests and parishes came into being in the early days of Christianity.

10. What is celibacy? When did it become universal in the Western Church, and what twofold purpose does it serve?

11. List and explain (a) two kinds of priests and (b) three kinds of religious communities.

Ministry of Deacons

12. Who are ordained deacons, and what are three services they perform for the Catholic community?

Church Organization

13. Identify the following: (a) Vatican, (b) Curia, (c) cardinal, (d) monsignor, (e) diocese, (f) parish.

Exercises

1. John Catoir makes this personal admission in his book *That Your Joy May be Full:*

> As a young man I felt a strong attraction for the priesthood, but I held back. . . . It took about seven years of inner turmoil from high school through college and military service . . . to say "yes" to God's call. I never regretted my decision.

Interview a priest, a sister, a brother, or a deacon about his or her vocation. Ask: When did you first experience the call? What was your first response to it? What moved you to eventually say yes to God? Have you ever regretted your decision? What do you think is the best age for a decision of this type? Explain.

2. Saint Francis Xavier was a fine athlete at the University of Paris. There he felt the call to the priesthood, responded to it, and became a missionary to India. In a letter from India, he wrote to a friend:

> *The native Christians here have no priests. There is nobody to say Mass for them, nobody to teach them. . . . Many people are not becoming Christian for one reason only: there is nobody to make them Christians. Again and again, I have thought of going round the universities of Europe and crying out like a madman [for young people to come help me].*

List some reasons why you think there is an even greater shortage of vocations to the priesthood, sisterhood, and brotherhood in our day.

3. Imagine that you have been hired by a team of professional advertising consultants. The team has been commissioned to design a one-minute television commercial to run just before the half of the Super Bowl. Its purpose is to invite young people to consider the religious ministry.

What "gimmick" would you suggest the team use to get the attention of the young viewers they want to reach? What would you suggest they say to them once they had their attention?

4. Recall a "good experience" you had with a priest, a brother, or a sister. Also recall a "bad experience." What do you look for most in a priest, a sister, a brother, or a deacon? Explain.

Personal Reflection

Thomas Merton was one of the great spiritual writers of our time. In his autobiography, *The Seven Storey Mountain,* he tells how he made his decision to become a priest. It was after a night on the town. About four in the morning, he and two friends returned to his apartment and sacked out on the floor. They awoke around eleven the next morning, "half stupified." Later Tom went out to get some breakfast. He writes:

> *While we were sitting there on the floor playing records and eating this breakfast the idea came to me: "I am going to be a priest." I cannot say what caused it. . . . It was not the music, not the fall air. . . . It was not a thing of passion or of fancy. It was a strong and sweet and deep and insistent attraction that suddenly made itself felt.*

That night Tom headed for Saint Francis Xavier Church on New York's Sixteenth Street. He writes:

> *The church was full of lights and people and the Blessed Sacrament was exposed in a monstrance on the altar. . . . I looked straight at the Host . . . and I said: ". . . I want to be a priest, with all my heart I want it. If it is Your will, make me a priest—make me a priest."*

The rest of the story is history. Thomas Merton went on to become one of the most influential priests of our time.

Have you ever felt God's presence or a "spiritual experience" in some "unspiritual setting," such as Tom did? Describe the setting and what you felt. Have you ever experienced a kind of call (or even a slight nudge) toward the priesthood or religious life? Explain.

Bible Reading

Pick a passage. After reading it prayerfully, write out a brief prayer to God that reflects your personal thoughts or feelings about it.

1. Jesus the priest   Hebrews 4:14–5:10
2. Peter the leader   Acts 1:15–26
3. Bishops and deacons   1 Timothy 3:1–13
4. Presbyterate ordination   1 Timothy 4:6–16
5. Paul and celibacy   1 Corinthians 7:32–35

Part Three
Catholic Morality

Looking Back
WORSHIP:
God's Ongoing Initiative of Love

Looking Ahead
MORALITY:
God's Invitation to Love

To the eye of the casual observer,
a skillfully carved imitation acorn
could pass for a real one.
In reality, an infinite gap separates the two.
The real acorn contains the power
to send a tree soaring skyward.
The imitation acorn does not.

Pope Pius XII had something like this in mind
when he said of the liturgy:

It is not a cold and lifeless representation
of the events of the past. . . .
It is rather Christ himself . . .
ever living in his Church.
MEDIATOR DEI, 165

And the Second Vatican Council had something
similar in mind when it said of the risen Jesus:

He is present in the sacrifice of the Mass. . . .
He is present in the sacraments,
so that when [anyone] baptizes
it is really Christ Himself who baptizes.
He is present in His word. . . .
He is present, finally,
when the Church prays and sings.
CONSTITUTION ON THE SACRED LITURGY, 7

When she was seven,
Saint Teresa of Avila ran away from home,
intending to go to Morocco to die for Christ.
As she grew older,
her spiritual fervor gave way to material things.
At seventeen, a serious illness
and some serious reading restored her fervor.
She went on to become a great saint.
Saint Teresa reminds us in her writings:

Christ has no body now on earth but yours.
Yours are the only hands
with which he can do his work. . . .
Yours are the only eyes
through which his compassion can shine
upon a troubled world.
Christ has no body now on earth but yours.

In Part Three we will explore
our response to God's invitation
to love and live as Jesus did:

17 Morality
18 Moral Life—1
19 Moral Life—2
20 Moral Decision Making
21 Life Models

17 Morality

In his novel *The Source*, James Michener re-creates a time in history when people worshiped many gods. In one scene, he portrays the people of Makor sacrificing infants and young children to their new god, Melak. Then Michener explains why the people threw out their old gods and adopted a new god.

> [It was] partly because
> his demands upon them were severe . . .
> and partly because
> they had grown somewhat contemptuous
> of their local gods
> precisely because they were not demanding.

A Gallup poll shows that many modern Christians are like the people of Makor. They do not think their religion is very demanding. That poll raises a question: Why do many modern Christians think Jesus' teachings are not demanding?

On a scale of one (not very) to seven (very), how demanding do you think Jesus' teachings are? Why do you think many people feel that Jesus' teachings are not very demanding?

Jesus' Teachings

One high school girl answered the above two questions this way: "Many modern people don't feel Jesus' teachings are very demanding because they do not really understand them or they don't take them seriously." She gave this example:

> Take the Sermon on the Mount.
> There Jesus said:
> "Love your enemies,
> do good to those who hate you,
> bless those who curse you,
> and pray for those who mistreat you. . . .
> Do for others
> just what you want them to do for you."
> LUKE 6:27, 31

> How many people
> really understand those teachings
> or take them seriously?
> On a scale of one to seven,
> I'd give Jesus' teachings about a six.
> They're terribly demanding.

Assuming the girl is correct—and many agree with her—why did Jesus make his teachings so demanding? Was it because he wanted to challenge us? Or was there a more profound reason?

To answer this question, we need to go back to the beginning of time. We need to go back to the creation itself.

Creation

The Bible teaches *that* God created the universe. It does *not*, however, explain *how* God created it. In other words, the biblical writer did not intend the creation story to be a scientific explanation or an eyewitness report of what happened. Thus, the Bible leaves unanswered how such things as the following first appeared on earth:

- water, soil, minerals;
- countless varieties of plants;
- myriads of insects, birds, animals;
- different races of people.

To what extent were these things created individually by God? Did God simply create the basic form from which the myriads of variations gradually emerged? Or did God—as Saint Augustine suggested fifteen hundred years ago—simply create the "seed" or "seeds" from which creation emerged gradually?

When you ask scientists *how* the universe came to be, they answer, "The 'big bang' theory is probably pretty close to the truth." This theory holds that a giant "fireball" was once poised in space. It exploded, flinging its contents outward,

Eternal Life

These questions have been answered by Jesus. He said that human life is *not* at the end of the process. The final quantum leap lies ahead of us. It is the leap from *human* life to *eternal* ("divine") life. Jesus said:

> *"I have come*
> *in order that you might have life—*
> *life in all its fullness. . . .*
> *For what my Father wants is*
> *that all who see the Son and believe in him*
> *should have eternal life.*
> *And I will raise them to life on the last day."*
> JOHN 10:10; 6:40

And so Jesus teaches that the last stage of life still lies ahead. It is the quantum leap into "life in all its fullness": *eternal* life.

Before life reached the human stage, creation seems to have advanced from one quantum leap to the next *randomly.* Some parts of creation made the leap. Others did not; they remained where they were. In other words, individual life forms did not have the *freedom* to choose to make the leap or not.

Now that life has reached the human stage, all this is changed. God gives to each human being the freedom and the help to choose to make the leap to eternal life or not.

It is against this background that we should view Christian morality.

eventually forming our stellar system. Then over billions of years, by a series of "quantum leaps," the rest of creation appeared on planet Earth.

The series of quantum leaps (breakthroughs into higher forms of creation) would reflect the makeup of the universe. For example, the leaps conceivably went from—

- nonlife to vegetative life,
- vegetative life to sense life,
- sense life to conscious life.

In any event, once life reached the *human stage,* something remarkable happened. Creation became conscious of itself. For the first time, it could *consciously* ponder the past and speculate on the future. It could *consciously* ask, Where did we come from and where are we going? It could ask these mind-boggling questions: Is human life the end of the quantum leaps? Or is there yet another leap ahead of us? If so, what will it be?

Christian Morality

Imagine that the deterioration of the environment made it necessary for us to abandon the planet Earth within ten years. What would we do?

Immediately we would begin a frantic search to find another planet that is capable of supporting life. Suppose that we found one and that it was very different from earth; but with drastic modifications in how we live, we could adapt ourselves to the new planet.

Then engineers would reproduce here on earth the conditions we would encounter on the new planet. Under simulated conditions, we would learn to live under the new conditions.

This fanciful exercise helps us understand what Christian morality is all about.

Old age and illness make it impossible for human beings to survive indefinitely on planet Earth. Jesus has revealed, however, that there is another planet, so to speak, beyond this one: heaven. Life in heaven is totally different from life on earth. Yet, it is within our capacity to adjust to this new life and prepare for it while still in this world.

Simulated conditions on earth preparing astronauts for survival on the moon.

And this brings us to Christian morality. Christian morality has to do with making the quantum leap to *eternal* life. It has to do with freely choosing to share in the fullness of life that Jesus came to bring.

Christian morality may be described as *accepting God's invitation to live life on earth in such a way as to make the leap to eternal life.* What Moses said to the Israelites, God says to each human being:

> *I am now giving you the choice*
> *between life and death . . .*
> *and I call heaven and earth*
> *to witness the choice you make.*
> *Choose life.*
> DEUTERONOMY 30:19

And so our job in this world is to accept God's invitation. It is to choose life. Our job is to plant the seeds that will yield the harvest of eternal life in the next world. Listen to Saint Paul:

> *A person will reap exactly what he plants.*
> *If he plants*
> *in the field of his natural desires,*
> *from it he will gather the harvest of death;*
> *if he plants in the field of the Spirit,*
> *from the Spirit*
> *he will gather the harvest of eternal life.*
> GALATIANS 6:7–8

> *What I say is this:*
> *let the Spirit direct your lives. . . .*
> *The Spirit has given us life;*
> *he must also control our lives.*
> GALATIANS 5:16, 25

And so, borrowing Saint Paul's imagery, our job in this world is to open ourselves to the Spirit. Then we will be able to plant the seeds that will lead to the harvest of eternal life in the next world.

Here we should point out that Paul's vision of planting the seeds in this life to yield the harvest of eternal life involves seeing everything in this life as being closely related to eternal life. It means involving ourselves totally in God's *re-creation* of this world. More specifically, it means working for peace, justice, and harmony in every area of human society and at every level of human existence.

This brings us to an *alternate,* more *personal* way of describing Christian morality.

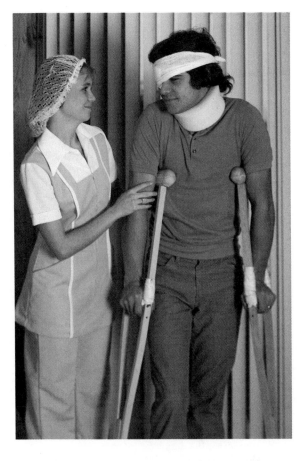

We Are to Live As Jesus Did

At the Last Supper Jesus washed the feet of his Apostles. When he had finished, he said:

> *"You call me Teacher and Lord,*
> *and it is right that you do so,*
> *because that is what I am. . . .*
> *I have set an example for you,*
> *so that you will do*
> *just what I have done for you. . . .*
> *Love one another, just as I love you."*
> JOHN 13:13, 15, 17; 15:12

And so an *alternate,* more *personal* way of describing Christian morality is as follows: It is *accepting Jesus' invitation to live and love as he did.*

It means seeing God's work on earth as our own work. It means seeing every activity in human society as being inseparably related to God's Kingdom—just as seeds are inseparably related to plants.

Christian Morality Is a Challenge

Living and loving as Jesus did is not an easy task. It is a challenge. This is because original sin has *flawed* human intellect and human will. As a result, we are not always able to do what we would like to do. Saint Paul speaks for all of us when he writes:

> *Even though the desire to do good is in me,*
> *I am not able to do it.*
> *I don't do the good I want to do;*
> *instead, I do the evil*
> *that I do not want to do. . . .*
> *What an unhappy man I am!*
> *Who will rescue me from this body*
> *that is taking me to death?*
> *Thanks be to God, who does this*
> *through our Lord Jesus Christ!*
> ROMANS 7:18–19, 24–25

And so Christian morality is a challenge. We can meet it successfully only by remaining united with Jesus. Jesus said:

> *"A branch cannot bear fruit by itself;*
> *it can do so only if it remains in the vine.*
> *In the same way you cannot bear fruit*
> *unless you remain in me.*
> *I am the vine,*
> *and you are the branches. . . .*
> *You can do nothing without me."*
> JOHN 15:4–5

Moral Growth

Christian morality involves an ongoing growth process. It is a journey that begins in childhood and continues all of our life. It never ends.

One attempt to describe this ongoing process was formulated by theologian Soren Kierkegaard. He said it moves forward gradually through the following three stages:

- the self-centered stage,
- the other-centered stage,
- the God-centered stage.

Here we need to keep in mind that any attempt to describe the human growth process is at best a guide. This is especially true of *moral* growth. In a sense, every human being follows a unique path that has its own twists and turns, its own dips and rises.

What Kierkegaard's formulation does is give us a better appreciation of the *general* dynamic involved in moral growth.

Self-centered Stage

Our moral growth begins with the self-centered stage. During this stage we live largely under the influence of our senses and our emotions. Our main concern is with our own enjoyment and our own concrete needs.

At this stage we are basically selfish. We want to be free to do whatever we want. We do not realize it, but we are anything but free. We are slaves to our passions and prejudices.

In the self-centered stage we view *God's law* as a *restriction* to our freedom. It is something that cramps our style or holds us back. Likewise, we view *sin* as a *violation* of a restriction. It is breaking a law, nothing more.

Kierkegaard said that as long as we remain at this stage, we are doomed to unhappiness. Constantly seeking one fleeting pleasure after another, we are condemned to ultimate frustration. We can resolve this unsatisfying situation only by moving to a more responsible level of human behavior.

Other-centered Stage

We progress to the next stage of moral growth when we decide to break out of our self-centered world and relate to other people. We do this by assuming social obligations, such as friendships and commitments.

By accepting these responsibilities, we take a giant stride toward our personal freedom. Kierkegaard held that we can become free only by abandoning our self-centeredness and relating responsibly to others.

In the other-centered stage we view *God's law* not as a restriction (to freedom) but as a *guide* (to growth). It has value. Likewise, we view *sin* not as a violation (of a restriction) but as *infidelity* (to personal growth). It is living irresponsibly.

God-centered Stage

We progress to the final stage when we discover our personal relationship with God. This discovery leads to a personal awareness of—

- our *identity* (we are God's children) and
- our *destiny* (we are called to eternal life).

In this God-centered stage we also discover Jesus Christ, the Son of God. We discover why Jesus came into the world. He came to communicate to us the fullness of life: *eternal* life. At this stage Jesus Christ becomes the central figure in our life.

In this stage we also discover the true relationship between law and love. Law is an invitation to love God. Jesus said:

*"Whoever loves me
will obey my teaching.
My Father will love him,
and my Father and I will come to him
and live with him.
Whoever does not love me
does not obey my teaching."*
JOHN 14:23–24

And so in this God-centered stage we view *God's law* neither as a restriction (to freedom) nor as a guide (to growth), but as an *invitation* (to love). And we view *sin* as a *refusal* to love. It is saying no to God and to our brothers and sisters.

Reconciliation

Just as we view law and sin according to the stage of our moral growth, so we view the sacrament of Reconciliation in a similar way. At the self-centered stage, we view it as a *distasteful task* of having to confess our sins to a priest. At the other-centered stage, we view it as a *valuable tool* to help us grow as persons. Finally, at the God-centered stage, we view it as a *celebration of reconciliation* with God and God's family.

The following diagram sums up our views of *law, sin,* and the *sacrament of Reconciliation* at each of the three stages of moral growth: *self*-centered, *other*-centered, *God*-centered.

	Law	*Sin*	*Reconciliation*
Self	restriction to freedom	violation of restriction	a distasteful task
Other	guide to growth	infidelity to growth	a valuable tool
God	invitation to love	refusal to love	celebration of reconciliation

Recap

Christian morality is accepting God's invitation to live life on earth in such a way as to make the leap to eternal life. Or, to put it in a more personal way, it is accepting Jesus' invitation to live and love as he did.

Christian morality involves an ongoing growth process. It is a journey that begins in childhood and never ends. It moves forward gradually through the following three stages:

- the self-centered stage,
- the other-centered stage,
- the God-centered stage.

Our view of law, sin, and the sacrament of Reconciliation varies according to the stage of our moral growth.

Understanding Morality

Review

Jesus' Teachings

1. Explain (a) why the "big bang" theory does not contradict biblical teaching concerning creation, (b) by what series of "quantum leaps" human life appears to have emerged, (c) what remarkable change took place in creation with the emergence of human life, (d) what important questions surfaced with the emergence of human life.

Eternal Life

2. Explain (a) how Jesus answers the question about another quantum leap that still lies ahead of us, (b) how individual life forms made a quantum leap before life reached the human stage.

Christian Morality

3. Give two ways that Christian morality may be described.

Moral Growth

4. List and describe the three stages by which Kierkegaard says we grow to moral maturity.

5. Explain how our view of *law* and *sin* changes as we grow through these three stages.

Reconciliation

6. Explain how our view of the sacrament of Reconciliation changes as we progress through the three stages of moral growth.

Exercises

1. In her book *Pilgrim at Tinker Creek*, Annie Dillard writes:

> *Somewhere I read about an Eskimo hunter who asked the local missionary priest, "If I did not know about God and sin, would I go to hell?" "No," said the priest, "not if you did not know." "Then why," asked the Eskimo earnestly, "did you tell me?"*

How would you answer the Eskimo hunter?

2. A friend of yours finds herself viewing *law, sin,* and the *sacrament of Reconciliation* in terms of the first stage of moral growth. She is not hostile to the Church but wants to deepen her appreciation of all three of these realities.

What advice would you give your friend? For example, how would you help her see that the sacrament of Reconciliation is not a "distasteful task" but a "valuable tool" for personal growth? How would you help her see that it is a "celebration of reconciliation"—the restoration of a friendship with God and the community?

3. A young Hindu and a Christian seminarian were attending the same week-long seminar on Christian morality. During the week the two became good friends. At one point the young Hindu confided to the seminarian that there was much about Christianity that he admired. His problem was that he thought Christian morality was far too lofty for ordinary people to live out.

What response would you make to the young Hindu?

4. Manette O'Neill was a teacher on New York's Lower East Side. One day she gave a math test to her grade school class. When she corrected the papers, she found that twelve boys had given the same unusually wrong answer to the same problem. She had the boys stay after school. She didn't ask any questions. She didn't make any accusations. She simply wrote twenty-three words on the chalkboard and had the boys copy them one hundred times.

Here is what Ms. O'Neill wrote:

The measure of a man's character is what he would do if he knew he would never be found out.—Thomas Babington Macaulay

Years later, author Jerome Weidman recalled the incident, saying:

I don't know about the other eleven boys. Speaking for the only one of the dozen with whom I am on intimate terms, I can say this: it was the most important single lesson of my life.

Why would you agree or disagree with the statement Ms. O'Neill wrote on the chalkboard? Describe in writing an episode from your life that taught you an important lesson about morality (what is right and wrong).

5. Hubert Courtney appeared before a federal commissioner on a charge of interstate auto theft. To try to help his case, Courtney removed his shirt and showed the commissioner his chest. There in a maze of tattoos were the words "Crime Doesn't Pay." The commissioner was unimpressed. Knowing the truth and not doing it is as foolish as writing a letter and not mailing it. It is as foolish as buying gas and not putting it in the tank.

List three things that you find yourself doing fairly regularly, even though you know you shouldn't do them. If you had a close friend who was doing these things and wanted to change, what would you suggest to her or him? Explain.

Personal Reflection

Christian morality may be described as living in this world in such a way as to plant the seeds that will lead to the harvest of eternal life in the next world. Another way of expressing this same idea is found in a section of *The Spiritual Exercises of St. Ignatius*. A paraphrase reads:

1. I believe that we were created to share our lives and loves with God and one another forever.

2. I believe that all the other things on the face of the earth were created to help us attain the lofty goal for which we were created.

3. I believe, therefore, that we should use the other things that were created insofar as they help us attain our goal and abstain from them insofar as they hinder us. It follows therefore that we should not prefer some things over others. That is, we should not value, automatically—

- *health over sickness,*
- *wealth over poverty,*
- *honor over dishonor, or*
- *a long life over a short one.*

4. Our sole norm for preferring one thing over another should be this: that it helps us better attain the goal for which God created us.

What are your thoughts and reflections on this statement? Which of the four conclusions under the third paragraph would you find hardest to accept and why?

Bible Reading

Pick a passage. After reading it prayerfully, write out a brief prayer to God that reflects your personal feelings or thoughts about it.

1. I am in the Father — John 14:1–14
2. Remain in me — John 15:1–11
3. You are like light — Matthew 5:1–16
4. Set your heart on heaven — Colossians 3:1–17
5. We will share God's glory — Romans 8:18–30

18 Moral Life—1

How might an evening television news team do a "live" report from Mount Sinai shortly after Moses received the Ten Commandments from God?

ANCHOR: Good evening. I'm Joel ben Isaac. The Hebrew leader Moses just came down the mountain with a lightning bolt: ten commandments from God. Our roving reporter, Rebecca, is at the scene. What's the mood there, Rebecca?

REPORTER: Ugly, Joel! That lightning bolt has this crowd up in arms. Pro-choicers call it a criminal attack on human freedom.

ANCHOR: How are these laws likely to affect the average people, Rebecca?

REPORTER: That's hard to say right now. But one camel trader put it this way: "It's going to take more than ten rules to change habits that have built up over the centuries."

ANCHOR: Rebecca, how is all this likely to affect Moses' leadership of the people?

REPORTER: As you know, Joel, he's been taking his lumps lately. This could be the straw that breaks his back. He could be history.

ANCHOR: Thank you, Rebecca. . . . When we return, a look at how today's events could affect your future.

(inspired by Jeffrey Rubin)

A high school girl said to her teacher:

I'm confused about the Ten Commandments.
You quoted Saint Paul as saying,
"No longer do we serve in the old way
of a written law,
but in the new way
of the Spirit" (Romans 7:6).
Then you said that the new way is love.
Where does that put the Ten Commandments?
What purpose do they serve
now that Jesus has come?

How would you answer the girl?

The Commandments

On one occasion, Jesus was asked, "What good thing must I do to receive eternal life?" Jesus answered, "Keep the commandments." The person asked, "What commandments?" Jesus answered:

"Do not commit murder;
do not commit adultery;
do not steal;
do not accuse anyone falsely;
respect your father and your mother;
and love your neighbor as you love yourself."
MATTHEW 19:18–19

On another occasion, Jesus was asked, "Which is the greatest commandment?" Jesus answered:

" 'Love the Lord your God
with all your heart,
with all your soul, and
with all your mind.'
This is the greatest
and the most important commandment.

"The second most important commandment
is like it:
'Love your neighbor as you love yourself.'

"The whole Law of Moses
and the teachings of the prophets
depend on these two commandments."
MATTHEW 22:37–40

The Christian Scriptures make it clear that Jesus did not do away with the commandments. He fulfilled the commandments (Matthew 5:17) and placed them at love's service. They serve—

- as *invitations to love* and
- as *guides to love.*

The commandments serve as *invitations to love* in that they call forth love from us when we do not respond with love as we should. They

First Commandment

A reporter asked Cecil B. DeMille, film director of *The Ten Commandments,* "What commandment do people break most today?" DeMille answered, "The first commandment: 'Worship no God but me.' It's the one that Israel broke first, and it's the one that we still break most."

DeMille hastened to explain that we do not fashion idols out of metal or stone and bow down before them. "Rather, we make idols of flesh and money and bow down before them."

Somewhat related to the worship of idols is *superstition,* which attributes *godlike* powers to ordinary things. In an age of science and reason, it is incredible that some airplanes have no "row 13" or "seat 13," and that some hotels skip from "floor 12" to "floor 14"—all because some people feel uneasy about the number *13.* This is evidence that superstition still plays a surprising role in some people's lives.

Somewhat related to superstition is *divination,* which seeks to learn the future from palm readers, fortune-tellers, and horoscopes. Such practices are regarded as evil in both the Hebrew Scriptures (Deuteronomy 18:10–11) and in the Christian Scriptures (Acts 16:16).

A final practice that relates to the first commandment is *spiritism,* which seeks to communicate with the dead through mediums and seances. Again, the Bible prohibits such practices (Leviticus 20:27). Commenting on spiritism, Thomas Higgins says in *Man As Man:*

> *While most spiritistic mediums*
> *may be laughed at as frauds . . .*
> *not all the phenomena of modern spiritism*
> *may be dismissed as hokum.*
>
> *Some truly genuine effects are wrought.*
> *The explanation of some of these effects*
> *may be traced*
> *to occult but natural causes,*
> *whereas others . . .*
> *can be due only to diabolical intervention.*

In general, sins against the first commandment vary in gravity, depending on circumstances.

serve as *guides to love* in that they indicate a course of action when we are not sure what response love invites us to make.

And so the commandments should be seen in this perspective: as *positive* guides (to happiness) and invitations (to love), not as *negative* restrictions (to freedom).

Let us now see how the Ten Commandments serve as *invitations* and *guides* to help us better love—

- God (commandments 1–3) and
- neighbor (commandments 4–10).

(This chapter treats the first five commandments. The last five are discussed in the next chapter.)

Michaelangelo's Moses.

The Ten Commandments

Moses called together all the people . . .
and said to them,
"People of Israel . . .
at Mount Sinai the LORD our God . . .
spoke to you
face-to-face from the fire [saying] . . .
'I am the LORD your God. . . .

" '[1] Worship no God but me. . . .
[2] Do not use my name for evil purposes. . . .
[3] Observe the Sabbath and keep it holy. . . .
[4] Respect your father and your mother. . . .
[5] Do not commit murder.
[6] Do not commit adultery.
[7] Do not steal.
[8] Do not accuse anyone falsely.
[9] Do not desire another man's wife . . .
[10] or anything else that he owns.'

"These are the commandments
the LORD gave to all of you. . . .
Then he wrote them on two stone tablets
and gave them to me."

DEUTERONOMY 5:1-22

The Israelites cherished the commandments. They viewed them as signs of God's special love for them. The psalmist prayed:

Your word, O LORD, will last forever. . . .
How I love your law! . . .
How sweet is the taste of your instructions—
sweeter even than honey! . . .
Your word is a lamp to guide me
and a light for my path.

PSALM 119: 89, 97, 103, 105

Second Commandment

Someone said, "When I misuse God's name, I don't mean anything by it. It's just a *bad habit* I have." Try using that excuse when a traffic officer stops you for speeding or when your supervisor catches you arriving late for work.

The second commandment prohibits dishonoring God's name. Common ways in which people dishonor God's name (and therefore God) are by cursing, swearing, and perjuring oneself.

Cursing is calling upon God to inflict evil or harm on someone. It dishonors God gravely, because it attempts to make God a partner to evil. We should note, however, that the expression "God damn you," normally, is not used to ask God to inflict harm on someone. Rather, it is simply used as an expression of anger or frustration. Such an utterance is not a curse.

Swearing is taking an oath. It is calling upon God to witness to the truth of something. Swearing abounds in the Bible (for example, Abraham in Genesis 21:24 and Paul in Romans 1:9). Even Jesus was placed under oath by the Jewish Council (Matthew 26:63). Jesus, however, taught his followers that they should be so truthful as to make swearing unnecessary. He said, "Do not swear" (Matthew 5:34).

In a society where lying is commonplace, courts require people to swear that their testimony is true. In cases like this, swearing is permissible. To *lie* after taking an oath is to be guilty of *perjury*. It dishonors God gravely by asking God to witness to a falsehood.

Third Commandment

It is not uncommon to find a pamphlet by some religious sect saying that Christians should observe the Sabbath, rather than Sunday. A few early Jewish converts to Christianity made the same point. But Saint Paul taught otherwise (Colossians 2:16).

This raises a question. If the third commandment says we should "observe the Sabbath and keep it holy," why did Jesus' first followers change their observance to Sunday?

There are many reasons. Two major reasons are that Jesus rose on Sunday (John 20:1) and the Spirit descended on Sunday ("day of Pentecost," Acts 2:1). These two events gave new significance to this day. They signaled the sunset of the Old Testament era and the sunrise of the New Testament era. And so, guided by the Spirit, the followers of Jesus chose Sunday as the day to celebrate the Lord's Supper (Acts 20:7–11) and referred to this day as the Lord's Day (Revelation 1:10).

From the beginning, Sunday was observed in a special manner by the early Church. Modern Church law spells out its observance this way:

> *On Sundays*
> *and other holy days of obligation,*
> *the faithful are obliged to assist at Mass.*
> *They are also to abstain*
> *from such work or business*
> *that would inhibit the worship*
> *to be given God,*
> *the joy proper to the Lord's Day,*
> *or the due relaxation*
> *of mind and body.*
> CANON LAW 1247

Besides Sunday, the Church also observes the ancient practice of setting aside holy days for special observance. In the United States, these holy days are—

- *Mary, Mother of God* (January 1),
- *Ascension* (forty days after Easter),
- *Assumption* (August 15),
- *All Saints* (November 1),
- *Immaculate Conception* (December 8),
- *Christmas* (December 25).

By gathering for worship on Sundays and holy days, we proclaim to the world what Jesus proclaimed: that God is our origin and our ultimate destiny. God must therefore be at the heart and center of all human life and activity.

Christian responsibility to proclaim this binds us gravely, unless we are excused for a serious reason. This means that when we are otherwise faithful in our Mass attendance, we need not worry or feel guilty when something (for example, sickness, unusually exhausting work, or a vacation) makes it really difficult for us to assist at Mass on that particular day.

Trust Me!

Teenagers find themselves in an especially critical situation. They are moving toward adulthood and independence, but have not yet reached either.

This situation calls for special respect and trust—both on the part of parents and on the part of teenagers. The young person, especially, needs to keep in mind the reason for this special respect and trust. Stressing this point, actor Ricardo Montalban once wrote to his son:

> *We are father and son by the grace of God,*
> *and I accept that privilege*
> *and awesome responsibility. . . .*
> *I am not your pal. . . .*
> *I am your father.*
> *This is 100 times more than what a pal is. . . .*
> *Whatever I ask you to do is motivated by love.*
> *This will be hard for you to understand*
> *until you have a son of your own.*
> *Until then, trust me.—Your Father*

Fourth Commandment

The fourth commandment—"Respect your father and your mother"—recalls that we are *communal* or *social* beings. This means that we do not enter the world or grow up in it by ourselves. We do this with the help and guidance of two communities, especially:

- our family and
- our country.

The Family Is the Key Community

Years ago, Alvin Toffler made this sobering statement in his popular book *Future Shock:*

> *The family has been called*
> *the "giant shock absorber" of society—*
> *the place to which*
> *the bruised and battered individual returns*
> *after doing battle with the world,*
> *the one stable point*
> *in an increasingly flux-filled environment.*
> *As the superindustrial revolution unfolds,*
> *the "shock absorber" will come in for*
> *some shocks of its own.*

What Toffler predicted has come to pass. And the shocks to the family community have been so great that some social critics say it is heading toward "complete extinction."

Not everyone agrees with these critics, but all *do* agree that the situation is serious. All agree that family members have an obligation—more than ever before in history—to contribute to family stability.

Concretely, Christian parents must take to heart—more than ever—Saint Paul's words, "Raise [your children] with Christian discipline and instruction" (Ephesians 6:4). And children must take to heart—more than ever—Saint Paul's words, "Obey your parents. . . . 'Respect your father and mother' " (Ephesians 6:1–2).

God intended the family to be one of God's greatest blessings and gifts. Our gift back to God is to help the family become what God made it to be: the sign and instrument by which human society matures into the Kingdom of God.

The State Is Also Important

Closely related to the family community is the civil community. Because we share the blessings of the civil community, we owe it special loyalty. Jesus made this clear when he told his disciples, "Pay to the Emperor what belongs to the Emperor" (Luke 20:25).

Later on Paul told Christians in Rome to obey and respect civil authorities, because these authorities derive their right to govern from God (Romans 13:1).

On the other hand, the state must also respect the rights of citizens. Citizens do not exist for the state; the state exists for the citizens. No state may trample on the natural human rights of an individual or family. If it does, citizens have not only the right but also the obligation to refuse to obey, saying with Saint Peter, "We must obey God, not men" (Acts 5:29).

Fifth Commandment

Albert Diianni has traveled widely in such places as South America, Central America, and the Philippine Islands. These travels have had a profound effect on him. Writing in *America* magazine, he says:

In my visits
to Peru, Brazil, Mexico, and the Philippines,
I have seen peoples and lands ravaged
by the corruption of political leaders
and the uncaring greed
of multinational corporations.
I have shivered at the burials of infants
who died because their parents lacked
the rudimentary education to provide them
simple hygienic or medical care.

Diianni's words put flesh and blood on these otherwise cold statistics:

- 2 billion people in the world have incomes below $500 a year,
- 900 million people are illiterate,
- 600 million people have no full-time job,
- 450 million people suffer from hunger and malnutrition.

It was with these millions of human lives in mind that the bishops of the Second Vatican Council wrote:

There must be made available to all . . .
everything necessary
for leading a life truly human,
such as food, clothing, and shelter. . . .
[People] are obliged
to come to the relief of the poor,
and to do so not merely
out of their superfluous goods. . . .
This sacred Council urges all . . .
to remember the [early Christian] saying . . . :
"Feed [those] dying of hunger,
because if you have not fed [them]
you have killed [them]."
PASTORAL CONSTITUTION ON THE CHURCH
IN THE MODERN WORLD, 26, 69

This shocking statement jolts us out of our complacency. It makes us realize that when brothers or sisters are dying of hunger, we have a grave obligation to feed them, insofar as we are able. To turn our backs on them and walk away is to share, to some degree, in the very cause of their pain and suffering—even their death.

This brings us to the fifth commandment, which deals with respect for human life.

Human Life Is Sacred

The destruction of innocent human life is called *murder* and is one of the gravest crimes a person can commit. No Christian questions this. Every person has a right to life and a right to preserve life. This includes the right to kill an unjust aggressor, if this is the *only* way to preserve one's life.

What is true of individuals is also true of groups of individuals, for example, a nation. Thus from early times, Christians have tolerated war in certain circumstances.

In modern times, however, many Christians are finding it harder and harder to tolerate war in any circumstance. This is becoming even more and more the case now that countries are stockpiling nuclear, chemical, and biological weapons. It was with this in mind that the bishops of the Second Vatican Council said of modern war:

Any act of war aimed indiscriminately
at the destruction of entire cities or
of extensive areas along with their population
is a crime against God and [the human family].
It merits unequivocal
and unhesitating condemnation. . . .

The arms race
is an utterly treacherous trap for humanity,
and one which injures the poor
to an intolerable degree. . . .

It is our clear duty, then,
to strain every muscle
as we work for the time
when all war can be completely outlawed
by international consent.
THE CHURCH IN THE MODERN WORLD, 80–82

As never before, Christians are becoming aware of their responsibility to be peacemakers in the spirit of the Sermon on the Mount:

Happy are those who work for peace;
God will call them [God's] children!
MATTHEW 5:9

If we do not take seriously these words of Jesus, John Kennedy's warning, that we must put an end to war or war will put an end to us, becomes frighteningly ominous.

Human life is a gift and must be respected and protected in every area of human activity.

What about Suicide?

Closely related to taking another's life is taking one's own life. It too is forbidden by the fifth commandment. A question arises, however, concerning such actions as hunger strikes. Are they also forbidden because they involve the possibility of taking one's own life? There are three kinds of hunger strikes: those in which the striker—

- *does not intend death* but *will accept it,* if necessary;
- *does not intend death* but uses the *possibility of it* to "push" the other side;
- *intends death* as a means to some important end.

The first two cases involve the *indirect* killing of oneself. We say *indirect* because in neither case does the striker intend death. In fact, the striker hopes and prays it will not occur. Both cases, therefore, are morally permissible *when the importance of the end is proportionate to the risk to the striker's life.*

The third case, however, is totally different. It involves the *direct* killing of oneself and is objectively indefensible, no matter the motive.

What about Capital Punishment?

In the past, people have tended to view capital punishment as a "last resort" measure taken by society to defend itself against hard-core criminals. Today, however, many Christians are finding capital punishment harder and harder to justify. Some of the reasons for this view are that capital punishment—

- tends to erode respect for life and to dehumanize all concerned;
- risks executing the innocent, especially the poor who can't afford quality defense (over half of those on death row are minorities, most of whom are poor);
- frustrates the primary purpose of punishment: rehabilitation;
- leads to incredible court delays that diminish its effectiveness as a deterrent (the major reason given for justifying it).

Those who hold this view also maintain that modern prisons effectively protect society from hard-core criminals.

First, there is *direct* abortion, which is an action whose *direct* intent is to kill an unborn fetus. Direct abortion is forbidden by the fifth commandment.

Second, there is *indirect* abortion, which is an action whose *direct* intention is *not* to kill the fetus but to save the life of the mother. For example, let us suppose that to save a pregnant mother's life, a doctor must remove a diseased uterus. The abortion of the fetus that follows *indirectly* from this operation is totally unwanted and uncontrollable.

To underscore the *intent* of indirect abortion, we might add that every effort to preserve the life of the fetus is made. Removing the uterus in this situation is permissible, even though it leads *indirectly* to the death of the fetus.

Abortion has far-reaching social effects. Touching on this point, Dr. Bernard Nathanson says:

> *Abortion strikes at the heart*
> *of the integrity of family structure*
> *and sexual mores.*
> *It affects virtually every person*
> *in this country to some extent.*
> *It also reflects the state of moral health*
> *of this society.*

What about Abortion?

Abortion was widespread in ancient pagan society. Early Christians' response to abortion was militant opposition. For example, around A.D. 80, the *Didache,* the oldest known Christian document apart from the Christian Scriptures, says bluntly, "You shall not practice abortion."

Under the influence of Christianity, abortion was eventually outlawed by civil authorities. Not until the twentieth century did it become so widespread again.

Opposition to abortion is based on the belief that the fertilized egg will develop into a human person and must therefore be protected. In dealing with the issue of abortion, however, we need to make an important distinction.

What about Euthanasia?

The word *euthanasia* comes from the Greek word *euthanatos,* which means "easy death." As with abortion, an important distinction must be made here.

First, there is *direct* euthanasia (traditionally referred to as "mercy killing"). This is a deliberate act (for example, administering a lethal injection or withholding medicine) that brings about the death of someone, usually a person who is suffering greatly from very old age or an incurable illness. *Direct* euthanasia is always gravely wrong, no matter how noble the motives.

Second, there is what some people call *passive* euthanasia, which is totally different from *direct* euthanasia. In fact, it is not euthanasia at all. It is simply allowing something that is morally permissible: allowing an aged or incurably ill patient to die naturally rather than prolonging their death needlessly and indefinitely by using *extraordinary* means.

What about Drugs and Alcohol?

Some religious groups consider the drinking of alcohol to be a sin. They contend that the original Greek word that the Christian Scriptures use for *wine* means something nonalcoholic. There is absolutely no scholarly basis for this contention.

The danger of alcohol comes when the user abuses or misuses it. It is gravely sinful to deliberately drink to excess, seriously impairing one's ability to function both physically and mentally. The pain and suffering brought on by such irresponsible behavior can be seen daily.

It must be noted, however, that the abuse of alcohol often stems from alcoholism, which the medical profession lists as a disease. Those suffering from this disease have a grave obligation to seek help. Moreover, we have a duty to help them in any way we can.

Related to the abuse of alcohol is the abuse of drugs. Again, the tremendous suffering brought about by drug abuse is one of the horrendous tragedies of modern times.

A serious abuse of drugs for mind-altering or recreational purposes is gravely wrong. As with those who suffer from alcoholism, those who suffer from drug addiction are gravely obliged to seek help, if they are aware of their affliction.

Recap

The Ten Commandments act as *invitations* to love by calling forth love from us when we do not respond with love as we should. They act as *guides* to love by indicating the proper course of action when we are not sure what response love invites us to make.

Specifically, the first three commandments invite us to make love of God the center of our lives, and they give us guidelines for doing this.

The fourth and fifth commandments invite us to love our neighbor as ourselves. They, too, give guidelines for doing this, especially when it comes to respect for authority and reverence for human life.

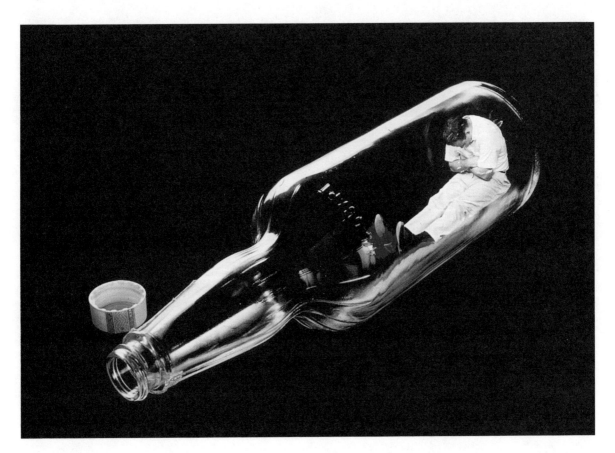

Understanding Moral Life

Review

The Commandments

1. List and explain the twofold way that the Ten Commandments serve love.

First Commandment

2. Identify (a) idolatry, (b) superstition, (c) divination, (d) spiritism.

Second Commandment

3. Identify (a) a curse, (b) an oath, (c) perjury.

Third Commandment

4. List two major reasons why Christians observe Sunday rather than the Sabbath.

5. List the six holy days that Catholics in the United States observe.

6. Explain the twofold way Catholics are to observe Sunday and the holy days.

Fourth Commandment

7. Why is cooperation between family members more important today than formerly?

8. Why does Paul say we must obey civil authorities? When do we have a right and a duty to oppose them?

Fifth Commandment

9. Explain when it is permissible to kill another person in self-defense.

10. Explain why modern Christians are finding it harder and harder to tolerate (a) war, (b) capital punishment.

11. Using the example of a hunger strike, explain the difference between the direct and the indirect taking of one's life. Under what circumstances is the indirect killing of oneself morally permissible?

12. Explain the difference between (a) direct abortion and indirect abortion, (b) direct euthanasia and so-called passive euthanasia.

13. Explain (a) when indirect abortion is permissible, (b) when passive euthanasia is permissible.

Exercises

1. Ann Landers received a letter from a young woman who had gone to a fortune-teller. The fortune-teller told her that she would never have a child of her own. The young woman was devastated. She said, "I cried all the way home." Then to the young woman's great joy, she became pregnant. But her joy soon turned to fear when she recalled what the fortune-teller had said. She fully expected a miscarriage or something worse. But the baby arrived on schedule and healthy. The young woman ended her letter by pleading with Ann's readers, "If there is anyone out there who is tempted to go to a fortune-teller, save yourself the money, needless worry and pain."

You may have heard the statement, "Something is not bad because it's a sin; it's a sin because it's bad." Explain how the woman's fortune-telling experience illustrates the point of this statement. What are two concerns that you have about the future? Explain.

2. A high school boy wrote:

I had a job at a drugstore, and everything was going nicely. My parents were trusting me, and I could do almost anything I wanted to do. Then I was fired for stealing money from one of the registers. The reason I did this is because I was getting below the minimum wage, which is wrong. So I decided to do what everyone else was doing. Well, I got caught. The owner called my parents and I got killed. Worse yet, they won't trust me anymore. My problem is that now I can't get my parents to believe me and to trust me again. I just don't feel like I belong if I'm not trusted. I want to be trusted again, but how do I go about it?

If this student were a good friend of yours, what advice would you give him? Recall a time when something similar happened to you.

3. A report in *USA Today* says that "alcohol claims 100,000 lives a year" and costs our nation "more than $117 billion a year in everything from medical bills to loss of time in the work place." Commenting on ancient abuse of alcohol, poet William Shakespeare said, "O God. That man should put an enemy in their mouths to steal away their brain."

On a scale of one (not much) to seven (very much), how big a problem is alcohol abuse among your friends? Drug abuse? How do you account for the degree of the problem of each?

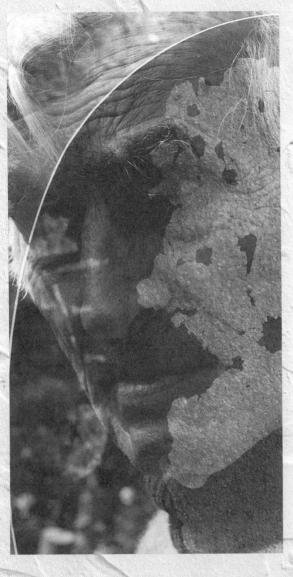

thought of writing the networks and complaining. But this would have little effect on sponsors (who bankroll the shows). Finally, the writer decided to join an organization of viewers who are telling sponsors that they will boycott their products if the sponsors continue to back such shows. Apparently a lot of viewers are taking this approach, because suddenly we are hearing "howls of protest from networks, squeals of anguish from producers, and screams of indignation from performers."

On an unsigned sheet of paper, answer the following questions:

- On a scale of one (negatively) to ten (positively), how do you think television is influencing people's morals?
- What one nonsport program do you think is having a *negative* influence? A *positive* one?
- What two nonsport programs do you usually watch?
- How many hours a week do you watch television?

Collect the sheets, tally, and discuss the results.

Personal Reflection

The following is excerpted from an unknown author:

1. *I drank for sociability and became argumentative.*
2. *I drank for friendship and made enemies.*
3. *I drank for relaxation and got the shakes.*
4. *I drank for courage and became afraid.*
5. *I drank for confidence and became doubtful.*
6. *I drank to feel heavenly and ended up feeling like hell.*

If you drink (or used to drink), which three points from the above list best explain why you started drinking? To what extent did drinking have a similar effect on you? Add three points of your own to the list.

Bible Reading

Pick a passage. After reading it prayerfully, write out a brief prayer to God that reflects your personal feelings or thoughts about it.

1. Worship God only   Deuteronomy 4:15–20
2. Keep the Sabbath holy   Nehemiah 13:15–22
3. Keep the Temple holy   Matthew 21:12–16
4. Respect authority   Ephesians 6:1–7
5. Avoid sexual immorality   Romans 1:18–28

4. A girl you know and like is beginning to smoke pot on a regular basis. You can see her changing into a totally different kind of person. You've already talked to her about it, but she doesn't want to discuss the matter.

What should you do?

5. A writer got fed up with network TV shows that cater to violence, sex, and materialism. First, the writer thought of boycotting the shows by switching channels. But this would do little to inform producers how the writer felt about their shows. Second, the writer

19 Moral Life—2

The so-called *Playboy* philosophy once viewed sex as recreation and sex partners as instruments of pleasure. Today most people reject this philosophy. Most agree that sex must be *responsible:* it must be based on love. But this brings up a question: What is love? In other words, what do we mean when we say, "Mary and Ron love each other"?

How would you answer that question?

Love

There is a lot of confusion about what people mean by love. One writer alludes to part of this confusion, saying that love is not a *feeling* but a *commitment:*

> *[Feeling] is the high-voltage,*
> *circuit-blowing infatuation we've all experienced*
> *when we connect with someone new.*
> *It is the intoxication*
> *of being accepted and desired.*
> *It's the thrill of taking a leap,*
> *shedding clothes and inhibitions,*
> *being dazzled by the private magnificence*
> *of another. . . .*
> *[Feeling] is awesome and enthralling,*
> *but in the end, sadly,*
> *it's an emotional sprint. . . .*
>
> *[Commitment], by contrast,*
> *is a marathon of the heart.*
> *It requires training, discipline,*
> *endurance and work.*
> *It is not a spectator sport or an event*
> *whose outcome can be decided in seconds.*
> *It is pushing up hills*
> *and suffering pain*
> *and resisting the temptation*
> *to drop out. . . .*
> *When love is viewed as an act of will . . .*
> *it can survive*
> *as long as your heart beats.* *

This brings us to what people mean by *responsible* sex. They mean sex that is born of commitment. They mean sex that expresses and celebrates three beautiful mysteries:

- love,
- life, and
- faith.

Sex Celebrates Love

Responsible sex is not yielding to a "circuit-blowing" feeling. It is not taking "a leap" and "shedding clothes and inhibitions." It is not engaging in an "emotional sprint," no matter how "awesome and enthralling."

Responsible sex is a celebration of love. It celebrates a love that is committed to "pushing up hills and suffering pain . . . as long as your heart beats." Responsible sex is the ultimate celebration of committed love.

Here we need to keep in mind that sex is not the only expression of love between two people. Rather, it is the *crowning* expression of a marathon of prior expressions. These prior expressions take a variety of forms. Saint Paul refers to some of them when he says:

> *Love is patient and kind;*
> *it is not jealous or conceited or proud;*
> *love is not ill-mannered*
> *or selfish or irritable;*
> *love does not keep a record of wrongs;*
> *love is not happy with evil,*
> *but is happy with the truth.*
> *Love never gives up.*
> 1 CORINTHIANS 13:4–7

In other words, Paul is saying that love expresses itself in a multitude of down-to-earth, everyday, concrete ways. The crowning expression, however, is the sexual union.

---

*Art Carey, "In Defense of Marriage," *The Philadelphia Inquirer Magazine* (February 20, 1983).

Sex Celebrates Life

Responsible sex also celebrates the mystery of life. Concerning this point, someone once said that every birth begins with a love story. This is simply another way of describing responsible sex. It is a way of saying that sex joins together in the same loving embrace the two ends for which God ordained it. God intended the sexual union to be both—

- unitive and
- procreative.

First, God intended the sexual union to be *unitive*. This means that God ordained sex to be the way for a married couple to celebrate and strengthen the love bond that *unites* them.

Second, God intended the sexual union to be *procreative*. This means that God ordained sex to be the way a married couple cooperates with God to bring new life into the world.

The unitive and procreative ends of sexual union are like the body and soul of a person. God joined them together and intended them to remain together. In this sense responsible sex is not only a celebration of *love* but also a celebration of *life*.

Sex Celebrates Faith

Many married couples testify that at the height of sexual union they sometimes soar beyond themselves. They are caught up in an experience that they can only describe as being mystical: one that goes to the heart of their marriage.

This "mystical" experience is a deep faith experience of God—especially God's presence in the love bond that unites them. It is a faith experience of the fact that Jesus blessed the love of a husband and wife in the most remarkable way imaginable. He raised it to the level of a sacrament. Commenting on this, one author writes:

In Christian marriage
God covenants with the couple. . . .
God promises to stand by the couple . . .
so that they can initiate a union . . .
and bring it to maturity in love.
Ladislas Orsy

Sixth and Ninth Commandments

Saint Paul likened the love of a husband for his wife to the love of God for Israel and, also, to the love of Christ for his Church (Ephesians 5:25–33). And it is *only* with this in mind that we can appreciate the sixth and the ninth commandments that God gave to the Israelites at Mount Sinai. God said to them: "Do not commit adultery. . . . Do not desire another man's wife."

This brings us to the traditional teaching of the Catholic Church concerning responsible sex. It general, it may be summed up in the following six statements:

1. Sex is a gift from God to be treasured exclusively as celebration of love between a husband and a wife.

2. Sex celebrates the gift of one's total self to another. This gift demands such a commitment and dedication that it cannot be made except with the help of the grace that God makes available through the sacrament of Marriage.

3. The sexual union between a husband and a wife must always respect both the unitive and the procreative purposes for which God ordained it.

4. All voluntary sexual activity or pleasure (thoughts, words, and actions) outside of the marriage is objectively and gravely wrong. Subjectively, however, the gravity of an act may be diminished because of circumstances. For example, someone watching a movie may be caught by surprise by an unanticipated sequence that is sexually exciting. This could result in a powerful sexual reaction that was neither foreseen nor intended. On the other hand, to watch a movie primarily because it is sexually stimulating and exciting is objectively and gravely wrong.

5. Young people, especially, should not lose heart or become discouraged when it comes to the problems and the moral failures they experience in matters related to sex. They should learn to speak maturely and frankly about these problems with a parent, a counselor, or a priest.

6. All Christians should realize that temptations against the sixth and the ninth commandments are not a sign of depravity. Rather, they are a sign of our humanity and our need for the healing and the forgiveness that Jesus came to bring us. We should never forget that God is more willing to forgive than we are to ask for forgiveness—no matter how repeatedly we fall victim to temptation and sin.

Seventh and Tenth Commandments

A camera store in New York City has reduced thefts drastically by posting this sign for all customers to see: "Your picture has been taken four times in the last thirty seconds. We have a front view, two side views, and one from the rear."

The seventh and the tenth commandments deal with stealing and with desiring another's property.

Stealing is one of the most disturbing problems that stores and banks face. It involves not only customers but also employees. For example, one reliable survey (documented by lie-detector tests) shows that 72 percent of store employees and 83 percent of bank employees engage in some form of stealing (often minor).

Technically, stealing may be defined as taking something from another *against his or her reasonable will.* The phrase "against his or her reasonable will" is important, because it would not be stealing if, for example, we took food to stay alive.

Presumably, the owner of the food would not object if she or he knew of our circumstances. (To object under such circumstances would be "unreasonable.") The gravity of stealing depends on two factors:

- the circumstances involved and
- the value of what is taken.

An example will clarify what this means. If an employee of a successful business steals five dollars from the cash register, the theft is sinful but not gravely so. But if the employee intends to continue to steal over a period of time, the thefts can add up to a grave matter.

Before we can be forgiven a sin of theft in the sacrament of Reconciliation, we must restore, or intend to restore, what we took. If it is extremely difficult or impossible to return it without revealing our identity and, perhaps, losing our job, we can presume that the one from whom we stole would be agreeable to our giving to charity the equivalent of what we stole.

In rare cases we may be excused from restitution (restoring the stolen goods) because it would cause grave hardship—substantially graver than that inflicted upon the injured party. The willingness to make restitution is a concrete sign of repentance.

What about Cheating?

A study conducted by Cornell University indicates that the average ten-year-old has already developed a "noncondemning attitude" toward cheating. Experts say that children pick up this attitude from adults and peers.

Cheating—whether it be to acquire money, grades, or a scholarship—is doubly sinful. It involves, in some sense, both *stealing* and *lying*. Take cheating on an examination, for example. Our action involves taking an answer from another (stealing) and claiming it to be our own (lying).

The gravity of cheating depends on the circumstances of the situation. To knowingly and willingly cheat another out of a scholarship, for example, is clearly a grave sin. On the other hand, to cheat on a quiz would fall into a lesser category of sinfulness.

What about Stealing?

Stealing originates in the heart with greed or desire. Repeatedly, Jesus taught his disciples to guard against these two attitudes, saying:

> *"Happy are those
> who know they are spiritually poor;
> the Kingdom of heaven belongs to them! . . .
> Happy are those
> whose greatest desire is to do
> what God requires;
> God will satisfy them fully!"*
> MATTHEW 5:3, 6

Jesus recognized that inequality exists when it comes to material wealth. Some people are more talented and earn more money. Some have more luck and acquire more wealth. Some are simply born into a wealthy family.

But Jesus also made it clear that with greater wealth comes an obligation to help those who are not so fortunate. The Parable of Lazarus and the Rich Man (Luke 16:19–31) and the Last Judgment narrative (Matthew 25:31–46) leave no doubt about this obligation.

What about Gambling?

Gambling may be described as betting or taking a chance on an uncertain outcome. State lotteries and betting on sporting events are examples. They are so widespread that some sources estimate that over 60 percent of the adult population engages in some form of gambling.

When gambling is comfortably within one's means, it may be considered entertainment and, therefore, morally permissible. But gambling can quickly become immoral when it ceases to be—

- within our means or
- under our control.

First, gambling becomes sinful when it ceases to be within our means. Irresponsible gambling has brought untold suffering upon people and families.

Second, gambling becomes a problem when it ceases to be under our control. When we become aware that gambling has a compulsive hold on us, we have an obligation to seek help.

Compulsive gambling is so widespread in the United States that numerous organizations, like Gamblers Anonymous, are now springing up to deal with the problem.

Describing the grip that compulsive gambling can get on us, one person says:

*The first time
I had a dollar in my pocket
that I could call my own
was when I was forty-six years old.
By that time I had wrecked a business
and put out of work a couple of hundred people
who depended on me for a living.*

Compulsive Gambling

There are nearly five million compulsive gamblers in the United States. To help these victims, Gamblers Anonymous operates over seven hundred groups.

The seriousness of compulsive gambling is illustrated by the fact that 70 percent of the people who come to Gamblers Anonymous have considered suicide. Twenty-two percent of the women who come have actually attempted suicide.

According to a *Chicago Tribune* report, "A study in California showed that about 6 percent of the adolescent population is involved in pathological gambling. It is partly due to the lottery."

Gamblers Anonymous offers twenty questions to help people decide if they (or someone they know) are a compulsive gambler. Here are five of the questions.

- After you lose, do you feel the desire to return as soon as possible to win back your losses?
- After you win, do you experience a strong urge to return in order to win more?
- Have you ever borrowed money to gamble?
- Do you ever gamble longer than you had originally planned?
- Do arguments, disappointments, or frustrations cause you to want to gamble?

If you answered yes to any two of these five questions, you may have a problem.

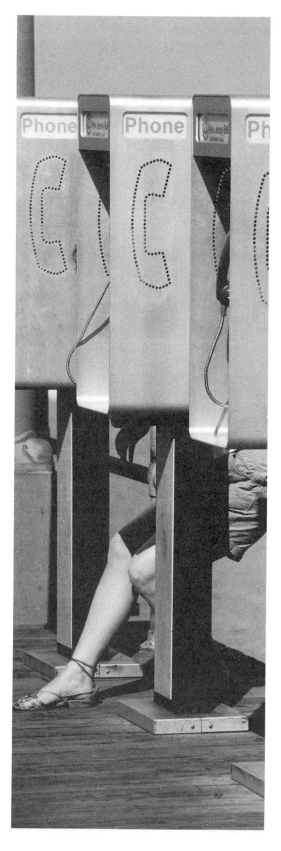

Eighth Commandment

In July 1975, American and Soviet astronauts docked together 140 miles above the planet Earth. The docking made spectacular television coverage. Yet, a few days later, the *Chicago Tribune* carried a front-page story about people who refused to believe that the event actually took place.

NASA said it was not surprised. It routinely receives letters from skeptics, like the person who claimed that the first moon walk was "staged on a back lot at Warner Brothers."

These two examples illustrate the serious crisis of trust in our world. This crisis has been created by violations of the eighth commandment, which instructs us to be truthful.

Lying Erodes Trust

Human society is built on mutual trust between individuals and nations. Nothing erodes or destroys trust more than lying. When trust breaks down, society breaks down.

A lie may be defined as communicating to another something that we know to be false. The Hebrew Scriptures were especially hard on liars. For example, the Book of Sirach says:

> *Lying is an ugly blot*
> *on a person's character. . . .*
> *A thief is better*
> *than a habitual liar.*
> SIRACH 20:24–25

Lying is especially destructive when it involves people who have a special claim to our trust, like family or friends. One of the most destructive forms of lying, however, is lying to oneself. For example, we can deny that we sin. Commenting on the need to be truthful to ourselves, one poet penned these memorable lines:

> *This above all,—*
> *   to thine own self be true;*
> *And it must follow, as the night the day,*
> *Thou canst not then be false to any man.*
> William Shakespeare, HAMLET

Lying Can Destroy Lives

One of the most vicious lies is one that destroys another's good name. Concerning this lie, one poet says:

> *Who steals my purse, steals trash;*
> *'tis something, nothing;*
> *'Twas mine, 'tis his,*
> *and has been slave to thousands;*
> *But he that filches from me my name*
> *Robs me of that which not enriches him*
> *And makes me poor indeed.*
> William Shakespeare, OTHELLO

A person who injures another's name has an obligation to repair the damage, if possible. But trying to repair the damage is often as difficult as trying to unring a bell.

Detraction Can Destroy Lives

A person's reputation or good name can also be destroyed by *detraction*. Detraction may be described as broadcasting another's private faults, failures, or sins without sufficient reason. The most common way this is done is by gossip. A fitting commentary on this sinful practice is this excerpt:

> *I maim without killing.*
> *I break hearts and ruin lives. . . .*
> *The more I am quoted*
> *the more I am believed. . . .*
> *My victims are helpless. . . .*
> *To try to track me down is impossible.*
> *The harder you try,*
> *the more elusive I become. . . .*
> *I topple governments and wreck marriages. . . .*
> *I make innocent people cry in their pillows. . . .*
> *I am called Gossip.*
> *Office gossip. Shop gossip. Party gossip. . . .*
> *Before you repeat a story ask yourself:*
> *Is it true? Is it fair? Is it necessary?*
> *If not—SHUT UP.*
> Anonymous

Recap

The Ten Commandments act as invitations to love by calling forth love from us when we do not respond with love as we should. They act as *guides* to love by indicating the proper course of action when we are not sure what response love invites us to make.

Specifically, the sixth and the ninth commandments invite and guide us in loving our neighbor as ourselves in matters relating to sex; the seventh and the tenth commandments, in matters relating to the property of others; and the eighth commandment, in matters relating to truthful communication.

Understanding Moral Life

Review

Love

1. Explain what people mean when they say that love is a *commitment,* not a *feeling.*

2. Explain in what sense sex is not the only way to express love, but rather, is "the crowning expression of a marathon of prior expressions."

3. List and briefly explain the twofold end for which God ordained the sexual union.

Sixth and Ninth Commandments

4. Express briefly and in your own words the six statements that summarize traditional Catholic teaching concerning responsible sex.

Seventh and Tenth Commandments

5. What is the technical definition of stealing?

6. List and explain the two factors that enter into determining the gravity of stealing.

7. What do we mean by restitution, and what is our obligation to make restitution when we have stolen something?

8. Explain (a) how cheating, in some sense, involves both lying and stealing, and (b) when cheating becomes gravely sinful.

9. What are the two conditions that make gambling immoral, and what obligation does a compulsive gambler have?

Eighth Commandment

10. Explain (a) the difference between *lying* and *detraction,* (b) how lying and detraction injure another person, and (c) the obligation we have to repair this injury.

Exercises

1. At one point in life we can become plagued by sexual fantasies. We can even begin to thumb through pornographic magazines and perhaps even to buy such magazines. Finally, we can begin to watch adult movies. When we reach this point, we may become alarmed for three reasons. First, this is not the way a Christian should act. Second, it suggests that the next step will involve actions. Finally, pornography tends to destroy our ability to focus on God. We might try to change but can't. Our willpower is no match for our temptations. When one young person reached this

point, she turned to the Bible for help. These words struck her: "Decide today whom you will serve" (Joshua 24:15). She wondered, was God telling her not to fight the battle *at the point of temptation,* but *before the temptation?* It seemed so. Right then and there the young woman prayed aloud to God: "I choose to serve you." That decision was the turning point in the young woman's battle. She still experienced temptations occasionally, but she also experienced the new help of grace that flowed from her decision.

Using the above example, review the three steps that sometimes lead us to alarm concerning our sexual curiosity. *Why* would the fourth step, logically, involve actions? Why does pornography tend to destroy one's focus on God? Explain the difference between fighting the battle "at the point of temptation" and "before the temptation." What advice would you give to a friend who seems to be addicted to pornography?

2. Lori Magraw was a college student working part-time in a Seattle shoe store. One day she was told to package defective shoes and return them to the manufacturer. She was also told to use a knife to damage perfectly good shoes that had been returned by dissatisfied customers and could not be resold. When she refused, she was fired. Lori filed a complaint with a city agency and received a small cash settlement and a promise from the shoe store that the practice of purposely damaging shoes would be stopped.

Describe a time when you were asked to participate in something that you considered to be wrong. Explain your feelings and your response.

3. A survey of over one hundred universities showed that over half of the students cheated regularly. What was even more alarming was that the cheaters seldom had any sense of wrongdoing. This raises a question: Besides being against the seventh commandment, why is cheating wrong? A discussion of this question by a group of students netted the following results.

■ Cheating hurts ourselves. We get into the habit of taking the easy way out. We also pave the way for cheating on a bigger scale later. It involves us in both stealing and lying. We *steal* answers from another and *lie* to our teachers, making them think that the answers are ours.

■ Cheating hurts others. When we cheat, we deprive honest people of a class rank they have worked hard to deserve. We may even deprive them of a scholarship. Cheating also hurts others in that a doctor who got through med school by cheating is a danger to patients.

On an unsigned sheet of paper, answer the following questions:

- Do you cheat now?
- On the average, how often do you cheat in the course of a week?
- On a scale of one (not very) to ten (very), how guilty do you feel when you cheat?
- Why do you cheat?
- Do you cheat only in schoolwork? Explain.
- Do you plan to cheat in college? Explain.

4. A worried mother wrote the following letter to a columnist who deals with family problems.

The other day I found some pictures of nude women in the pockets of my fifteen-year-old boy's pants, as I was preparing to throw them in the washer. I was shocked and crushed. He knows I found them and is terribly embarrassed. He is a good boy, gets excellent grades, and is very good with his younger brothers and sisters. My husband and I thought we had brought him up well, but now this! I feel I must say something to him, but I don't know how to approach the subject or what to say.

What advice would you give this mother?

Personal Reflection

Four girls tell what they dislike in a boy:

KIM: The little-boy type! Never serious! Always goofing around and treating you like one of the guys.

KRIS: I hate a guy who's wrapped up in himself—the superior "God's-gift-to-the-world" type.

MARY: I don't like a guy who puts on a front, even though he gets away with it for a while. Sooner or later people will find out.

AMY: Spare me the macho jock.

Four boys tell what they like in a girl:

JOE: I like honesty—not in the sense of not lying, but in the sense of not pretending to be someone she isn't.

MARK: I like a girl I can share my ideas and inner thoughts with.

MIKE: I like a girl who respects me as much as she respects herself.

TODD: I like a good friend, someone I enjoy and someone who enjoys me.

List three things you like in the opposite sex and three things you dislike.

Bible Reading

Pick a passage. After reading it prayerfully, write out a brief prayer to God that reflects your personal feelings or thoughts about it.

1. Punishment for lying	Ezekiel 13:6–16
2. Punishment for cheating	Amos 8:4–10
3. Punishment for stealing	Exodus 22:1–14
4. Punishment for illicit sex	Deuteronomy 22: 13–30
5. Jesus forgives an adulteress	John 8:1–11

20 Moral Decision Making

In her book *Winning by Letting Go,* Elizabeth Brenner describes how farmers in rural India catch monkeys.

First they cut a hole in a box. Then they put a tasty nut inside the box. The hole is just big enough for the monkey to put its hand through. But once it grabs the nut, its fist is too big to withdraw. So the monkey has two choices: release the nut and go free, or keep it and stay trapped.

But the monkey wants the nut so badly that it usually delays in making the decision. While it is delaying, a farmer rushes up and grabs it.

Decision making is difficult. It is especially difficult when it comes to moral decisions: deciding what is the right, wrong, or better thing to do in a certain situation.

Recall a time when you were not sure what was the right, wrong, or better thing to do in a situation. How did you come to a decision on the matter?

Moral Decisions

A fifteen-year-old boy and his father were driving past a tiny airport in a small town in Ohio. Suddenly a low-flying plane spun out of control and nose-dived into the runway.

The boy yelled, "Dad! Dad! Stop the car!" Minutes later the boy was pulling the pilot out of the plane. It was a twenty-year-old friend of the boy. He had been practicing takeoffs and landings. The friend died in the boy's arms.

That night the boy was too shocked and crushed to eat supper. He went to his room, closed the door, and lay on his bed. The fifteen-year-old had been working part-time in a drugstore. Every penny he made he spent on flying lessons. His goal was to get his pilot's license when he turned sixteen.

The boy's parents wondered what effect the tragedy would have on their son's decision to continue flying. They discussed it with him, but they told him that the decision had to be his.

Two days later the boy's mother noticed an open notebook in her son's room. It was one he had kept from childhood. Across the top of the page was written in big letters, "The Character of Jesus." Beneath it was listed a series of qualities:

- Jesus was humble,
- he championed the poor,
- he was unselfish,
- he was close to God.

The mother realized that in her son's hour of decision he was turning to prayer and to Jesus for guidance.

Later, she asked her son, "What have you decided?" The boy looked into his mother's eyes and said, "With God's help, I *must* continue to fly."

That boy was Neil Armstrong. And on July 20, 1969, he became the first human being to walk on the moon. The millions of people who watched him on television had no idea that one reason he was walking on the moon was Jesus. They had no idea that it was from Jesus that he drew strength and guidance to make a teenage decision that was responsible for what he was now doing.

The story of Neil Armstrong illustrates an important point: not all moral decisions are easy to make. In other words, there are times when we are not sure what we should do. When a difficult decision arises, we should do what Neil Armstrong did. We should—

- ponder it in light of Jesus' teaching,
- consult appropriate people about it,
- pray for guidance.

These three steps should precede every difficult moral decision.

In general, there are three kinds of difficult moral decisions. They may be described in everyday language as—

- clear-cut decisions,
- clouded decisions,
- contrary decisions.

Clear-cut Decisions

The movie *A Man for All Seasons* is based on the life of Saint Thomas More. More rose to prominence when King Henry VIII appointed him Chancellor of England in 1529. But tragedy soon struck his life.

Henry divorced his queen and remarried. To combat civil and religious opposition to his marriage, Henry ordered certain high dignitaries of the state to sign a document, swearing that his marriage to the queen had been invalid and should be annulled. Henry passed word along that if they refused, the dignitaries would be tried for treason.

A dramatic scene occurred when Lord Norfolk presented the document to Thomas More to sign. Thomas refused. Norfolk appealed to Thomas to reconsider in the light of his love for his family and his friends.

But Thomas knew that a more important love was at stake: his love of God. He could not swear in God's name to something he knew to be false.

Shortly afterward, Thomas was arrested. After being imprisoned for fifteen months in the Tower of London, he was executed for treason.

The decision Thomas More faced was as clear to him as it was difficult. He knew Jesus' teaching on the matter. He had discussed it with his family and he had prayed over it.

More's greatest need was for the courage to do what his conscience told him he must do. The role that prayer played in giving him this courage is evident from a letter to his daughter, Meg. Commenting on what he would do if fear threatened to shake his resolve, he wrote:

I shall remember
how Saint Peter at a blast of wind
began to sink
because of his lack of faith,
and I shall do as he did:
call upon Christ and pray to him for help.
And then I trust
he shall place his holy hand on me
and in the stormy seas hold me up
from drowning. . . .
And therefore my own good daughter,
do not let your mind be troubled.

And so the first kind of moral decision is one that is clear-cut. It is one in which it is perfectly clear what we must do. Such a decision, however, can be extremely hard to make because it can exact such a great personal price from us, as it did from Thomas More.

Clouded Decisions

When Hitler began his march across Europe during World War II, Franz Jägerstätter was a young Austrian farmer. He had a wife and two small children. He also had the distinction of being the only man in his village to vote against Austria's political merger with Nazi Germany.

In February 1943, Franz was ordered to report for military service in the German army. He faced a dilemma. How could he fight in what he regarded as an immoral war waged by an immoral government?

Franz consulted his parish priest and his bishop. Both suggested the possibility of serving in the medical corps, which would excuse him from bearing arms. But he felt uneasy about this, saying that wearing a uniform could be interpreted as a sign that he approved of the government and the war.

When a state-appointed lawyer asked Franz why he was having such a problem with military service when millions of German Christians had no problem, he responded:

> *I guess they don't have the grace to see it.*
> *But I do have the grace to see it,*
> *so I cannot serve in the army.*

So it happened that, after pondering Jesus' teaching, consulting the appropriate people, and praying for guidance, Franz felt compelled to follow his own conscience.

On August 9, 1943, Franz was executed. History has since honored him as a hero and a saint.

Jägerstätter's decision is a good example of a *clouded* decision. It involves making a decision about a situation that is so complex that it is not clear to all what Jesus' teaching invites us to do.

Because this kind of moral decision is so critical, consider yet another example.

Imagine that you are Joan, the mother of three children, ages six, nine, and eleven. Your eighty-year-old grandmother lives with you. She is mentally alert, pleasant, and dearly loved by your children. But she has severe arthritis and is beginning to need more and more attention. This is starting to take its toll on you and the family.

One day, after a very trying experience, your husband reluctantly suggests that maybe it is time to move "Granny" into a nursing home. Suddenly the two of you realize that you are faced with a clouded moral decision, for it is not clear what love (Jesus' teaching) invites you to do in Granny's case.

The correct procedure for making such a decision is to follow the three steps mentioned earlier. You should—

- ponder Jesus' teaching concerning it,
- consult appropriate persons about it, and
- pray for guidance.

The second step of this process is especially important in Granny's case. It involves consulting not only with Granny and the children but also with professionals, like the family doctor and your pastor.

Once we have taken these three steps, we may choose with a clear conscience whatever our intellectual judgment, guided by grace, seems to indicate to us.

Contrary Decisions

The most difficult moral decision of all is one that puts us at odds with a particular moral teaching of the Church. This is the most serious moral decision a Catholic can make. To illustrate why it is so serious, consider these words of Jesus to his disciples:

> *"I have been given all authority*
> *in heaven and on earth.*
> *Go, then, to all peoples everywhere . . .*
> *and teach them to obey everything*
> *I have commanded you.*
> *And I will be with you always,*
> *to the end of the age."*
> MATTHEW 28:18–20

Consider also these words of Jesus to Peter:

> *"I tell you, Peter: you are a rock,*
> *and on this rock foundation*
> *I will build my church. . . .*
> *I will give you*
> *the keys of the Kingdom of heaven;*
> *what you prohibit on earth*
> *will be prohibited in heaven,*
> *and what you permit on earth*
> *will be permitted in heaven."*
> MATTHEW 16:18–19

Finally, consider what Jesus said to his disciples just before returning to his Father:

> *"I have much more to tell you,*
> *but now it would be too much for you to bear.*
> *When, however, the Spirit comes,*
> *who reveals the truth about God,*
> *he will lead you into all the truth."*
> JOHN 16:12–13

The above passages explain why a moral decision that is contrary to an official teaching of the Church is so serious. It is because of the twofold *charism* that Jesus bestowed on his Church. He—

- authorized and empowered his Church to teach in his name, and
- assured his Church that the Holy Spirit would guide it in its teaching role.

In other words, to act contrary to an official teaching of the Church is to act in opposition to the special charism that Jesus bestowed on it.

Having said this, however, we must understand that the Church is made up of human beings, and that the Holy Spirit guides it accordingly. This means that the Holy Spirit does not short-circuit human intelligence, insight, and learning. The Holy Spirit guides the Church in keeping with the laws of human nature. Thus it happens that the Church receives clarity on certain moral and doctrinal matters gradually and by stages, depending upon—

- its openness to the Spirit and
- the complexity of the matter.

The Church Teaches at Two Levels

Because the Church does not enjoy the same clarity on all moral and doctrinal matters, it teaches at two different levels.

At the first level the Church teaches as one possessing absolute certitude on a matter. For example, when it teaches that the Eucharist is really the Body of Christ, the Church does so with absolute certitude. Consequently, we give this teaching a full "faith assent." If we did not, we would no longer be Catholic.

At the second level the Church teaches as one possessing less than absolute certitude on a particular matter.

A kind of biblical parallel to this second level of teaching occurs in Paul's First Letter to the Corinthians, where he writes:

> *Now, concerning what you wrote*
> *about unmarried people:*
> *I do not have a command from the Lord,*
> *but I give my opinion*
> *as one who by the Lord's mercy*
> *is worthy of trust.*
> 1 CORINTHIANS 7:25

A modern example of second-level teaching is the Church's teaching on artificial birth control, as set forth in the Church's document *Humanae Vitae* ("Of Human Life"). Traditionally, the *magisterium* (supreme teaching authority of the Church) has taught, and continues to teach, that artificial birth control is gravely immoral.

The Church has the responsibility to give guidance on this and other moral issues of this kind—just as Paul had the responsibility to give guidance to the Corinthians on a question that was bothering them.

Likewise, we have the responsibility to give "religious assent," rather than a full "faith assent," to the Church's second-level teachings. Giving religious assent means that we should accept the reliability of the Church's teaching on such issues because—

- Jesus authorized and empowered his Church to teach in his name, and
- Jesus assured us that the Spirit would guide the Church in its teaching role.

For these two *religious* reasons, we accept the reliability of this teaching. Hence the expression "religious assent."

Formation of Conscience

Acting contrary to the Church's teaching on artificial birth control is a grave matter, for it means we act in opposition to the twofold charism that Jesus bestowed on his Church to assist it in its teaching ministry.

It is also a grave matter because it is so easy to delude ourselves into believing what we would like to believe. Saint Augustine had this in mind when he wrote:

> *If you believe . . . what you like*
> *and reject what you don't like,*
> *it is not the Gospel you believe, but yourself.*

The Church, however, does leave open to us the possibility of forming our own conscience. Five steps are involved in forming our conscience on a moral matter that puts us in opposition to the Church's teachings. These steps are as follows:

1. We have a grave reason for doing so.
2. We have pondered the Church's teaching on the matter and the reasons for it.
3. We have sought without success alternative solutions to our moral problem.
4. We have prayed diligently for guidance.
5. We do not think we are doing wrong.

Therefore, it is possible that after following these five steps faithfully, a Catholic couple honestly finds itself in a conflict of duties (for example, reconciling conjugal love with responsible parenting, with schooling children already born, or with a mother's health). Concerning such a couple, the Canadian bishops wrote:

> *In accord with the accepted principles*
> *of moral theology,*
> *if these persons have tried sincerely*
> *but without success*
> *to pursue a line of conduct*
> *in keeping with the given directives*
> *[Church's teaching]*
> *they may be safely assured*
> *that whoever honestly chooses the course*
> *which seems right to him*
> *does so in good conscience.*
> Response to HUMANAE VITAE, September 27, 1968

After Pope Paul VI read the Canadian bishops' statement, his spokesperson informed the bishops that the Holy Father was satisfied with the way it was expressed.

Recap

Moral decision making has to do with deciding what is the morally right thing to do in a given situation. We may distinguish three general kinds of moral decisions:

- clear-cut decisions, like the one Thomas More made;
- clouded decisions, like the one involving Jägerstätter;
- contrary decisions, like the one a Catholic couple may face.

Each of these decisions is heart-wrenching and difficult in its own way. Each involves serious study, thorough consultation with appropriate people, and prayerful discernment.

Understanding Moral Decision Making

Review

Moral Decisions

1. List the three kinds of moral decisions that we may be called upon to make.

Clear-cut Decisions

2. Explain (a) who Thomas More was, (b) what clear-cut moral decision he was called upon to make, and (c) why a clear-cut moral decision can be hard to make.

Clouded Decisions

3. Explain (a) who Franz Jägerstätter was, (b) what clouded moral decision he was called upon to make, (c) what a clouded moral decision is, and (d) the three steps we should follow in making such a decision.

Contrary Decisions

4. What is a contrary moral decision, and why is it so serious?

5. What twofold charism did Jesus bestow on his Church to assist it in its teaching mission?

6. Explain (a) the two levels at which the Church teaches, (b) the kind of assent that we must give to the teaching of each level, and (c) the difference between these two kinds of assent.

Formation of Conscience

7. List the five steps we must follow in forming our own conscience about a moral matter.

Exercises

1. Bubba Smith was a college and a pro football star. In the early 1980s he became famous for his beer commercials. In October 1985, Michigan State honored Bubba by making him the grand marshal of their homecoming parade. Bubba was thrilled to be back at his alma mater. As he rode through the student-lined streets, one side started shouting, "Tastes great," and the other side shouted back, "Less filling." It was obvious that Bubba's beer commercials were a hit. But that night Bubba became deeply disturbed by the number of students at the parade who were clearly "drunk out of their heads." Then and there he made a decision to stop making the commercials. He felt the ads were influencing young people to do something he didn't want to be a part of. The decision cost Bubba a small fortune, but he thought something greater was at stake.

Into which of the three groups of moral decisions did Bubba's decision fall? Discuss the pros and cons of Bubba's decision.

2. The *Louisville Courier-Journal* carried a story about a seven-year-old youngster who accidentally swallowed a crayon while playing on a school bus. It lodged in the windpipe and was slowly choking the youngster. Seeking a speedier ride to the hospital, the driver tried to flag down a motorist. When no one stopped, the driver finally blocked the traffic lane, forcing the next car to stop. The motorist refused, saying, "I don't want to be late for work." When the child finally reached the hospital, surgery was ordered. But it was just minutes too late to save the youngster.

Into which of the three groups of moral decisions did the motorist's refusal to help the child fall? Explain.

3. You are the mother of three children, ages five, seven, and nine. Your oldest child has a poor self-image and needs a lot of home support. Your husband, Bob, spends about ten hours a day at the office just to make ends meet. You are offered an excellent forty-hour-a-week job.

What would you decide to do and why?

4. Bill Quinlan and his eighteen-year-old nephew, David, sailed out of San Diego Harbor for Ecuador. Ten days later, a tropical hurricane destroyed their sailboat, leaving them with a rubber raft that began losing air. It became clear that they had no chance of survival because of a limited water supply. Bill scratched out a loving message to his wife and children on an empty water can. Then he handed his wedding ring to David, saying, "Give this to my son when he's old enough to understand." David accepted the ring, too exhausted to argue. Then Bill slipped into the water, swam out about fifty yards, and smiled at David. It was obvious that he had decided to improve his nephew's chances of survival. That was the last time David ever saw him. After his uncle was out of sight, David became overwhelmed with guilt and began to cry hysterically. Two days later he drank his last can of water. Then he lapsed into a deep sleep. Sometime later a Portuguese fishing boat spotted him adrift and picked him up.

Granted that Bill's action was courageous, was he guilty of suicide? Explain. In which of the three groups of moral decisions did Bill Quinlan's action fall?

his wife. He dropped from the team. As it turned out, his wife was late in giving birth and the American canoe team won the gold medal. Bill could have competed and still arrived home for the birth of his son, Frank. Frank grew up. Bill never said anything to him about being disappointed that he missed the Olympics. Years passed. Then one day in July 1952, a cablegram arrived from Helsinki, Finland, where the Olympics were in progress. It read: "Dad, I won. I'm bringing home the gold medal you lost while waiting for me to be born." Bill's son, Frank, had just won the Olympic single's canoe competition.

Describe a time when you made a hard decision that had a happy ending such as the one in this story.

Personal Reflection

A free-lance writer in *USA Today* wrote that all guns—toy and real—are banned in the writer's home. Violent cartoons are also banned. The writer asks: "Who am I kidding? Do I really think I can make a difference by imposing these rules on my children? But I have to start somewhere." The writer is making the same point that Pearl Buck made years ago when she said:

> *This country is divided into two halves: the people who build, and the people who break down. It's time for each of us to stand up and be counted on the side of the people who add to our spiritual health rather than subtract from it. . . . Each day things happen which make the wheel turn. And it's up to each one of us which way it goes.*

Compose a prayer to God on some moral decisions you face in your life right now. Ask God to help you to take a stand as the free-lance writer did. Ask God to give you the courage "to stand up and be counted on the side of the people who add to our spiritual health rather than subtract from it."

Bible Reading

5. A member of the American canoe team, Bill Havens, was scheduled to compete in the 1924 Olympics in Paris. In those days there was no jet travel across the ocean. Thus, when the doctor said Bill's wife would have their baby sometime during the games, Bill considered dropping out and letting his alternate go in his place. His wife urged him not to do it, assuring him that she would be fine. But the more Bill pondered the question, the more he thought his place was with

Pick a passage. After reading it prayerfully, write out a brief prayer to God that reflects your personal feelings or thoughts about it.

1. Clear-cut decision	1 Corinthians 5
2. Clouded decision	1 Corinthians 8
3. Clouded decision	Romans 14
4. Postponing a decision	Acts 5:27–39
5. Landmark decision	Acts 15:1–21

21 Life Models

The catacombs were underground burial places used by early Romans. They consisted of a maze of tunnels, cut through soft clay that hardened when exposed to the air. The sides of the tunnels contained "shelf" graves in which the dead were buried, one on top of the other. During times of religious persecution, Christians met secretly in these underground passageways to celebrate Mass together.

Years ago, five boys were playing in a catacomb outside Rome. Suddenly the battery in their flashlight died. For two days they groped about in darkness, unable to find their way out. Then one of the boys felt a smooth path running along the rough floor of the passageway. He reasoned that it had been worn smooth by the feet of ancient Christians filing in and out of the secret tunnels for Mass. The boys followed the path—to safety.

A high school girl observed, "That story makes a good parable to illustrate how ancient saints can still serve as guides and life models for modern Christians."

Assuming the girl is right, who/what would the following stand for: the failure of the boys' flashlight; the boys' groping about in the darkness; finding the path and following it to safety?

Saints

Saint Francis of Assisi was born into a wealthy Italian family. As a teenager, he was a spendthrift and a "party" person. In 1202 he became a soldier and marched off to battle. He was taken prisoner and spent a year in chains.

After his release, it took Francis a full year to regain his health. The ordeal changed him forever. He left the wealthy surroundings of his family, put on a peasant's garb, and set out to find God. His new home was an abandoned church on the outskirts of Assisi. There he spent hours alone in prayer.

Two biblical teachings, especially, began to haunt Francis. The first was that every person is created in God's image (Genesis 1:26–27). The second was that whatever we do for the least person, we do for Jesus himself (Matthew 25:45). Through his meditation on these two teachings, Francis developed a deep love for the rejects of society.

One day he came upon a leper. Although Francis had a dreadful fear of leprosy, he embraced the man. This moving incident dramatized

Catacombs may still be visited outside Rome.

the extent to which the teachings of Jesus had taken root in his heart.

Not long after this incident, Francis was attending Mass. The Gospel reading recalled Jesus' instruction to his disciples to go forth into the surrounding towns to preach the Good News. Jesus told his disciples not to take any money with them, but to trust in God for their material needs (Matthew 10:5–15).

This instruction touched Francis deeply. He lived in a time like our own, when people were drifting from the teachings of Jesus. So Francis went forth into the towns of Italy to preach the Gospel anew. His charismatic personality soon attracted other young people to join him. And so the Franciscan order (religious community) was born.

Saints Are Dangerous People

In the novel *Anthony Adverse,* Hervey Allen says of Francis and saints like him:

> *Brother Francis and his kind . . .*
> *have always made Christianity*
> *a dangerous religion.*
> *Just when the Church is about to be taken*
> *as a decorative and snugly woven cocoon . . .*
> *poof!—that cocoon bursts*
> *and the beautiful psyche of Christianity*
> *emerges.*

The "psyche" that emerged in Francis is captured in this moving prayer that he wrote:

> *Lord,*
> *make me an instrument of your peace.*
> *Where there is hatred, let me sow love;*
> *where there is injury, pardon;*
> *where there is doubt, faith;*
> *where there is despair, hope;*
> *where there is darkness, light;*
> *and where there is sadness, joy.*
>
> *Grant that I may not so much*
> *seek to be consoled as to console;*
> *to be understood as to understand;*
> *to be loved as to love;*
> *for it is in giving that we receive;*
> *it is in pardoning that we are pardoned;*
> *and it is in dying*
> *that we are born to eternal life.*

What Is a Saint?

A saint may be described as a person who takes seriously the Gospel's invitation to love and live as Jesus did. A saint is a living reminder that God's grace can work miracles in us, if we but open our hearts to it.

The word *saint* comes from the Latin word *sanctus,* which means "holy." Literally, the word *saint* means "holy one." These words recall God's command: "Keep yourselves holy, because I am holy" (Leviticus 11:44).

Early Christians referred to one another as saints. They did this not in a self-righteous sense, but in the sense that this was what they were called to be. Thus, we find the word *saint* (sometimes translated as "God's people" or "holy ones") used over sixty times in the Christian Scriptures (for example, Matthew 27:52 and Acts 9:13).

With the passage of time, however, the word *saint* was reserved exclusively for those Christians who were martyred for their faith or who had lived extraordinary, holy lives.

At first, a person was declared to be a saint by those who had seen the person martyred or who had witnessed the person's holy life. Beginning around the year 1000, however, Pope John XV set up a more exacting and more objective process for declaring a person a saint. Called *canonization,* this process involves a rigorous investigation of every aspect of a person's life.

Saint Francis.

Communion of Saints

A question that non-Catholics ask is this: Why do you Catholics pray to saints? Why don't you pray directly to God?

The answer is that we do pray directly to God in every Mass. No relationship is more important than our relationship with God.

But our relationship with our Christian brothers and sisters is also important. We are all members of the Body of Christ. We are community. We are family.

The seriousness with which we have always taken this relationship with one another is seen in the Apostles' Creed, which dates back to the earliest days of Christianity. One of the twelve articles of the Creed reads: "We believe in the communion of saints." (The word *saints* is used here in the biblical sense of referring to followers of Jesus.)

The "communion of saints" professes our faith in the belief that we belong to a larger community or family than the *faith* family or the *human* family here on earth. We belong to those who have gone before us. The "communion of saints," therefore, includes three groups:

- the Church in pilgrimage (on earth),
- the Church in purgation (in purgatory),
- the Church in perfection (in heaven).

Early inscriptions in the catacombs witness to the fact that early Christians prayed for the dead and asked the dead to pray for them. They believed that if they prayed for one another on earth, why shouldn't they continue to do so now that their loved ones are dead. Loved ones do not cease to be family just because they now live in different dimensions of reality.

Catholic attitude toward the saints who have died is summed up in this prayer to God:

You are glorified in your saints. . . .
In their lives on earth
you give us an example.
In our communion with them,
you give us their friendship.
In their prayer for the Church,
you give us strength and protection.
This great company of witnesses
*   spurs us on to victory,*
to share their prize of everlasting glory.
PREFACE FOR HOLY MEN AND WOMEN—I

Famous thousand-year-old Black Virgin *at Monserrat, Spain.*

Mother of Jesus

From the dawn of Christianity, one saint has stood out above all others. That saint is Mary, the mother of Jesus. Mary's specialness flows from the fact that God chose her to be the mother of Jesus. The angel Gabriel said to her:

> *"Peace be with you!*
> *The Lord is with you*
> *and has greatly blessed you! . . .*
> *You will become pregnant and give birth to a son,*
> *and you will name him Jesus. . . ."*
> *Mary said to the angel,*
> *"I am a virgin.*
> *How, then, can this be?"*
> *The angel answered,*
> *"The Holy Spirit will come on you,*
> *and God's power will rest upon you.*
> *For this reason the holy child will be called*
> *the Son of God. . . ."*
> *"I am the Lord's servant," said Mary;*
> *"may it happen to me as you have said."*
> LUKE 1:28, 31, 34–35, 38

Mary's words, "I am a virgin," testify to her virginity. The child she conceived in her womb was not of human origin, but of the Holy Spirit. Thus Mary is traditionally referred to as the "Virgin Mother of God." Moreover, tradition teaches that she remained a virgin throughout her life.

Mother of God

The title "Mother of God" startles some people. This expression does not mean that Mary is God's mother from all eternity. It simply means that Jesus is God *according to the flesh.* It is in this sense that Catholics honor Mary with the title "Mother of God."

Historically, the title "Mother of God" dates from the Council of Ephesus (A.D. 431). It came about when the council faced the problem of declaring that Jesus had two natures (divine and human) but was not two persons, as some theologians erroneously taught.

To correct this error, the council declared that while Jesus had two natures, he was only one person. To stress that Jesus was only "one" person, the council added that Mary, therefore, could be called the Mother of God. For, indeed, Jesus was God *according to the flesh.*

Immaculate Conception

Catholics also honor Mary under the title "Immaculate Conception." To understand this title, we need to recall that the first sin "flawed" the human race. We refer to this flawed condition as the state of *original sin.*

The title "Immaculate Conception" expresses Catholic belief—handed down by tradition—that, from the instant of her existence as a human person, God preserved Mary from original sin in preparation for her calling to be the mother of Jesus. Tradition also teaches that Mary remained sinless throughout her life. In the words of Scripture, Mary was "most blessed of all women" (Luke 1:42). In the words of the poet William Wordsworth, she is "our tainted nature's solitary boast."

Apparitions of Mary

In 1858 a fourteen-year-old French girl, Bernadette Soubirous, reported having a vision of Mary at a hillside in Lourdes, France. Civil and religious authorities scoffed at her claim. When she continued to visit the hillside to pray, she was threatened with punishment.

One day Mary told Bernadette to dig into the ground with her hands. She did and a spring bubbled up. Miracles began. A blind man washed there and regained his sight. A mother bathed her paralyzed child in the waters, and the child was restored to health. (Fifty-four years after Bernadette died, that same child, then a seventy-seven-year-old man, was an honored guest at her canonization ceremony in Rome.)

Today, the Medical Bureau of Lourdes has on file records of over 1,200 recorded cures that have taken place there. Before a cure is accepted by the bureau, it must be certified by an international commission of doctors and surgeons of all faiths.

A highly publicized cure took place in the 1970s. It involved an ex-serviceman, twenty-three-year-old Vittorio Michel of Italy. He had contracted bone cancer, and doctors had given up hope of his recovery. In desperation, his family and friends took him to Lourdes. There he was washed in the spring waters. Within a week, his pain vanished and the bone repaired itself.

There have been reports of other apparitions or visions of Mary over the centuries. Because of the possibility of deception, the Church exercises extreme caution in dealing with such reports. Each case is investigated thoroughly (sometimes for years) before it is declared worthy or unworthy of credibility. The Church is even more cautious of "messages" reportedly received during an apparition. If, after an investigation and study, a message is declared "credible," this does not mean we must believe it. It simply means that it contains nothing contrary to faith or morals.

Assumption

When Catholics speak of Mary's assumption, they refer to their belief—also handed down by tradition—that she was taken up to heaven at the end of her life in the totality of her person. In other words, she went directly from an earthly state to a heavenly state, without her body undergoing decay, the penalty of sin (Genesis 3:19).

Belief in Mary's assumption is a corollary of Mary's Immaculate Conception. Because she was sinless, she did not fall under its penalty.

Mary's assumption is a beautiful reminder that we too are destined to be in heaven someday in the totality of our person, soul and *body,* just as Mary is.

Touching on this mystery, Paul compares our body before death to a seed; he compares our body after death to the plant that emerges from the seed (1 Corinthians 15:36–38). Continuing this metaphor, Paul says:

> *When the body is buried, it is mortal;*
> *when raised, it will be immortal. . . .*
> *When buried, it is a physical body;*
> *when raised, it will be a spiritual body.*
> 1 CORINTHIANS 15:42, 44

Model Disciple

Catholics look upon Mary as the "model disciple." This means that they look upon Mary as being the model of what they should strive to become. Two characteristics, especially, stand out in Mary's life:

- her spirit of service and
- her spirit of prayer.

Someone said, "My life turned around when I stopped asking God to do things for me and asked God what I could do for him." Mary had this same kind of *spirit of service.*

Mary's spirit of service showed itself when the angel announced to her that she was to be the mother of Jesus. She answered, "I am the Lord's servant; may it happen to me as you have said" (Luke 1:38).

Her spirit of service showed itself again when she learned that Elizabeth was pregnant with John the Baptist. She went immediately to help her cousin and to share her joy (Luke 1:39–45).

Finally, Mary's spirit of service showed itself in a touching way at a wedding in Cana. When she learned that the newly married couple had run out of wine, she immediately sought Jesus' help (John 2:1–5).

The second characteristic, Mary's *spirit of prayer,* is also evident. It showed itself in her song of praise to God shortly after arriving at her cousin's home (Luke 1:46–55).

Mary's spirit of prayer also manifested itself at the birth of Jesus. Concerning the remarkable events surrounding Jesus' birth, the Gospel says Mary "remembered all these things and thought deeply about them" (Luke 2:19).

Finally, Mary's spirit of prayer showed itself in her anticipation of Pentecost. Luke says that she and Jesus' disciples gathered "to pray as a group" in preparation for the coming of the Holy Spirit (Acts 1:14).

Mother Teresa of Calcutta said, "Prayer enlarges the heart until it is capable of containing God's gift of himself." Prayer did this for Mary and the saints. It can also do it for us, if we follow their example.

Recap

A *saint* may be described as a person who takes seriously the Gospel's invitation to live and love as Jesus did. Of all the saints, the Virgin Mary is special because God chose her to be the mother of Jesus. We therefore give her the title "Mother of God." We also give her the title "Immaculate Conception," because she was preserved from original sin. Finally, because Mary was sinless, she did not fall under its penalty, but was assumed into heaven in the totality of her person. Mary's *assumption* is a pledge that we too will join her in heaven in the *totality* of our person, if we strive to be like her, especially in her spirit of prayer and service to others.

Continuing the Faith Journey

God, who began this good work in you, will carry it on until it is finished.
PHILIPPIANS 1:6

A farm boy had a fear of the dark. One night his father told him to go to the barn to feed the animals. The boy turned pale. When his father saw this, he stepped onto the porch, lit a lantern, and held it up. "Son," he said, "how far can you see?" The boy said, "I can see halfway to the barn." The father said, "Walk halfway to the barn."

When the boy reached the halfway point, the father called out, "How far can you see now?" The boy said, "I can see the barn." The father said, "Good! Walk to the barn door, open it, and tell me what you see." When the boy got to the barn door, he opened it and shouted back to his father, "I can see the animals!" The father said, "Good! Now feed them."

That story makes an excellent point. The lantern did not light up the whole barnyard. It lit only a part of the path leading to the barn. But that was enough to get the boy started down the path. The rest took care of itself.

Path through Catholicism is like the lantern. It does not light up everything there is to know about the Catholic faith. It lights up only "a part of the path." But it is enough to get us started down the path. The rest will take care of itself.

This brings us to four brief guidelines for continuing the faith journey we have begun.

First, remain open to God's grace. For as the hymn "Amazing Grace" says: " 'Tis grace hath brought me safe thus far, / And grace will lead me home."

Second, reach out to others. One way God graces us is through other people. We do not journey to God alone, but in community with other followers of Jesus.

Third, keep in touch with Jesus through prayer. "I am the vine, and you are the branches," said Jesus. "Whoever remains in me, and I in him, will bear much fruit" (John 15:5). Begin with just a few minutes of prayer each morning or night. Let the Holy Spirit take it from there.

Fourth, be filled always with hope—and joy. For as Saint Paul says:

There is nothing in all creation that will ever be able to separate us from the love of God which is ours through Jesus Christ our Lord.
ROMANS 8:39

Understanding Life Models

Review

Saints

1. Explain (a) what ordeal changed the life of Saint Francis of Assisi, (b) what two Scripture readings gave him a love for society's rejects, (c) what Scripture reading inspired him to preach the Gospel, and (d) how the time in which Francis lived was similar to ours.

2. Explain (a) how a saint may be described, (b) the origin and meaning of the word *saint,* (c) how early Christians used the word differently than we do, and (d) what *canonization* means.

Communion of Saints

3. What do we mean when we say in the Creed that we believe in the "communion of saints"?

4. What three groups make up the communion of saints?

5. Why do Catholics pray to saints?

Mother of Jesus

6. Explain (a) what gives Mary her "specialness" and (b) what tradition teaches concerning Mary's virginity.

Mother of God

7. Historically, how did Mary receive the title "Mother of God," and what exactly does the title mean?

Immaculate Conception

8. Explain (a) what we mean when we call Mary the Immaculate Conception and (b) what tradition teaches concerning sin in Mary's life.

Assumption

9. Explain (a) what we mean by Mary's "assumption," (b) how it relates to the title "Immaculate Conception," and (c) how it reminds us of our own destiny.

Model Disciple

10. Explain in what sense Mary is the "model disciple."

11. What two characteristics, especially, that Mary had should we try to imitate? Give two examples from Scripture to illustrate each of these characteristics.

Apparitions of Mary

12. Explain (a) the origin of the springs at Lourdes, (b) how Lourdes became a place to which people came for healing, (c) why the Church is so cautious about reputed apparitions, and (d) what the Church means when it says that a reputed "message" during an apparition is *credible.*

Exercises

1. In the 1930s Dr. Alexis Carrel, a New York surgeon and Nobel Prize winner, went to Lourdes to investigate firsthand the cures that were being reported there. He himself had no religious faith at all.

While en route by train to the French village, Carrel was called several times to treat an extremely sick girl, also on the same train to Lourdes. He told someone that if she were cured at Lourdes, he would become a religious believer.

When the train arrived at Lourdes, Carrel accompanied the girl to the shrine. In his book *The Voyage to Lourdes,* he describes what happened at a prayer service after the girl was bathed in the famous spring waters. (For professional reasons, he changed all names and called himself Lerrac.)

> *Suddenly, Lerrac felt himself turning pale. The blanket which covered Marie Ferrand's distended abdomen was gradually flattening out. . . . He watched the intake of her breath and the pulsing of her throat. . . . "How do you feel?" he asked her. . . . "I feel weak, but I feel I am cured . . ." Lerrac stood there in silence, his mind a blank.*

Later, Carrel and two other doctors examined the girl carefully. Their conclusion was unanimous: she was cured. Carrel still did not believe, even though he had seen everything with his own eyes.

That night Carrel went for a long walk. He ended up in the back of a church and prayed for the gift of faith. At about three o'clock in the morning, he returned to his hotel. As he sat down to record his thoughts before going to bed, he "felt the serenity of nature enter his soul. . . . All intellectual doubts vanished." At that moment Dr. Alexis Carrel became a believer. He went on to become a prominent Catholic.

Why do you think Dr. Carrel doubted, even after seeing the miracle? Why do you think fewer miracles are apparently taking place at Lourdes today than there once were?

2. In the 1980s a series of Marian apparitions was reported at Medjugorje, Yugoslavia. Two reports—"What I Saw at Medjugorje" by Jack Wintz and "Medjugorje: Pro and Con" by Peter Toscani—appeared in the November 1988 *Catholic Digest.* Have a librarian help you get photo copies of the article. Then team up with another person, make a report on Medjugorje to the group, and share your personal thoughts and feelings about the reputed apparitions.

Saint Elizabeth Ann Seton.

3. Elizabeth Ann Seton was the first native-born American saint. At nineteen, she married into a wealthy family. Before her husband died at the age of twenty-nine, they had five children. Two years after her husband's tragic death, Elizabeth and the children embraced the Catholic faith. She became a teacher and opened a school for girls in Maryland in 1808. The following year she founded the American Sisters of Charity, which pioneered the Catholic school system in the United States. Elizabeth Ann Seton was canonized in 1975. Other U.S. saints include Mother Frances Xavier Cabrini (canonized in 1946), Bishop John Neumann (canonized in 1977), and Mother Katherine Drexel (canonized in 1988).

What factors made Elizabeth Seton an unlikely candidate for sainthood? Why do you think God often chooses *unlikely* candidates? Prepare a brief oral report on a saint or a contemporary Catholic and present it to the group. If the *Catholic Digest* is available in your school or parish, you might check out one of the following:

- "Mother Teresa's Sisters Help AIDS Victims" (January 1987)
- "Five Frontier Women" (January 1987)
- "The Vision of Father Clements" (December 1987)
- "This Jesuit Runs a Circus" (August 1989)
- "Sister Jeannette and Her Children" (August 1990)
- "The Saint Who Hid Priests" (August 1990)
- "They Pray to St. Jude" (September 1990)
- "Soulmate to St. Francis" (October 1990)

Personal Reflection

A college student was talking to a priest while on retreat. The conversation drifted to Mary. Suddenly the student said, "Let me read you a poem I wrote about Mary." Then the student flipped open a small spiral notebook. The poem went something like this:

> *Today I saw a water lily growing in a pond.*
> *It had the freshest yellow color I'd ever seen.*
> *The lily—a precious treasure—was unconcerned*
> *about whether anyone noticed*
> *its astounding beauty.*
>
> *As I sat there,*
> *watching it unfold its petals noiselessly,*
> *I thought of Mary pregnant with Jesus.*
> *She, too, was a precious treasure.*
> *She, too, was unconcerned about whether*
> *anyone noticed her astounding beauty.*
>
> *But to those who did, she shared a secret.*
> *Her beauty came not from herself,*
> *but from the Jesus life within her,*
> *unfolding its petals noiselessly.*

Reread the poem prayerfully. Compose a poem or a prayer of your own concerning Mary. Make it honest and from the heart. If you prefer, base your poem or prayer on some saint, perhaps the saint whose name you bear.

Bible Reading

Pick a passage. After reading it prayerfully, write out a brief prayer to God that reflects your personal feelings or thoughts about it.

1. You will bear a son   Luke 1:26–38
2. All will call you blessed   Luke 1:39–56
3. Sorrow will break your heart Luke 2:22–35
4. Do whatever he tells you   John 2:1–12
5. Behold, your mother   John 19:23–27

INDEX